Also C

Praise for Street Legends

"In this gripping gangstaography, Seth Ferranti, manages to once again take you somewhere you don't want to go." **Susan Hampstead, Don Diva Magazine**

"Street Legends is gangsta with a capital 'G'." **Wahida Clark, Essence Bestselling Author of the Thugs series and Payback is a Mutha**

"Street Legends is what every hood novel aspires to be, the Realness. This is history in the making." **Kwame Teague, Bestselling Author of the Dutch Trilogy and The Adventures of Ghetto Sam**

"Many try to claim authenticity when it comes to knowledge of the game and what goes on in the streets, but few come close to reality. Street Legends captures a rare account of the other side of the law and it's more in-depth than a full season of BET's American Gangster." **Eyone Williams, Bestselling Author of Fast Lane**

"Seth Ferranti possesses the zeal of a strong investigative reporter with the street smarts of a hustler. Even though I've been writing about street crime for nearly a decade, I can always count on Seth to surprise me." **Ethan Brown, Bestselling Author of Queens Reigns Supreme: Fat Cat, 50 Cent and the Rise of the Hip-Hop Hustler**

"Seth provides a unique perspective of the gangster's creed from the Belly of the Beast. Few writers of any caliber can claim such firsthand access to men as feared and dangerous as those found in Street Legends." **Curtis Scoon, Producer of BET's American Gangster**

"Seth Ferranti's writing is informative, intense and extremely powerful. Street Legends is like riding shotgun with a hood icon." **Ben Osborne, Editor-in-Chief, Slam Magazine**

"Seth's stories are strong and they resonate with a sense of truth that needs to be expressed, especially dealing with the delicate topic of snitching. There is a profound difference between a witness who has no vested interest in criminal activity and a snitch who benefits greatly." **Kenneth "Supreme" McGriff, New York City Street Legend**

"Seth has earned the right to the title of Soul Man. He's been chosen from a higher authority to canopy the game in a digestible manner. Now those that seek understanding of the game will come to better understand the truth of their choices." **Walter "King Tut" Johnson, New York City Original Gangster**

"Seth Ferranti brings you the real and the raw of the streets live and direct from behind the wall. Street Legends is hood certified." **J.M. Benjamin, Author of Down in the Dirty and Ride or Die Chick**

"Street Legends chronicles the life, the legend and the lore of some of the biggest names in the history of the drug game. From Kenneth "Supreme" McGriff to George "Boy George" Rivera, Ferranti has left no stone unturned in his memoriam." **Elaine Watkins, www.urbanbooksource.com**

"Street Legends is a true epitome of street tales- that up-close, intriguing, naked excitement, untaught drama and unquestioned power- all that resides between these pages." **Terrell C. Wright, Author of Home of the Body Bags and 2 Live and Die in LA**

"The genre gets a boost of reality from author Seth "Soul Man" Ferranti in this all too real accounting of some of today's most notorious hood legends. Street Legends Vol. 1 strikes a chord with its intended readers." **O.O.S.A. Online Book Club**

"Seth Ferranti is a captivating, real, seasoned and experienced great writer. Seth is a criminal journalist who brings you the unadulterated certified stories of real life gangsters." **Kaywan from Flatbush, Original Gangster**

STREET LEGENDS

By Seth "Soul Man" Ferranti

ISBN 978-0-9800687-0-2

Printed in the United States of America

Second Printing: April 2010

Book Design by E-Moxie Data Solutions
www.e-moxie.com

Gorilla Convict Publications
WWW.GORILLACONVICT.COM

To order additional copies of Street Legends visit
WWW.GORILLACONVICT.COM

ISBN 978-0-9800687-0-2

ACKNOWLEDGMENTS

I'd like to thank and acknowledge all the following who have played a part, either minor or major, in the making of this book and the evolution of my writing career in general-

Don Diva, Feds, As Is, Street Elements, King, www.hoopshype.com, www.urbanbooksource.com, www.gorillaconvict.com, Slam, and all other publications that have published my writing.

My wife Diane, my parents and family, Kevin and Tiffany, Ben, Ethan, Wahida, Nikki, Kwame, Curtis, Sue, Elaine, Jorge, Eyone, Aisha, Lil Bob, Joe Black, Mike, Carole, Preme, Tuck, Bing, Tut, Fridge, Ant, Trouble, Najee, Gina, Panama, Rome, Prince, Pappy, Cat, Adee, AJ, the JBM, Boy George, Pistol Pete, Silk, Markell, Titi, Walt, Hameen, Cheesecake, Manny, Sop-Sop, Lop, Dee, Paco, Mark, Vincent, Johnny Oatmeal, Amin, Keith, Mushin, Ali, Mofid, Boobie, Donny, Skins, E, Trick, Vee, Black, Smooth, Dino, DJ, Thompson, Negro, Wise, Dread, De Aza, Big Pete, Roger, Jolisco, Dinero, Hot Rod, Esco, Killer, Bubba Sparks, Beeson, Will, Lou, Gerry, Manny, Gene, Rock, K, Twin and his brother, Stretch, Bobby, Big Reg, Henry Booker, Chavez, Big Hef, Mike Vargas, Big Jack, Khalial, Naim, Eric Milan, Perkins, Polo, Ron Jordan, Monkee, DJ, Matrix, Judge, Buck, Big Jay, Santana, Raheem, Outlaw, Parker, JB, Larry, Bucci, Dimitri, Max, Big Russia, The Magician, Gillie, Bizzel, Jeremy, Lima, Curt, Kaywan, Scott, Jason, John, Richardson, Pete, Al, Zack, Hurley, JM, Toni and O.O.S.A., Loko, Relentless, Caleb, Choke, Terry, June, Love, Billy, Dudley, Mr. Stern, Qawiy, Critter and anyone else I forgot.

This book is dedicated to the streets.

TABLE OF CONTENTS

FORWARD BY WAHIDA CLARK

Bumpy Johnson, Gotti, Al Capone, Luciano...they all chose a way of life that guaranteed fast money, power, respect and instilled fear. Their lifestyle included bloody murder, extortion, drugs, and was labeled 'organized crime,' so I'm told.

Supreme, Pistol Pete, Wayne Perry, Aaron Jones, Anthony Jones, Boy George Rivera...they too chose that same lifestyle and they added bling-bling, the 'ball until you fall' mentality and developed a player's code. When black men embrace the lifestyle its labeled 'black on black crime,' they tell me.

Everything we do we take it to another level. We can't help it. Whether we recognize it or not, being the best is divinely embedded in our genes. Whatever task we focus our minds on, be it golf, basketball, football, music, fashion, entrepreneurship, politics or hustling...we take it to the extreme.

Street Legends. According to the American Heritage dictionary, a legend is defined as *(1)* an unverified popular story, esp. one believed to be historical, *(2)* one of great fame or popular renown.

There are several *Street Legends* but only a small select few that lived by the code: Death Before Dishonor. Those are the true *Street Legends*. Study some other cultures of the world. They have men and women who will take their own lives before they dishonor themselves or their families.

In a country where the rich are getting richer and the poor are getting poorer, it is only natural for dissatisfaction to take root. The 100% dissatisfied will bring about a 100% change. Living in want and poverty is not an option when others around you are living large and in heaven, while telling you, you can't live in luxury until you die. Those days are long gone. We are no longer allowing ourselves to be hoodwinked or bamboozled. The black people of America are no longer buying into the fairy tale of getting the American Dream in the Hereafter. They want theirs here and now. There is no pie in the sky. When you combine an impoverished environment, desperation, a strong desire for success, a hungry and fearless hustling mentality, what you get is a, ruthless and oftentimes mean-spirited hustler.

Add the dope and crack. They both equal fast money. And fast money is addictive. Using fast money to provide for your loved ones, when before there were very little or no other options, is incentive enough to chance facing prison or death. And unfortunately once you're in the game, it's hard to get out.

Coming up in a dysfunctional family, where the father is more than likely absent from the home due to serving a prison sentence, a drug addiction or from simply being a dead beat dad; when a job is not cuttin' it or not even in the equation, some will either pick up a gun, or start slinging drugs. A stand-up person to the code has to step up to the plate and do what he has to do. And when you live by the code of the streets, you not only die by the code but you don't succumb to snitchin'. It sickens me to hear of men snitching on their grandmothers, mothers, baby mamas and their crew. If you can't do the time don't do the crime. I know women who stood up like I did and refused to snitch. Up until the day of my trial the government kept saying, "We want the girl! We want the girl!" I was the only female who stood trial on my case. They went from offering me 11 years to 3...providing that I would snitch. My husband, Yah Yah, taught me the code...Death Before Dishonor. So I ended up serving my 125 months sentence

We have to give respect to anyone who makes a conscious decision to face the fire and smile the same smile when they win that they smile when they lose.

Signing off,

Wahida Clark

The Queen of 'Thug Love' Fiction

INTRODUCTION

Now it's cool to be gangster and everybody in the rap game and hip-hop claims to be from the streets but if we talk about the real dudes, the legends of the streets, it's a given that they're either dead or in jail doing life. We have to look at these dudes as men who went all out and put their work in. They were real gangsters that lived by absolute rules. Rules of the drug game that were passed down from generation to generation. That's what they stood for and they rode it out to the end and took it all in stride like troopers. They are gangsters, they are what street legends are made of.

To live by a code, to embody that ideal, to be the real deal- that is death before dishonor. A lot of dudes talk about keeping it real and staying true to the game but when they get busted and snitch they say, "Charge it to the game." The drug game is fucked up, that's a fact. With Mandatory Minimums, the Federal Sentencing Guidelines and our government's War on Drugs snitching has become the norm. A man who sticks to his ideals is a rarity. A throwback to the past when principles, omerta and honor among thieves stood for something other than a rap video. This new "Stop Snitching" fad embraced by the hip-hop culture is all well and good but will it harken back to the times of old when men where men, gangsters kept their mouths shut and crossing your brother was obsolete?

Street Legends Volume 1, Death Before Dishonor featuring Kenneth "Supreme" McGriff, Wayne Perry, Anthony "AJ" Jones, Aaron Jones, Peter "The Pistol" Rollack and George "Boy George" Rivera, six of the most infamous and notorious gangsters of our times is the first in a new series of books by Gorilla Convict Publications. The criminal exploits and drug empires of these men who have been mythologized in countless hip-hop songs will be covered like never before. The lives, the territories, the crews, the M.O.'s- it will all be covered as the myths are examined and the legends explored.

Take a journey into a gangsta's paradise but realize the end result is always the same. Gangsta's don't live happily ever after. They die viciously or get served the big L, a life sentence in prison. The crimes range from running continual criminal enterprises to murder for hire to racketeering to execution style killings to large scale drug distribution and retail operations, which brought in millions of dollars. Basically, these men were running shit in their respective hoods or cities. They were not faking.

The fear, intimidation, respect and admiration they inspired was immediate and everlasting. They are the gunslingers of our times, the Billy the Kids, the Scarfaces, the Don Corelones. Their hoods remember them fondly with love in their hearts but also with apprehension because the reach of these legends is deadly and extends from the streets to the penitentiaries and back again. They lived by ideals and morals that went beyond their criminal exploits and even in the face of adversity they stood their ground and held true to the game that spawned them and to their beliefs even as those around them crumbled under the pressure of the law.

They always came correct and played by the rules with a gangster's mentality in the vicious and brutal drug game they courted. That's why Gorilla Convict has recognized these fallen soldiers with this expose. The Street Legends series will continue with more looks at the men and gangs from coast to coast that have inspired the myths that echo in hip-hop and popular culture. You've heard about the legends through your favorite rappers songs now read their true stories in the Gorilla Convict Publications Street Legends series starting with this book- Death Before Dishonor.

Title 21 § 848

§ 848 Continuing Criminal Enterprise

(a) Penalties; forfeitures

Any person who engages in a continual criminal enterprise shall be sentenced to a term of imprisonment which may not be less than 20 years and which may be up to life imprisonment.

(b) Life imprisonment for engaging in continuing criminal enterprise

Any person who engages in a continuing criminal enterprise shall be imprisoned for life and fined in accordance with subsection (a) of this section, if-

(1) such person is the principal administrator, organizer, or leader of the enterprise or is one of several such principal administrators, organizers, or leaders; and

(2) (B) the enterprise, or any other enterprise is which the defendant was the principal or one of several principals administrators, organizers, or leaders, received $10 million in gross receipts during any twelve-month period of its existence for the manufacture, importation or distribution of an illegal substance or narcotic.

(c) Continual criminal enterprise defined

(1) a violation which is a part of a continuing series of violations or ongoing conspiracy

(A) which are undertaken by such person in concert with five or more other persons with respect to whom such person occupies a position of organizer, as supervisory position, or any other position of management, and

(B) from which such person obtains substantial income or resources.

Chapter 1

Kenneth "Supreme" McGriff

KENNETH 'SUPREME' MCGRIFF

Supreme is a towering street legend immortalized in both hip-hop and hood lore. An infamous drug lord with ties to both major players in the rap industry and a notoriously profitable and ruthless drug crew, The Supreme Team, that ruled the same Queens streets that later produced platinum selling artists like Ja Rule and 50 Cent. To both law enforcement and a generation of rappers and hustlers, Supreme is a black John Gotti, a larger than life figure whose underworld reach seemed limitless. He was the only one of the renowned drug kingpins of the 80's to outlast the crack epidemic and law enforcement's pounding. But the feds finally got their man and *Queens Reigns Supreme* author Ethan Brown probably said it best, "By taking the storm and not flipping Preme secured his spot as one of the baddest guys ever to walk the streets of NYC."

Part 1- The Jump Off

Kenneth McGriff was born on September 19, 1960 in the southside of Jamaica, Queens. "He lived right across the street from the Baisley Projects," says Tuck, a former Supreme Team member and Queens native. "His pops was ex military, a strict disciplinarian. Preme grew up on Foch Boulevard and the Guy Brewer intersection in South Jamaica." An unremarkable area in the five boroughs of New York City at the time but an area that would go on to spawn some of the biggest crack lords in the city's drug lore.

"The brother Supreme grew up in the 60's and the 70's when guys in the life had a semblance of the principles," says T, a D.C. convict who befriended Supreme in prison. "He stays true to his word and always has. His whole family is square. All his brothers and sisters are professional people in their own lives." The future kingpin's beginnings were humble. He was raised in a blue-collar environment.

The working class neighborhoods of South Jamaica, St. Albans and Hollis where Supreme grew up lie in the 103rd precinct which is a 4.8 square mile imperfect box encompassing Van Wyck Expressway to the west, Hillside Avenue to the north, Francis Lewis Boulevard to the east and a jagged line that runs along the 110th Avenue to the south. Around 125,000 people live within its borders, 62 percent of them black. For all intents and purposes Supreme had a regular inner city childhood, coming of age in a two parent household. He didn't grow up in the projects but they were right next door. Both his parents were transit workers on New York's subway system. They worked hard to provide a better life for their children, who all attended school in New York City's public school system. Supreme was a talented student and an avid football player who was preparing for college, like any other ordinary kid coming of age in the 1970's.

But Supreme's future would be anything but ordinary.

His life was significantly altered when he discovered a new philosophy dictated by five percenter ideology. "God-Be and his brother recruited and organized us within the five percenter nation." Gerald "Prince" Miller, Supreme's nephew and future partner in crime said about their induction into the culture. "He been in that since he was 10," T says. The five percenters are a splinter group that broke away from the Nation of Islam in 1964 under Clarence 13X who was part of Mosque #7 under Malcolm X. Clarence 13X rejected the belief that NOI founder Wallace Fard was god. The five percent doctrine teaches that the black man is god and their women are earths. They believe that they are the chosen five percent of humanity, hence the name. They drop jewels and science, speak in cyphers and contend that 85 percent of the population lack knowledge and that 10 percent are devils, leaving the chosen five percent, which they claim.

"Supreme got his name in 1971 from his affiliation with the five percent nation," Lance Fuertado, another infamous Queens gangster said. The fiery teachings came slamming off the radio and boomboxes in the late 60's. It was hip-hop before hip-hop. The messages were delivered as a staccato street rap that mesmerized NY City youth and gave a name and a way of life to the young Kenneth McGriff who "doesn't smoke, drink or eat red meat," Tuck says in accordance with his beliefs. "You have a given name according to your characteristics." T says. "Supreme is his given name." And in five percenter doctrine, Supreme means the most high. But the five percenter affiliation led Preme to other vocations that would drastically affect his life. "What probably influenced him into the game was becoming a five percenter." T says.

"With most of them coming out of prison it had to influence his decisions." T concludes. The prison system was an important recruiting ground for the five percenter message and they actively recruited prisoners and ex-cons into their ranks. Five percenter imagery and lyrics have also taken their place in hip-hop. Rappers like Busta Rhymes, Wu-Tang Clan, Rakim, Nas and A Tribe Called Quest have all proscribed to the teachings and spread the message in their music and songs. "It really started with the five percenters, Preme and them were god bodies. That's like 1980. They wasn't selling drugs at that time. It was a religious thing." Bing, another Supreme Team member and hustler from the era says. "Peace God," was how five percenters greeted each other, earning Preme's crew that hung on Linden Boulevard the name Peace Gods. And out of all the Peace Gods, Supreme was the most promising. He was turning into a young proficient hustler with a whole crew behind him. "His whole crew were five percenters," T says and they would play a vicious part in the coming crack era that would engulf Queens and make headlines in New York's tabloid newspapers.

The role models for the young crew were guys on the street from the hood. The hustlers, the drug dealers, the players, the pimps, the stick-up kids and strong arm robbery specialists. By studying these guys Supreme picked up a lot. He started carrying himself like an older, more established hustler, emulating the guys he saw holding it down on the block. He studied the ghetto stars of his hood like Ronnie "Bumps" Bassett and acquired the swagger of a man on the hustle. Behind Supreme's two thousand dollar suits and crisp white shirts was a seriousness about hustling that made the youngster stand above his peers on the street, and the older dudes noticed and took Supreme under their wings. His charismatic smile, piercing green eyes, muscled physique and good looks gave him an image that certified him a hood star even before his time. As a youngster Supreme was becoming a larger than life figure and with his crew growing and backing him up with a fierceness born of the hood, rivals were aware that crossing Preme invited an attack from the much feared team, giving Preme Don Dada status in the streets of Southeast Queens. "Preme created an underground economy for us to thrive and flourish." Prince said. And as a young man Supreme transformed a group of local guys into a lucrative and brutal drug gang that served a legion of crack addicts in and around Baisley Projects. But first came Seven Crowns.

Part 2- Learning the Game

In Queens, the conflicting streets of private homes and grim city housing projects gave birth to another factor that proved pivotal in the young Supreme's life- The Seven Crowns. "Seven Crowns was a seventies thing," Bing says. "I was in Seven Crowns at the end. It was all on the southside, but different areas. It was all one gang. Everybody was in one gang before they started selling drugs. They had little gang fights but no major killings, little brawls, shit like that, regular shit, no gunplay. We came together against outsiders."

According to legend, Seven Crowns formed in the early 70's and started out selling marijuana and then graduated to cocaine. In 1979, the street gang split up, dividing up their turf into several territories and launching the careers of some of New York's largest urban drug dealers- including Lorenzo "Fat Cat" Nichols, Howard "Pappy" Mason, Tommy "Tony Montana" Mickens, The Corley Brothers, Pretty Tony, Supreme and his nephew Gerald "Prince" Miller. "We were a little street gang when we were younger." Lance Fuertado, Pretty Tony's brother said. "We grew up together. We lived on the same block. We knew each other since childhood. But we didn't carry guns. We believed in a beatdown." The future kingpins paid their dues, hustling, fighting, becoming men and learning about the life and the drug game from their elders.

"Niggas was always hustling. Before they were selling drugs they were robbing banks, burglarizing, shooting dice, sticking up dudes, gambling. Queens was always fly niggas, getting money niggas." Bing says. "That's how it started. I been knowing Preme since 79. I met him on the block. I was supposed to be in high school but I was hustling." Like the other Seven Crowns members

Preme gravitated toward the block, toward the action. The block was an area on 150th and 107th Avenue where all the hustlers congregated. "It was called the block, it's where niggas hustled at. It was turf of the Seven Crowns. Pretty Tony, Cat, the Corley brothers, Skinner, Danny, Early. Different muthafuckers would be down there selling drugs," Bing says. "Fat Cat had a store with a poolroom, it was a hangout spot. Preme was more with Fat Cat at the time. They were good friends. They were real close." Preme had an eye for success even then. By studying the older hustlers like Ronnie Bumps, who he guarded drugs and cash for at Southeast Queens stash houses and hanging with his mentor, Fat Cat, Supreme was learning the ropes of the game and laying the groundwork for his future empire. "At one time Cat and Preme were rivals," T says. "But a mutual friend between them both settled the rivalry and they became alright." Securing a bond that would last throughout the 80's.

"A lot of brothers and sisters didn't like the idea that we hustled because it was contrary to the lesson," Supreme Team member Knowledge said but the five percenter crew was now involved in drugs. Seven Crowns had split up and spawned the crews that would become legends. "Pappy Mason was with Fat Cat. Pappy's crew was the Bebos. Cat had 150th Street. Wall Corley had Forty projects and Supreme had Baisley Projects." Tuck says breaking it down. Supreme received his supply of coke and heroin from bigger dealers like Fat Cat. He became a meticulous organizer who formed strategic alliances and tended to use force coldly and carefully in order to preserve power. "Even as a kid Supreme was sharp enough to put things in place," T says. And the emergence of crack cocaine sparked a phenomenal crime wave in the 103rd district and nowhere did criminals more boldly seize upon the opportunities that the emergence of crack afforded to those willing to break the law than in the southside of Jamaica, Queens.

Part 3- The Come Up

The Supreme Team was a street gang organized in the early 1980's in the vicinity of the Baisley Park Houses in Jamaica, Queens, New York by a group of teenagers who were members of a quasi-religious sect known as the five percenters. Under the leadership of Kenneth "Supreme" McGriff, with Gerald "Prince" Miller his nephew, as second in command, the gang concentrated its criminal efforts on widespread distribution of crack cocaine, court records indicate. The Peace Gods became the Supreme Team. Under Supreme's direction they took control of Baisley Projects. Baisley Park Houses at Guy R. Brewer Boulevard and 116th Avenue in Jamaica was one of the largest public housing developments in Queens. The team sold small amounts of coke and heroin hand to hand on the street at first. They were hustling, getting money, coming up as they say. Emulating the older hustlers on the block and trying to get theirs. The first members of the crew called themselves the original seed and Preme was the first to see the benefits of merging Latinos and blacks into one unified crew.

"My uncle is an exceptional and natural born leader. Ever since I can remember Preme exemplified the qualities of a true gangsta with a capital G." Prince said. "He started the team like 83." Bing says. "A bunch of dudes that were five percenters started getting into the drug game on 150th Street and Sutphin Boulevard, Baisley was a hangout then." It was remembered as a good time by all. The come up before all the violence and before the crack epidemic. Bing remembers, "parties at the Rollerdome, Olympic Palace, Disco Fever, the Empire Rollar Skating Rink and Red Parrot. Kurtis Blow might come out and rap." And Preme was sponsoring sports programs for kids, helping community residents out when they were in financial troubles, funding turkey giveaways and bus trips for kids to amusement parks. "Preme is not the bad guy he is made out to be," said Teddy, another Supreme Team member. "He owned businesses before dudes were even thinking about it. He used to own a neighborhood store. He used to give away more food and diapers then he sold. People always hear the bad but the good is never mentioned." Preme supported the hip hop industry from day one too when they were nothing more then dudes spitting rhymes down on the block. "Preme used to book Run DMC, the Beastie Boys, LL Cool J." Russell Simmons said. "They would have big parties, every rapper played and he'd give every rapper one thousand dollars."

By 1985, the Supreme Team was on the rise. Their spots were bubbling and Preme would cruise Baisley Projects in a black Mercedes flashing the muzzles of high powered automatic weapons and waving thick wads of cash out the window. The violent crack trade was in full effect, from the impoverished sections of South Jamaica to predominantly middle-class sections like St. Albans and Springfield Gardens. And Preme had a piece of them all. The team was definitely rolling and Preme was the man on the streets of South Jamaica. "Supreme was held in a high standard. He was a major figure at the time," Bing says. "Everybody knew him everywhere he went. That's how well known he was. I was like a brother to him back then." Street legend has it that Preme once came upon a group of cops down in the projects surrounded by 50 or so members of the Supreme Team, who were hurling insults, bottles and trash at the frightened police officers. With just a word and a wave of his hand Supreme dispersed the mob, asked the officers if they were okay and had them escorted out of the projects safely. Supreme was the epitome of the classic gangster and a perfect gentleman to boot. Preme proved himself an able manager who knew how to work people and push their buttons. He was known as a charmer, quick to pass out wads of cash to those in need. He played the diplomat to his nephew's growing reputation as a shooter. "Preme was sharper than the average kid," T says. "He had grown up experiences. His life could have been a success story had not the first conviction came down." With Preme's growing notoriety it was only a matter of time before the police got the 411 on his activities.

"You had guys getting arrested, ending up right back on the streets," Bing says. "So they were giving info about us. One cabbie who got caught with guns supposedly gave up info on our whereabouts, certain cribs where we got guns, coke, money." Queens Narcotics division had a series of photographs that were tacked to a wall in their office with the words "Supreme Team" inscribed over them. Making Preme and his team prime targets. "They set up surveillance on us and got a no knock search warrant from the judge." Bing says. "Me and Preme got arrested in September 85 at an apartment in Cambry Heights. They confiscated guns, drugs, money, money counting machines, assault rifles, vests, counterfeit money, bulletproof shirts, jackets and coats." The official line differed slightly but still the end result was the same. The cops said the premises were used "to facilitate the sale, manufacture, transportation and distribution of a controlled substance."

The investigation started because a stash house at 155-47 116th Avenue was robbed of 80 grand of Supreme's money, Preme complained loudly in the streets of the robbery, letting it be known that he was unhappy and that the money should be returned due to his reputation but the wrong people heard about it and informed the cops. One informant told Sergeant Clyde Foster of Queens Narcotics of the robbery and of Preme's plans to head back to his base at 166-16 231st Street. With the addresses of the two stash locations, Sergeant Foster moved quickly. In the morning of September 10, 1985 Foster got warrants from Queens Criminal Court Judge Steven Fisher for both the 166-16 231st Street and 155-47 116th Avenue addresses. "I received info that allegedly a location at 231st Street and Linden Boulevard had been robbed of 80 grand and narcotics and this house belonged to Supreme," Foster told the judge who immediately signed the warrants.

"Be careful," the judge said noting that, "there's an excellent chance Supreme would be present in the apartment." When cops busted in 166-16 231st Street just after 9 p.m. on September 10, 1985 they found Supreme and his crew trying to dump coke into a sink and toilets. Eight pounds of heroin and coke were seized, over 35 grand in cash, several rifles, nine firearms and numerous packaging and cutting materials like scales and vials were found on the premises. Preme was arrested on the spot and the cops figured that they got their man and shut down the cutting and distribution operation in the process.

"In 1985, Preme had a state case. He got arrested in a house with drugs," Tuck says. "Bing was arrested with Preme on that case. They both got locked up." In Queens Court though, Preme's wizard of an attorney, Robert Simels, started working his magic. "He was sentenced to nine years to life," Tuck says. Preme was hit with drug and weapon charges by the city's special narcotics prosecutor. The sentence wasn't bad considering the harsh Rockefeller Drug Laws that New York had on the books. But the back end of life must have stung. Bing got sentenced to six years to life to accompany his man upstate. Just before they went to prison in 1985, Preme threw a birthday party for his nephew Prince. Preme also handed over a prime drug-dealing spot to his nephew and gave control of the team to Prince. Some members of the team didn't like Prince's ascension though and outrage grew when Prince put together a security team to make sure he stayed in power while Preme was in prison. He figured it was his right, Preme being his uncle and all. It was evident to everyone on the team and in South Jamaica that Prince was the heir apparent.

And 22 months later Supreme's attorney worked some more magic. He got the appeals court to throw out the conviction on a technicality involving the search warrants. Preme got his conviction overturned and got out after only doing 22 months. "He only served 22 months because an appeals court threw out the conviction." Tuck says. And just like that Supreme was back on the streets. "I went to jail in 85 with Preme. We ended up beating the case on appeal." Bing says. "We were selling heroin and coke first then we started selling crack. That shit was big." And the Supreme Team was big also. Growing in stature and notoriety, they surpassed Preme's and everyone else's expectations.

Part 4- Back on the street

Just before Preme was released from prison in August 1987 an informant told Queens Narcotics officer William Tartaglia that the jailed Supreme Team leader had been busily preparing the crew for his return. "He wanted to make sure all the members and various locations had their money ready," the informant told Tartaglia. According to the informant, each Supreme Team member was instructed by Preme to save a chunk of their profits for him. The burgeoning crack era, birthed at the same time as hip-hop in the mid 80's, created an opportunity for a serious come up for those with the know how, daring, muscle and brains to organize and get it. We're not talking chump change. There was big money to be made and Supreme made it. When he hit the streets in late August 87 he held a formal meeting with the Supreme Team at Baisley Projects outlining his goals and plans for the crew. He used the occasion to take a detailed inventory of the crew's resources. He wanted to meet new members and to know what type of guns, drug amounts, connects, money and locations they had. He also wanted to know what muscle and bodyguards the crew had. With 25 ranking members present he instructed them to lock shit down and get back all their spots. Preme wasn't playing. He had missed the streets and all they had to offer while in prison and he was ready to get his. He wanted to reassert his dominance over the team and Prince who had Queens in check with his shoot first mentality. "Prince was about that gun smoke," Bing says. "He didn't play."

The killings by Prince and other drug dealers like Fat Cat and Pappy Mason had driven the homicide rates in the Jamaica, Queens area to unprecedented heights and sparked the formation of TNT, the Tactical Narcotics Team, a co-ordinated city wide, multi-agency approach that covered the l03rd, 105th, 106th and ll3th precincts- 22 miles of Southeastern Queens. But the murder that would bring it all down and thrust the Queens dealers into infamy had yet to happen. Preme was sitting in the eye of the storm but at the time there was no way for him to know that.

"In 87, he came home on an appeal bond. He was home for two months and made like half a million." Tuck says. Under the red-brick towers of Baisley Projects an around the clock crack cocaine trade that operated more like a corporation than a drug outfit prospered, selling 25,000 crack vials a week and earning $200,000 a day at its 1987 peak. The Supreme Team controlled everything in Jamaica, from Liberty Avenue and 171, to Sutphin Boulevard, from 121 to Linden, which is ten blocks. It was crazy. The Supreme Team had shit on lock. And it was all orchestrated by Supreme. "When you see New Jack City it was just like that," Tuck says and once you crossed the tracks into the Baisley Projects it was a war zone. The Supreme Team patrolled the street in bulletproof luxury cars, used rooftop sentinels with two way radios to thwart police and issued instruction manuals on criminal activity to members. They would buy drugs from anyone willing to sell- Colombians, Dominicans or Americans. They were known for killing informants and murder, chaos and mayhem were a part of the era. Crack cocaine, dirty money and body counts defined the decade as crack exploded onto the scene.

At one point Supreme decided to sponsor a summer basketball tournament. The players knew the tournament by its proper name- Supreme's Nite International Fastbreak Festival. Cocaine dealers knew it by its acronym-

SNIFF. On July 30, 1987, Gregory Vaughn, a 33-year-old gym teacher at PS15 and former coach at Medgar Evans college refereed a Supreme league game at Baisley Pond Park. The teams were playing for $50,000 in prize money and crew members had bet even more. Vaughn, who was married to a cop and had a reputation for getting kids off the streets and into schools, made a controversial call at the end of the game. As fans watched he was beaten to death by a dude alleged to be a Supreme Team member, who jumped from the stands. The SNIFF tournament was disbanded.

By the fall of 87, the feds were working with Queens Narcotics in their investigations of the crew. They were frustrated that Preme had beat the 85 case and were determined to take him down. This time for good. All the major players of the Supreme Team were being watched and on November 6, 1987 a massive raid was conducted by FBI agents and Queens Narcotics cops on the Supreme Team's headquarters, Baisley Projects. When informed of the raid Preme told his crew to dump or move the coke. Some of it was moved but most was tossed out the windows or flushed down toilets. Locals said it was raining cocaine that day at Baisley Projects and the fiends were in their glory. The raid squad found heroin, coke, scales, measures, police scanners, walkie talkies, Supreme Team jackets and books with titles like *Methods of Disguise*, *The Silencer Handbook*, *Point Blank Body Armor* and *Improved Sabotage Devices*. This showed authorities how serious the team was.

The feds got Preme and nearly all his top people. Drug plagued Baisley Park Houses was free and clean, or so the authorities thought. "The feds came in and said they were tipped off. They got him in 87. They charged Supreme with CCE." Tuck says. "He copped out to 12 years. No co-defendants. The feds just wanted him." Supreme pled guilty before U.S. Judge Thomas C. Platt in the Eastern District of New York of engaging in a continual criminal enterprise, the kingpin statute. For all the hype that marked the Supreme Team's reign in Southeast Queens, Preme left the streets quietly in 1987. Mike McGuiness of Queens Narcotics simply rolled up on Preme at the corner of Foch Boulevard and Gabreaux Street in South Jamaica and arrested him. Preme admitted to being the organizer, supervisor and manager of the Supreme Team under his plea and went to federal prison. Preme broke the series of arrests and convictions down, "In 1985 NYPD Task Force executed a warrant for a house we had. I was arrested and sentenced to 9 years to life. My legal team got it overturned in 20 months on the premise that the warrant was bad. When I came home the feds promptly picked the case up. This was a pivotal point for me because I just beat the same exact charges in the state. I was adamant about proceeding to trial, but upon consultation with some O.G.'s I met in MCC I conceded to the situation. They advised me it would be prudent to relent and satisfy the government's thirst for blood than to engage in a drawn out battle with no assurances. I was sentenced to 12 years for running a continuing criminal enterprise." And the hood legend from the Southside Jamaica, Queens was off the streets.

"Supreme was the originator of the team. He brought it into existence." Tuck says, and his legacy remained. "I remember the name Supreme as someone who was highly spoken of. I don't know if it was out of fear or respect, but usually when people spoke that name they were speaking of something greater than themselves." Preme's CCE charge and kingpin status conferred by the feds immortalized him in the eyes of Queens's urban youth. In the hierarchy of the crack trade, the life Supreme had lived up to that point, was the stuff of Mafioso legends. As Supreme did his time, his name was still ringing bells in the streets, as the team he founded became a military-style organization under Prince that dominated its turf through intimidation and terror. As the Supreme Team ran wild under Prince, Preme's notoriety grew to heights unimagined. With hitman killings, one million dollar bails, drug related shootings and witnesses being shot, the much feared and tightly run crew of the convicted kingpin Supreme, turned into a violent and deadly gang capable of almost anything. Putting fear into the hearts of the whole Southside- gangsters, hustlers, police and citizens alike. And a common saying among team members was, "Word to Preme."

Part 5- The Legend

To understand the legend of Supreme you have to understand the man. For a criminal legend he is shorter and slighter than expected. He has pale green eyes which he says are a result of his "Irish blood," a cool professional air and an easy smile. He keeps his watch 55 minutes fast so he'll "always be on time" and thinks all the attention given to him "is unwarranted." The man is full of charisma and generally likes his fellow human beings. He is very humble and diplomatic. "Preme is a dude who will rationalize. Talk it out." Tuck says. "He's very intellectual and culturally conscious. Not bias or racial." A gentleman gangster who upholds the virtues of honor, integrity and loyalty. "He's not flamboyant and he's highly intelligent, ain't nothing slow about him." T says. Ethan Brown was amazed at Supreme's intelligence and depth, "He's incredibly intelligent and aware of what is going on in the world." He says.

"I been doing time for 30 years in the adult system," says Choke, another friend of Supreme. "And most dudes I meet that be high profile try to act like they like that. They look down on people. But Preme don't. He respect men. He's a respectful dude." Tuck agrees, "His reputation in prison is impeccable. He gets along with everyone, all different nationalities and geographical locations embrace him. He's respected among his peers and staff alike." T also concurs, "Supreme is respected because whatever he's gonna do, he's gonna do it 150 percent. He's competitive, athletic and always trying to win. He's always looking for your best game, be it basketball, casino, ping pong, handball or chess." But not a lot of dudes know Supreme.

"He don't fuck with a lot of dudes but at the same time he's very open to what other people have to say," T says. "There might be three guys who really know what he's about." That's the drawbacks of being a gangster celebrity and make no doubt about it, in prison and on the street that's what Supreme is. "I was in a cell with Preme," Tuck says. "He was my cellie so we kicked it a lot. I got to know him more so than on the street." About his tendencies Tuck says, "He might be playing cards and dude might get the better of him. Preme hates to lose but he doesn't lose his shit. He channels his anger. He's a thinker." Choke has fond memories also, "He always told me, 'You can learn a lot from a dummy.' He's a stand up dude. Straight forward. He values nothing but friendship, loyalty and respect. He got a platinum heart. Everybody like him. He's a people person."

Supreme passed his time in prison reading Donald Goines books. *Crime Partners, Black Gangster, Street Player, Inner City Hoodlum*- Preme read them all.

Goines was a Detroit hustler, one-time junkie and ex-con who wrote 16 books before he was murdered in 1974. His street tales mesmerized Preme and gave him a vision. He dreamed of turning the Goines novels- which were so popular in the feds- into big screen gangster epics like the Godfather. Since hip-hop in the post NWA/Chronic era mimicked the hood star qualities of Goines novels, Preme believed there'd be a substantial mainstream audience for a Goines movie, especially if a couple of big time rappers acted in the movie and contributed to the soundtrack.

"I met Supreme while we were incarcerated." Wayne Davis, a Harlem native said. "We were talkin' about what we were gonna do when we got home and he told me he wanted to bring Donald Goines to the movie screen. At that time I looked at him like he was crazy." But Supreme wasn't crazy, just maybe a little before his time. He had a vision but things in the streets of Southeast Queens were heating up and even though he was in prison there was an organization, his organization, to run. At its 1987 peak, the Supreme Team receipts exceeded $200,000 a day and the gang regularly committed acts of violence and murder to maintain its stronghold on the area's drug trade. After McGriff went to jail in 1987, leadership of the Supreme Team was assumed by Miller, court records indicate. Miller solidified his control by increasing the security force and employing it against rivals and against team members suspected of disloyalty. Supreme was the titular leader and during 1987 alone, Miller and the then incarcerated McGriff ordered at least eight homicides. The police also linked the Supreme Team to more than 20 murders and countless shootings. They were not playing. A quadruple murder where four Colombians were beaten to death, hogtied and sealed in garbage bags was attributed to the team, but never proven in court.

The Supreme Team narcotics operation used dozens of employees, including layers of drug sellers to insulate the gang's leaders from street level activity. Team members communicated in coded language and numerical systems. To thwart law enforcement efforts further, Miller used armed bodyguards and rooftop sentinels. The sophistication of the gang's operation enabled it to survive periodic targeting of various members for prosecution by the NYPD and the Queens County District Attorney's Office. The much-publicized killing of police officer Edward Bryne by Pappy Mason's crew changed everything; the police mobilized and were out for revenge. Prompted by the February 26, 1988 murder, 113 additional officers were deployed to fight drugs in Queens. By targeting the area bounded by 110th Avenue on the north, Sutphin Boulevard on the west, Merrick Boulevard on the east and Baisley Boulevard on the south, the TNT task force waged war on the Supreme Team and other area dealers and won a brutal victory against the drug barons.

"In 89, Preme was in FCI Talladega," Bing says. "Black Just was in charge of the family because Prince was in Rikers fighting a murder beef. Black Just used to go see Preme." The streets were never far away from Preme's grasp but the feds had no way to tie him in. It was alleged that he ordered hits from his jail cell but with no proof the feds couldn't indict. The upper echelon of his crew was snitch free so the feds couldn't get anyone to testify against him, so they went with what they had, Prince as top man. Bing was back and working too. "He came home in 89 and got down with us." Tuck says. "He had 121 and Sutphin. That shit was booming too." But Baisley Projects was where the main action was.

"The media try to portray like we had the projects hostage but it wasn't like that," Tuck says. "But it was headquarters. Five buildings, eight floors in each building. Baisley Projects, that's where I hustled at." The Supreme Team was retrofitted to 80's excess and significantly raised the stakes in the process. They were the new age hustlers and gangsters that the rappers in the growing hip-hop world emulated. In court, it was Leslie Caldwell that finally brought the gang down. Leslie was an Assistant U.S. Attorney in Brooklyn with just two years experience on the job. The cops loved Leslie, she wasn't afraid of anyone. To her, a criminal was a criminal. Leslie succeeded in shutting down and getting murder convictions for most of the heavies- Fat Cat, Pappy, Prince, the notorious killers who terrorized their communities and those responsible for killing the police officer. "We were very aggressive with them including arresting their mothers who were intimately involved in their drug operations," Caldwell explained. There was one key exclusion to the Supreme Team convictions, the gang's mastermind, Preme, an exception that would come back to haunt hip-hop in the Y2K era.

In early 93, the Supreme Team trial began. Prince and his crew were indicted on 14 counts, including nine murders and cocaine distribution charges. Tuck remembers the trial he was a defendant at, "Preme was released from his twelve year federal sentence around February 93, so he was home when our trial began. Our trial lasted exactly two months. During the testimony of one of the defense witnesses, Preme was sitting in the audience with a dude I grew up with. While the prosecutor was cross-examining the witness she shocked the whole courtroom by turning around and pointing to Preme (in the audience) and saying, 'Isn't that Supreme right there, sitting with the sunglasses on? Isn't he the founder and leader of the Supreme Team?' Of course the witness denied knowing anything about him being the leader of anything." About the trial T recalls Supreme telling him, "He said, 'I wasn't sharp enough at the time to say, I'm Supreme. I'm not on trial.'" But the accusation ran deep. The cop killing from Fat Cat and Pappy Mason's crew was brought up again but like Tuck says, "Pappy wasn't with us." And he wasn't with Supreme, but the negative aspects of the murder lingered. Over 110 Supreme Team members were arrested and convicted in the late 80's and early 90's to satisfy the government's bloodlust. Supreme escaped the 80's with a relatively light 12 year sentence and was paroled back to the streets. But with all his peers doing life sentences Preme was a prime target for law enforcement. He was associated with the cold blooded cop killing even if he wasn't guilty of it and the FBI, DEA, ATF, NYPD and IRS were all dying to get a piece of him. But the reality was like Preme said, "I was dead broke. Everybody from the original Supreme Team was home waiting like, 'Supreme whatever you say.' And I'm like good luck on y'all venture. I wanted to be able to walk on the street or go to the club by myself and not have security. I just wanted to be a regular person." But it wasn't like that and it would never be in Supreme's case.

Part 6- The Rebound

Preme was back on the street and realizing that everybody in the drug game either ended up in jail or dead so he decided to make a run at legitimacy. "In the 80's when he seen so many thousands of young guys that grew up similar to him that were never getting out he decided to do legitimate stuff," T says. "His first venture, Picture Perfect was selling bathing suit shots of women to prisoners, with his sister he also started a hair salon." After doing eight years of a twelve-year sentence, Preme was ready to do something different. But he was also intrigued by the burgeoning rap industry. He saw a little of himself in guys like Suge Knight, J. Prince and Jimmy Henchman that were building companies and careers of their own in the hip-hop world. Preme figured with his street rep he could get into a position with somebody in the entertainment world to make his dreams of a Goines movie come true, but it wasn't all smooth sailing.

"He was going back and forth on violations," Tuck says. "Out in 93, back in 95. At MDC in 95 he came to my floor. I laid him out. Gave him whatever. He had another violation and was back out in 97. He did time at McKean, Talladega, Allenwood and one of those joints in Florida." At one point in a *Don Diva* magazine interview Preme explained his origins, "It's a basic background, you know, I came outta the hood, an area called Baisley Projects in Queens. I was in the street for a little while before I got locked up. I did two years in the state and then I went to federal prison to finish my time. I served eight years." And explaining his vision for the Donald Goines books he said, "I was always good with reading, but Donald Goines reintroduced me to reading. Each of Donald's books captivated me, it was like I was in a dark alley or I was in the back room and I could see the blood dripping. That's when I decided that if I ever got the chance, I would do it. I would make the movie. I've read all of Donald's books and there is no comparison." And when that chance presented itself Supreme grabbed it just like he said he would.

Preme was stuck in a halfway house in Queens dreaming of making it in Hollywood. He knew he could go legit. He knew he had a bankable vision. He just needed to make the right connections because it wasn't who you were it was who you knew, and one day when he was standing outside a bodega in his old territory of Southeast Queens on Guy Brewer Boulevard an up and coming young producer called DJ Irv was doing a video for Cash Money Clicks single, *Get the Fortune*. "Preme comes out on the block and BJ, who is a good friend of ours says, 'Preme is here, he wants to meet you.'" Irv said. Irv who longed for the street credibility of a hustler like Supreme readily agreed to the introduction to the South Jamaica hustling icon. His initial impression was not what he imagined. "My first response to seeing Preme was shock." Irv explained. "This was the notorious Supreme? This guy was like five-foot-two, this little guy, this little green eyed motherfucker. So my first response was 'Wow, this is the guy everyone is talking about?'" Responding to this Preme said, "People always say that when they meet me. They think I'm gonna be 6-foot-8, 250 lbs." After the introduction Irv immediately called his brother.

"I get a call from my brother like, 'Yo, I just met Supreme.'" Chris Gotti said. "And I'm like 'Supreme, Supreme?'. And he says, 'Yeah, Supreme.'" To Irv it was an opportunity to hang with a real live gangsta but to Preme it was an opportunity to pitch his dream project to a person with connections in the hip-hop world. "I took a liking to him instantly," Preme said of Irv Gotti. And why not, Preme was coming out of the joint and Irv was an up and coming impresario in the rap industry. "He seen me shooting the video and he said, 'Hey, I got this movie idea,'" Irv remembered. "He had a dream about doing movies. He wanted to do something with Donald Goines, because when he was locked up Goines was his favorite novelist. He felt Goines movies was gonna be big with the urban world." Irv wanted to help out. The unexpected introduction was a minor but important step for the former drug dealer to realize his quest to go legitimate. Preme made his first real connection in the music biz and with hip-hop straining for street credibility, more like DJ Irv were sure to follow. Because Preme had street credibility to spare and he figured his future was made if he could stay out of the streets. But the easy money of the drug game would always be a big temptation for him.

Part 7- Respect

"We were the trendsetters, the rappers emulated what we did," Lance Fuertado said and he was right. The emerging hip-hop scene owed a deep debt to the streets. Their icons were hood stars not entertainment figures. Preme was a legend and he played the part perfectly. To the feds Supreme was public enemy #1, but to hip-hop artists he personified what it meant to be gangsta. His way of life was a motif for their songs and to a new generation of rappers and producers he was a true ghetto star. Thus Irv's fascination. Irv Gotti was born in Hollis, Queens in 1971 and became a minor star in Queens as a DJ and talent scout. Before he met Supreme, he was DJ Irv but shortly afterward, he rechristened himself Irv Gotti, in admiration of the Gambino family crime boss and formed Murder Inc., the world's most dangerous record label in homage to the Depression-era crime syndicate. Lyor Cohen of Def Jam took Gotti and Murder Inc. under his wing and in appreciation Gotti dubbed Cohen, Lanksy, as in Meyer Lanksy, the mobster who led Murder Inc. and ordered the killing of Bugsy Siegal. In Irv's mind it must have all been falling in place. He was riding shotgun with a hood legend.

Irv Gotti promoted and produced music that turned thuglife into a multi-million dollar business that set trends in popular culture for youths across America, plus he had Queens' most notorious gangster, Supreme by his side. Supreme partied nightly at NY clubs with the Gotti brothers. "Those are my brothers." Preme said. "We are family." It seemed Preme was living the high life depicted in Murder Inc. videos but according to Chris Gotti, "Some people think he had money stashed from back in the day but this guy was broke." Still with Irv Gotti he was making contacts and getting closer to realizing his goals of making a movie. But it was hard when he still had one foot in the streets.

"Supreme always said 'I'm not famous, I'm infamous.'" Tucks says. "Loved by many, hated by some but respected by all." And it was true. In the rap industry Preme was networking, meeting all kinds of people even Tupac before he got killed. "He got with several of the dudes that had the conflict with Tupac when he got shot and ironed out that situation." T says of Preme. "This led to an organization where Supreme was involved with Tupac in organizing a clean up program to clean up the community. Then Preme went back to jail on a violation and Tupac got killed. He would of been able to mediate the situation with Tupac just out of the respect he got."

Street credibility was no small factor in CD sales in the gangsta rap market and Irv Gotti gained credibility on the streets with Supreme at his side. "A lot of dudes getting legitimate money wanna touch gangsterism but when it comes time to help somebody realize their dreams they back off," T says. "Irv

Gotti didn't. He tried to help someone who was through with the life." And Gotti described himself as a loyal friend who did nothing more then help the financially strapped ex-con go straight. "Supreme said Irv was basically a very good friend. A dude that was willing to give him a chance." T says.

"That's my man," Irv said of Preme. "He knows my mother. My whole family. He was at my wedding." And when other rap industry figures saw the gangster hanging with Irv they were stunned. "I saw Supreme at Irv's wedding and I was shocked," Russell Simmons said. "I hadn't seen Preme in 15 years. I didn't recognize him. You mean Supreme from Jamaica? How? Why?" But Irv was undeterred. The promising mogul who got $3 million from Def Jam in 1999 as an advance wasn't hurting so he spread the love. "I run with real dudes and these guys are my friends," Irv said. With platinum albums and glitzy videos he and his artists Ja Rule and Ashanti became magazine cover stories and MTV staples. And he brought Supreme into this world with him from Queens to Hollywood. Supreme was living the life from the bullet-ridden streets of Southside Jamaica to the highest echelons of the music and movie industries.

"Anybody that succumbs to hip-hop or thuglife would actually like or want to be associated with somebody like Supreme because he was a real gangsta who did real time." T says. With Gotti's patronage Supreme made legitimate strides in the rap industry. He was an aspiring scriptwriter and film producer who took his Donald Goines vision and ran with it. He had a dream of producing movies and music. He saw himself succeeding in the entertainment world just as he had in the drug world. "He knew for the most part it ain't a black or white thing," T says. "It's a rich or poor thing." And with Murder Inc. in his corner Supreme hoped to make his name with the movie. The first project he did was with Chaz "Slim" Williams and Black Hand Entertainment. Preme optioned the rights from Hollaway House, the publisher, through his company Picture Perfect, to *Black Gangster* and *Crime Partners*. "He was passionate about making the film." Bentley Morris, the LA publisher who sold Preme the film rights for 135 grand said. Chaz and Preme set out to make the soundtrack to the first movie. The *Black Gangster* soundtrack was made at Black Hand headquarters on 139th Street in South Jamaica with Jay Z, DMX,

Ja Rule and 50 cent. Because *Black Gangster* was to be released independently Chaz was free to stick with the novel centered marketing scheme he and Preme came up with. *Black Gangster* would be sold not as a soundtrack but a concept album "based on the novel by America's #1 selling black author Donald Goines." This was a stride toward legitimacy but Supreme was still fucking around on the streets.

Part 8- The Struggle

Preme was coming up, striving to make it, but it was a struggle. He was trying to go straight in the music and movie business but when money was tight he still turned to what he knew best- hustling. Behind the scenes he was reviving his violent drug dealing career, authorities alleged. The *Black Gangster* album was a success selling over 150,000 copies but there was no interest from Hollywood for the movie so Preme decided to do another Goines title, *Crime Partners* and instead of Black Hand, he enlisted Murder Inc. as a partner. Irv Gotti went to Universal Music Group and told them, "Here's a guy getting out of a life of crime, can you help?" And Preme landed his *Crime Partners* soundtrack distribution deal for $1 million, $500,000 of which was paid upfront. Preme brought in his sister, Wayne Davis and John "Love" Ragin to be his partners to produce the film through Picture Perfect Entertainment. With Irv's help he got Snoop Dog and Ice-T to star in the movie. "It took 16 years," Wayne Davis said. "But he kept the same passion and the same commitment about his thing up until the year 2001 and when we got back together in the world we made it happen." It all looked good. Maybe too good. "Shit was good. He was going legit." Bing says of Preme's hookup with Murder Inc. "I was glad to see that. He was with a legitimate organization that was making millions of dollars. That was like hitting the lotto. Especially, how they looked up to him like they did." Supreme was flying high like a Trans Atlantic concord, but he was about to experience some turbulence.

In 1999, in an argument in Queens, Supreme's man Black Just was shot. Guns were pulled and allegedly Supreme's gun jammed and Black Just was shot by a wanna-be rapper that went by E-Money Bags. Preme rushed Black Just to the hospital in an SUV registered to his partner in the *Crime Partner* venture, Love's Tuxedo Rentals. Of the event it came out later in court that Supreme said, "I pulled a gun. It jammed. I ditched it at the scene and drove Blacky to the hospital." But it was too late. Black Just died at the Southeast Queens Hospital. Preme hoped to get through this situation but the streets were talking. When a street legend is involved in an altercation the buzz just reverberates. At around the same time Preme started working on the *Crime Partners* movie. So it was a trying experience. But Preme trudged on. There was no point in looking back. He bought the rights to four more Goines titles- *Black Girl Lost, Death List, Kenyatta's Revenge* and *Kenyatta's Last Hit-* with the money from the Def Jam deal. He envisioned a series of movies based on the Goines books and he was ready to see his vision through. But with the streets talking about Black Just's death and Supreme's name ringing the feds got involved.

"The first thing the feds say is that it's drug money," DJ, a friend of Preme says. "Everything he did when he came back to the streets was legal but still the feds say its drug money." And Supreme's lawyer had a similar defense. He said his client worked hard to make a legitimate life for himself in the entertainment world when he left prison and was unfairly targeted by investigators hell-bent to find criminal activity in the rap world. "Success would of been assured without interference from the feds," T says, but it wasn't to be. Even Preme said how "every rap related crime, they bring my name up." To make matters worse his partner Love got caught up in illegal activities involving his tuxedo rental service and other business fronts, for his credit card fraud and ecstasy-dealing ring. So whatever Preme was doing, legal or illegal, the spotlight was on him because of his associations. Due to his past, he was under a microscope.

The murder of Black Just and Love's credit card schemes cast a cloud of suspicion over the *Crime Partners* production but the worst was still to come. At the same time this was all happening a kid named Curtis Jackson from Queens took the moniker 50 Cent from a dead stick-up kid out of Brooklyn and started releasing a series of underground mixtapes including 2000's *Guess Who's Back*, which featured *Ghetto Qu'ran* and the following lyrics- *When you hear talk of the southside/you hear talk of the team/see niggas feared Prince and respected*

Preme/for all you slow muthafuckers I'm gonna break it down iller/see Preme was the businessman and Prince was the killer. This wasn't the first time the team had been celebrated in songs but the lyrics about Preme in his bulletproof BMW that reeled out a roll call of Supreme Team members like Black Just was the last thing Preme needed as he tried to pull it all together and go legit. And with 50 Cent's ode, authorities had reason to believe Preme was back underground up to his old tricks with his life imitating his art.

"It was good that he paid homage to us for who we were and what we did," Bing says of the verses. "But I felt different about it when I first heard that shit. It is what it is." Preme's legacy was now aired to the world and right at the most inappropriate time. The storied street dude was getting out of the life but the lines between hustling and hip-hop had blurred casting suspicion on his ventures. But 50 wasn't the first to rap about Preme. In Nas's *Memory Lane* on 1994's *Illmatic* he rhymes- *Some fiends scream about Supreme Team/a Jamaica Queens's thing.* And it wouldn't be the last as Murder Inc.'s Ja Rule joined the fray with his intro on the *Survival of the Illest* CD- *Funds unlimited/backed by Preme team crime representatives.* That was something that the feds would eventually pick up on. It seemed the rap lyrics struck a cord with law enforcement officials. While many of the figures heralded in hip-hop lyrics were either dead or in prison, Supreme was in the streets-a real live gangster. He was both a figure in raps lyrical lore and an upcoming hip-hop movie-maker. "Preme is a legend. He's proven and he's not a rat," Tuck says. "That fact alone in this day and time says a lot. Stand up men are no longer the rule they are the exception to the rule." The rappers 50 and Ja Rule's status was less clear, as they started beefing about a world that Supreme had known far better than either of them. "The Ja Rule/50 Cent beef was partly because Supreme spoke up for Ja Rule and 50 Cent took this as a rejection of him," T says. "Supreme thinks 50 cent is an angry young man that been venting, and his venting could be construed as ungangsta, because real men don't put stuff out in the public that could bring about an investigation." Adds T, "Supreme looks at 50 like he's confused. If half the things that are said about 50 and Preme are true than 50 needs to send half his loot to Supreme."

In the streets, it was also rumored that Supreme had something to do with

50 Cent's mother's death. Sabrina Jackson allegedly was a Supreme Team member who got strung out on crack and fucked up some of Preme's money. She was found dead in her apartment. Somebody had put something in her drink and turned the gas on. Her body wasn't found until four days later. In the streets it was seen as a message- Don't fuck with Supreme's money or product. "That's some bullshit." T says. "That's just something that got picked up on. Supreme couldn't even tell you what she looked like. She didn't have anything to do with the Supreme Team." But as rumors swirled and 50 Cent caught wind of them after he'd grown up he went on the offensive escalating the beef with Ja Rule and Murder Inc. He must have figured fuck Supreme, if he's not with me, he's against me. And that's how it played out. "I try not to entertain what spills out of his mouth," Preme said referring to 50. "Because I don't wish to engage in a war of words. I'm not at war with him nor did I ever have a beef with him. I never knew his mother. I knew of her and from what I know she was cool people."

A couple of physical confrontations that turned violent ensued. One at an Atlanta club that resulted in Ja Rule's chain being snatched and another at a Manhattan recording studio where Murder Inc. cronies assaulted 50. These confrontations fueled the beef and it was suggested by police that the *Ghetto Qu'ran* rap caused bad blood between 50 Cent and Supreme. "Men that have been in the life you just don't put their business on wax." T says. "Preme showing love to Murder Inc. ostracized him from their counterparts." But in reality T relates that, "Supreme never gave 50 Cent any thought because barking dogs don't bite and 50 never been in the life. He's a perpetrator to the death of the game."

50 Cent built his career on the feud though. He called Murder Inc. out for what they were, making references to their menacing acquaintances in magazine articles and in verse. His pre-superstar hit *Wanksta* was a thinly veiled attack calling Ja Rule a fake gangsta wannabe, perpetrating a tough guy image. And in a battle rap 50 gave his take on Irv Gotti- *Don't nobody respect you nigga/you Preme's son nigga/muthafucker been getting extorted since day one.* The feds took this to mean that Murder Inc. was bankrolled by Supreme. They listened to 50's lyrics like they would a wiretap. 50 Cent said the song *Ghetto Qu'ran*

was a memorial to the street legends he grew up idolizing but *The Source* magazine took an anti-50 Cent stance and labeled him a snitch. Supreme even said as much, "When we was coming up there was a code of conduct. You didn't speak about dudes who may still be in the streets."

And the truth of the whole matter was that Supreme was trying to squash the beef between 50 and Murder Inc. "I sat down with 50 and said, 'Listen man, this is nonsense.' But 50 loves to keep things going. He would say 'Yeah, all right Supreme, I respect you man' and then turn around and go totally contrary to what we talked about." And about Preme and the beef T says, "He's a very diplomatic individual who feels that violence is an option that can't be afforded. I think he feels if a situation can get to the point of physical violence and he knows both parties he would feel obligated to find a peaceful situation." And Supreme did just that as 50 cent pointed out, talking about the Murder Inc. beef, "I had a conversation with an older god body that was holding them down. He was like yo, leave this little nigga alone. You know they pussy but this is my food. I was like okay." And the god body 50 Cent was referring to was Supreme. "I was intervening to squash the issue because I thought it was meatball. I think he said Ja Rule didn't say hi or something. Plus security can't stop a real beef." Supreme said of the situation. But it all came to a head.

On May 24, 2000, as 50 and a friend sat in a car outside his grandmother's house on 161st Street in South Jamaica a gunman rolled up in a vehicle on his left side and pumped nine shots into his body, hitting him in the hand, hip, calf, chest and face. 50 Cent survived and went on to become a superstar but the shooting has always been connected to Supreme. After he recovered, 50 put out a song, *Fuck You*, that said- *50, who shot ya? You think it was Preme, Freeze or Tata?* And Jon "Love" Ragin said later that he met with Preme the day of the 50 shooting and Preme said, "I got him." Supreme, "Explained to me that they caught him coming out of his grandmother's house and he got into a car and that's when he got shot. There was a lot of blood." Love recalled Preme telling him. The *New York Post* ran the headline, *Slay Plot vs. Fitty*, indicting Supreme of the crime. But even in court the shooting was never pinned on Supreme.

The subject of 50 being a snitch has been hotly debated also. "This dude sensationalizes everything. All his statements are incendiary. The government believes every lyric- and then he says, 'Read my lyrics.' Where I come from that's dry snitching." Supreme said and on the whole beef with 50 he said, "Kid you've never been through nothing. I walked around wolves, man. I walked among giants." And he's right. Maybe 50 is a snitch, maybe not. "The chump 50 Cent wouldn't even be a factor in the rap game today if his lyrics weren't snitch oriented," T says. "He owe his success to the media and his beef with Murder Inc. 50 ain't never been nowhere but to boot camp. A place guys like Supreme wouldn't even go to. With dudes yelling in your face telling you to do 50 pushups. How gangsta is that?"

Part 9- The Fall

Preme's gangsta was in full effect though with his name being linked to every rap related crime. If it wasn't him, it was an associate of his and the media played up the whole Supreme Team connection. Every ex-con in the rap game was now an ex-member of the Supreme Team. "At first, I didn't think nothing of it," Bing says. "Because they were always putting his name out there, because of who he was. They linked him to everything because of his name. He was one of the main generals who represented Southside Jamaica, Queens to the fullest. He's a person the streets will always acknowledge as a legend. He repped the hood and made Southside Jamaica shine. They always gonna remember him as a top legend from the hood." But Supreme's notoriety would be his downfall as the feds always felt like he was the one who got away. He had a long arrest record, but had escaped heavy prison time and the feds wanted to nail him to a cross. Preme was treading dangerously and walking a tight rope. Even with the heavy scrutiny Preme wasn't finished with the streets or at least it seemed that way.

Preme was under a microscope and on July 16, 2001 at 9:45 p.m., four gunmen sporting white gloves and driving a Mercedes pulled up alongside Eric "E-Money Bags" Smith's Lincoln Navigator, which was parked near Witthoff Street and 111th Road in Queens with guns ready. The weapons were fired at such close range that 9 millimeter shell casings covered the SUV's interior.

Preme allegedly boasted that former Supreme Team member Black Just could finally rest in peace and the streets were humming about the revenge killing. Allegedly, Preme sent a friend a text message, "you missed the party," after the killing. Maybe it wasn't all entertainment as it seemed. The same month that E-Money Bags was killed, Supreme was pulled over in his BMW near a known drug spot in Harlem on 145th Street, when asked for his driver's license by officers he identified himself as Lee Tuten and said he was an executive at Def Jam. Cops found a .40 caliber glock pistol and $11,000 in cash. According to the arresting officer's statements McGriff told them, "These aren't meant for you. It's a tough neighborhood." About the money he said, "We were shopping. You caught me on a bad day. Usually, I'm carrying more than that." When he was arrested and charged with weapons possession, his true identity was revealed. The ATF traced the gun belonging to a relative of the Gotti's. "From what I know since he got home his life was tried four times," Chris Gotti said. "Once in broad daylight by a gas station. He might want to keep a gun on him."

More murders occurred in the next three months. It seemed like all Preme's old enemies were turning up dead. On August 20, 2001 Karon Clarret and Dwayne Thomas were found murdered execution style in Red Run Apartments on Wheelright Drive in Owings Mill, Maryland. Word on the street was that both were suspected of snitching on some of Preme's associates operating in Baltimore. The murders proved detrimental as cops investigating it discovered a stash house at 4314 Flinthill Drive. The cops found coke and heroin, 30 grand in cash, a certificate for a firearms training course in the name of Lee Tuten and a video tape depicting surveillance footage of E-Money Bags 20 minutes before his demise. *Crime Partners* promotional material and Supreme's fingerprints were also discovered at the stash house. It wasn't looking good for the ex-con with ties to the hip-hop industry. The feds were actively building a case that Supreme had switched from a retail drug business to a wholesale one. And on October 28, 2001 E-Money Bags' partner Troy Singleton was killed outside a sports bar, the Club Van Wyck on Liberty Avenue in South Jamaica. All this along with the Jam Master Jay killing, which was initially linked to Supreme and the 50 Cent situation sparked a major investigation. The feds were looking into Preme's activities in both Baltimore and New York. And the chatter in the streets didn't help. Dudes in B-more were talking about how, "Preme was sending them things down and making niggas rich." Word on the streets was that he, "put his gorilla down in B-more."

In January 2002, FBI agent Gregory Takacs started investigating Supreme's ties to Murder Inc. by calling NYPD hip-hop patrol Detective Derrick Parker and asking about Supreme. Detective Parker had a lot of information and the FBI agent found that plenty of ex-felons were associated with Murder Inc. "He became a player in the hip-hop industry after he got out of prison," the FBI agent said but he contended that Supreme still had a foot in the streets. As he saw it Supreme was "Murder Inc.'s hired muscle" that enjoyed "perks in the form of SUV's, hotel suites, plane trips and more, all billed to Murder Inc." And with Murder Inc.'s studio in SoHo called Crackhouse Studios and their Murda Management Company representing Preme's and their various ventures it was a little too much for the lawman to take. To him it screamed criminal organization. He was incredulous that career criminals and young black men from the ghetto were making money by purporting to be gangsters. Two affidavits heightened the investigation. The first prepared by Special Agent Francis Mace said, "Gotti is the public face of the label and McGriff was the true owner of the company." The affidavit alleged that Supreme used the label to launder drug money and linked him to the Owings Mill, Maryland double murder.

The IRS sought forfeiture from Supreme's Picture Perfect Film company. The second prepared by Detective William Courtney, who was with the NYPD's High Intensity Drug Trafficking task force linked Supreme to the 2001 Queens Village slaying of E-Money Bags, which they claimed was a revenge killing for the earlier murder by E-Money Bags of Supreme's partner, Black Just. With the two gun charges he was facing, one stemming from the 2001 Harlem traffic stop and one for the firearms certificate found at the Maryland stash house in the same alias, Lee Tuten, Preme knew he was facing time, he just wasn't sure how much. As a suspect knowing that the feds were out to get him, Preme must have been wondering what would come to light and what would remain hidden in darkness. But it was like he said, "I am the usual suspect." It was a trying time for the legend. But nothing he hadn't faced before.

Before going to prison though, he went to see his nephew who was doing six life sentences in the feds. Prince was at USP Beaumont at the time and Irv Gotti stepped in and paid for the trip. "Whatever you want to say about Prince, he could be the most notorious dude ever, but to Preme this was his little nephew," Irv said. "And at the time Preme knew he had to go to jail for the gun charge. Every time he goes in he always feels like it could be his last. All he wanted was to see his nephew again." Preme pled guilty in 2002 to the NY state gun charge and while awaiting sentencing he took off to Miami, but with the fed gun charge for the firearms certificate coming down and the Jam Master Jay murder fresh the feds didn't want to leave Supreme on the street. On December 28th, 2002, they captured him at Loews Hotel in Miami Beach and charged him with the Maryland shooting range training certificate charge. "They locked him up and gave him 37 months for shooting on a firing range," T says. "They didn't have any video. They just found a certificate and got him off the street for 37 months." In effect the feds were putting Supreme on ice as they investigated all the murders that were being linked to him along with the Murder Inc. situation. The feds wanted to know if it was life imitating art or vice-versa. Was the *Crime Partners* production coming to life?

With Supreme in check the feds moved against both his *Crime Partners* co-producer Love and Murder Inc. on January 3rd, 2003. They raided Love's offices at 175-20 Wetford Terrace in Queens and Murder Inc.'s Manhattan office where the feds carted away computers and documents looking for evidence of money laundering, gang ties and drug dealing. "They was acting like I was John Gotti," Irv said. But all Irv shared with the Mafioso was a last name. The feds believed Murder Inc. and Supreme were crime partners. It was the Donald Goines novel coming to life. March 25, 2003, the day the *Crime Partners* DVD was released, should have been Supreme's happiest. But it wasn't. His dream came true, but as Preme sat in a Baltimore jail and Murder Inc. was raided, everything to do with *Crime Partners* was seized by the feds. The money from Def Jam, everything. By the spring of 2003 FBI agents investigating Murder Inc.'s connections to Supreme were interviewing Queens's hustlers on the street and in the prison system. It was an all out war for information about Supreme. And the feds were putting down a mean press game.

"They painted this picture themselves." Antoine Clark, the publisher of *Feds* magazine said. "There's something that comes behind bringing in a kingpin to ride with you. There's a certain ghetto pride and ghetto respect but there's also a police investigation." For more than two years, law enforcement officers and agents from the NYPD, IRS, FBI, and ATF, all the alphabet boys, investigated Supreme, and they alleged that upon his mid-90's release from prison he rebuilt his violent drug organization with several new members, since the Supreme Team were all in jail. The feds actively built a case that Supreme never left the drug game. "In Supreme's situation he is a perfect target, because of his past and because the hip-hop generation accepted him and put him on a pedestal as an example of what a gangsta should be," T says.

"It was a vendetta against Preme," Tuck says. "Dudes change but with the feds it's like once a drug dealer always a drug dealer. These days being a drug dealer is worse than being a rapist." The investigation overseen by U.S. Attorney Roslynn R. Mauskopf, saw the feds work two angles to the case. First, in November 2003, they indicted Ja Rule's manager and a Murder Inc. accountant with laundering more than one million in cash. They alleged Supreme would send bags of cash to Murder Inc.'s headquarters on 8th Avenue in Manhattan. Then, in a separate indictment, a Queens's couple was charged with the E-Money Bags slaying. The feds had pinpointed where the surveillance tape of E-Money Bags last moments was made and moved in on the couple who lived in the apartment from where it was filmed. "It's like Supreme said, 'They could have easily not been on the indictment by saying what the cops wanted them to say,'" T says. And at first they didn't. Supreme's former lawyer Robert Simels accused the government of pushing cooperating witnesses to falsely implicate the ultimate targets of the probe, namely the reputed cocaine kingpin who had history of murder, mayhem and hitman killings- Supreme.

Jon "Love" Ragin, Supreme's co-producer on the *Crime Partners* venture turned government stooge first, rather than face a 15-19 year sentence for his credit card scheme. "This creep, nothing he said had any validity. He started a lot of this when he went on the run and got caught in the forgery ring. The feds seized the film company due to this dudes lies." T says. Preme pled guilty in April 2003 for taking target practice at the Glen Burnie, Maryland firing range and on November 4, 2004, he was sentenced for the Harlem traffic stop gun charge. He received a five year concurrent sentence that would have put him out in the summer of 2005. But it wasn't to be.

Part 10- The End

On January 26, 2005, a 37 page, 13 count indictment that charged nine individuals and two corporations with racketeering, trafficking in cocaine, heroin and crack, money laundering and murder was handed down by the U.S. Attorney's office in New York. It charged that Irv Gotti had used his position to press Def Jam executives to pay tens of thousands of dollars to cover Preme's travel expenses and that Gotti persuaded Def Jam to finance *Crime Partners* by providing a $500,000 guarantee that was secretly backed by drug money. "We will not tolerate violent drug organizations and those who help them prosper by laundering their illicit proceeds," said U.S. Attorney Mauskopf in the press release announcing the indictments. FBI agent Fred Snelling added, "They don't call it gangsta rap for nothing." A sneering, hypocritical attitude that has long haunted the genre. The feds contended that Supreme was responsible for Mafia style murders while moving kilos of cocaine and heroin in multiple states following his release from prison in the mid-90's, after his twelve year bid in the feds. The government sought the death penalty, alleging Supreme directed conspirators to kill associates in Maryland and that he arranged other murders in New York City. Supreme was linked to nine murders in total according to the feds. "That man is a drug dealer and murderer," Assistant U.S. Attorney Jason Jones said referring to Supreme. It was a vicious assault, no holds barred, and the feds were gunning for the legend trying to get him in a deadly chokehold.

"It's like a desperation grab," Preme said. "I've never been known as a murderer and all of a sudden I'm this psychotic killer." After Murder Inc.'s case was severed from Supreme's and the Gotti brothers were acquitted of money laundering charges on Friday December 2, 2005, it looked good for Supreme. But somebody flipped the script. After numerous delays and several severances, Supreme stood alone, facing the death penalty with no co-defendants. All of them had flipped. "My entire trial existed because of snitches. A rat is the lowest life form known to man. They gave out 11 deals to convict one person. Six of these snitches testified at my trial." Preme said. "You have to have heart to be in the game." Teddy said. "That is why there are so many snitches. These dudes now want to be like Preme but they can't stand up. There isn't anything pretty about the street game." And there isn't anything pretty about facing death or getting a life sentence. It's an ugly business. The feds, facing reality, dropped the hip-hop hoopla and money-laundering charges and went for the jugular.

"The man sitting in the courtroom is one of the most dangerous, feared, ruthless gangsters in all Queens," prosecutor Carolyn Pokorney said to start Preme's trial for multiple murders in which the feds were seeking the death penalty by portraying Supreme as a caricature of one of Donald Goines's characters in January 2006. "And when Supreme gets in a fight with somebody he doesn't go to the cops. He doesn't hire a lawyer. He hires a hit team to assassinate them, to blow them away, so that their moms can barely recognize them when they go down to the morgue." The case was built on a combination of text messages and cooperation testimony. Like most high profile cases in the feds these days, hard evidence was lacking. There was very little physical evidence produced. *Feds Press New Case vs. Kingpin*, the *Daily News* headline on January 10, 2007 and Prosecutor Jeffrey Rabkin said, "The defendant wanted these men dead in part to maintain his reputation as a feared and ruthless gangster." The feds were going full force. They weren't pulling any punches. "The government with a renewed vigor used my past history to discredit and vilify me as a monster with no conscious," Preme said. "What aggravated the feds was that I actually made a film based on a Donald Goines book with an all star cast. You see the feds are vindictive in nature, they believe that once a bad guy, always a bad guy and that you don't deserve to be prosperous. Long before I came along the feds viewed hip-hop as a criminal entity." But hip-hop wasn't on trial, Supreme was.

"It was a tough situation for Supreme," Ethan Brown says. "He faced the death penalty and the feds kept adding superceding indictments to his case. He also faced a number of uncharged allegations including the shooting of 50 Cent." And the papers picked up on this, *Slay plot vs. Fitty* ran the *New York Post* headline in September 2005 right before the original trial began. And 50 Cent added his own two cents saying, "They should let him out so he can die in the streets like he's supposed to." As he was awaiting his turn to be judged by twelve, despite the media circus, Preme said, "All is well as can be expected under the circumstances. The fix is in, the government is sparing no expense to eliminate me. But I remain undaunted and resolute in my stance, head up and chest out. I am in the box and have been. It only strengthens my resolve." And Supreme added, analyzing the feds tactics, "By the time my trial commenced their initial premise was recalibrated numerous times. I was superseded four times. They formulated their case as they went along until they discovered some rats that would make it all fit."

The government's main evidence centered around Supreme allegedly paying 50 grand to have two rivals, E-Money Bags and Troy Singleton, gunned down in 2001. "This is about a man with the power and the will to get people murdered," Prosecutor Jason Jones told jurors in opening statements in the Brooklyn court. "He wanted those men erased to settle an old score and to show Supreme was not to be crossed." About this contention Supreme countered, "There was no enterprise and I never paid anyone $50,000 to kill two street corner hustlers. The President could be assassinated for that." The admitted hitman in both murders, Emmanual "Manny Dog" Mosely, testified against Supreme. Manny Dog began cooperating in the spring of 2006 with the government against Supreme. He put together and led the hit squads on both Singleton and E-Money Bags. "The feds ain't letting no black man win no federal trial, no murder case," Bing says. "Especially a dude like Preme with his history." But still Preme fought. His attorney David Ruhnke contended that "the government is prosecuting somebody who just doesn't exist anymore." He argued that *Crime Partners*, "was an effort to make money legitimately, to change the direction of his life." Ruhnke said both murder victims were known street thugs who were armed at the times of their deaths. He alleged the government built its case on the false testimony of admitted criminals hoping to see their prison time reduced. Supreme was resolute in his stance too.

"I'm gonna stick to my values and face certain death. Every shooting they point the finger at me, the bad guy." He said. "You can put the death penalty on me. I've lived my life already. I've done everything I wanted to do." *Facing Supreme Penalty – Druglord Could Get Death Sentence*, the *New York Post* trumpeted. But the judge threw out the death penalty frustrating prosecutors on the case. "There's no chance in the world there would be a death penalty verdict in this case," U.S. District Court Judge Frederic Block said. And Karen Cameron, the mother of one of the victims said, "Death is not the answer." It didn't look good for Supreme though. The hitman Manny Dog testified that during the summer of 2001 Supreme approached him about the contracts. Supreme wanted to kill Singleton for fucking with Murder Inc. and because he fucked with E-Money Bags. The E-Money Bags thing was just a plain and simple retribution killing for Supreme's man, Black Just. According to Manny Dog he took the payment from Supreme at a Pita shop in downtown Manhattan.

"There is a profound difference between a witness who has no vested interest in a criminal activity and a snitch who benefits greatly." Supreme said. And unknown to Supreme, Manny Dog was a 5K1 frequent flyer. It came out in trial that Manny Dog had snitched in a mid-90's Pennsylvania drug conspiracy when he was facing 20 years. How Supreme didn't know that is remarkable. "All the rats had numerous murders, drug dealing and horrendous crimes," Preme said. "They will be released in 5 to 10 years just so the government could get a conviction on me. These guys testified under oath that they would lie, have lied and would do what was necessary to receive a deal." And that's the real deal. It's vicious in the game nowadays and Preme found out the hard way. The ideals of honor, integrity and loyalty were out the window with the younger generation. "I feel for him," Bing says. "But if you chose to live that life, you got to suck it up. Dudes getting life every day. Everybody got to fight his battle. A life sentence is not a good thing but when you choose that lifestyle its one of the consequences."

The prosecutors laid out the numerous murder and drug conspiracy counts and operations in New York and Baltimore. More dudes from Manny Dog's hit squad like Barry "Mungo" Broughton, Alvin Smiley and Climente Jordan, the rat who started it all, testified against Supreme. "Cliemente 'CJ' Jordan was the catalyst. He was doing 15 years in Delaware and he decided to cut his sentence at my expense," Supreme said. The videotape Nicole Brown made of E-Money Bags, 20 minutes before he died was played for the jury. Michael Todd Harvey told the jury how he was involved selling large amounts of cocaine and heroin to Supreme in the mid-90's and John "Love" Ragin, Supreme's supposed partner testified to many things, among them how Preme told him the E-Money Bags slaying, "was like the forth of July." Prosecutor Carolyn Pokorney related how, "Supreme's finger prints were actually lifted from the drug stash house where the Baltimore detective found this tape (referring to the E-Money Bags tape). His fingerprints are all over that stash house, and not only the stash house, but from inside the exact bag where the detectives found this tape. There's heroin, there's crack, a gun, scales, thousands of vials, thousands of gel caps. A bag of tapes with the surveillance video of Eric Smith."

Prosecutors went way overboard portraying Supreme as this super evil gangster who couldn't possibly have been involved in any legitimate business ventures. His portrayal by them to the jury bordered on cartoonish. In his defense his attorney argued, "What we don't have on these murders is wiretaps, we don't have anybody discussing murder over a wiretap, we don't have finger prints that matter. No fingerprints that matter. No fingerprints associated with the murder at all. Fingerprints or something related to the crime. No eyewitnesses, somebody who explains they were on the street corner and they saw McGriff and Mosely. They don't have DNA. Firearm matches, nothing compares to anything. No matches, no ballistics, nothing." But it didn't matter. On February 1, 2007, the jury after two and half hours of deliberations found Preme guilty of murder conspiracy and drug dealing. The 46-year-old Supreme, wearing a three piece dark business suit with a tie and glasses, looked back and smiled at his three rows of supporters including Ja Rule and Irv Gotti, who he flashed smiles and the peace sign at when the verdict was issued.

He knew it was over and the *News Day* headlines read, *Hired Hit Rap Pinned on Drug Dealer*. He had his run but finally it was over. The jury came back with a 9-3 split for life. *Ex-Druglord McGriff Gets Life In Prison*, the newspaper headline read on February 10, 1997. As he was led from the courtroom he smiled again at his supporters and tapped his heart. It was the closing act for the legend. "This entire case against me was inconsistent," Preme said. "I was convenient in nature and background and my past put me in a precarious position. This case was about some prosecutor's lofty ambitions and about closing a chapter." Closing the chapter on Supreme and burying him in Supermax. The last of the crack era's druglords was finally out of commission.

Kenneth "Supreme" McGriff was sentenced to life and shipped off to federal prison for the last time, but his notoriety remains. "The streets will always respect Preme for who he is." Bing says. "We always been good. Everybody has their good and their bad ways to them but Preme is a brother to me. I have no complaints. He was always good to me. We lived the life. I'll love that nigga forever." And Supreme will be remembered forever as a sort of gangsta philosopher, an eloquent deep thinker who knew more then he let on, who almost made the jump to legitimacy that so many gangsters before him dreamed about, but never attempted. But his supposed beef with 50 Cent lingers. It seems 50 can't let it go. 50 told New York papers to, "release Supreme so he can die on the streets." Also on the Wendy Williams show after Preme was found guilty, 50 Cent boasted, instructing listeners at the jail to go wake up Supreme and tell him 50 Cent is on the radio mocking him. But recent reports indicate that 50 Cent fears Supreme trying to get revenge on him. And in truth 50 will never be a legend like Supreme. "I've never been fascinated by money." Preme said. "What fascinates me is Nelson Mandela on Robben Island breaking stones, eating bread and drinking water. Nat Turner being in a cell, captured after he led the slave revolt. That's what fascinates me, the struggle. The struggle is what defines a man." And Supreme's struggle has defined him, as one of the best to ever do it in the dope game.

chapter 2

Wayne "Silk" Perry

WAYNE 'SILK' PERRY

Wayne "Silk" Perry is the most infamous gangster to ever walk the streets of Washington D.C. aka Drama City. He's been called the Michael Jordan of the murder game. A professional head hitter and alleged killer. The streets hold a definite respect, a curious awe and a healthy amount of fear for the man they called Silk. "Wayne was one of those niggas that lived by the code, but played by his own rules." Says E, a gangsta who came up under Silk. In the Chocolate City it was by any means necessary and Silk took this attitude to new extremes with his boldness in the face of adversity and challenges. Nobody was off limits to Silk and nothing was undoable. According to police, Silk was legendary for his willingness to kill at will- in broad daylight, up close and personal, in front of the police- it didn't matter if you were on his hit list you could be killed anywhere in front of anyone. There was nowhere to hide, it's alleged that Silk would lay in wait for his prey all night until he got his opportunity to strike. Murder, robbery, drug dealing and extortion were said to be his business and he took it seriously. He prided himself as a man that could put his mind to whatever he wanted, as he conquered all aspects of the game.

Wayne Perry is the man who protected self-proclaimed Harlem drug lord and notorious snitch Alberto "Alpo" Martinez. Working as an enforcer for the so-called Martinez organization, a powerful DC-based drug ring, Silk acted as bodyguard and hitman for Alpo, who after he was apprehended by the law and arrested snitched on his too loyal right hand man, Wayne and countless others. But Silk didn't get down like that. He took his on the chin and kept on fighting. He held true to the code of the streets that spawned him. He's gone down in infamy, as one of the top soldiers from the Murder Capital. A true warrior and hustler who lives by the creed of death before dishonor. The *Washington Post* called him one of the District's most heinous murderers, and almost fifteen years after his rise, the streets are still talking about him.

Part 1- The Making of a Gangster

Wayne Perry was born November 14, 1962. He grew up on L Street in Southwest Washington D.C., in the area known as 203. "I was raised in D.C. but I spent a lot of the summers of my childhood in Georgia," Wayne says. "I even put fools in the dirt down there and back then it was super racist. Crackers used to call me boy." A sign of the times but Wayne moved through all of that and in his native D.C. as he grew into a teenager, sports became his passion. "I was real small back then. I was the best baseball player in D.C. too. I've been in the *Washington Star* several times about baseball. I grew up on sports. I lived across from the boys club in Southwest. I boxed, played basketball, baseball and football and I was always the MVP, but I was caught up in that gangster stuff." He says. "I got the name Silk from my extended brother Lop. I was real smooth in sports and with the girls when I was a kid. I think I was twelve or so when Lop gave me that name." Wayne says. "Lop was my idol, the roughest and baddest joker I ever knew." And Wayne was coming up under dudes like Lop, a well-known local D.C. street guy.

"I started hanging up 17th Street NW gambling. I was also hangin on 14th Street and 7th and T, NW. I was hanging with older guys back then, watching their backs while they hustled. You know what's funny, all the older dudes that was gangsters when I was a kid, I became their leader when I became a teenager." And Silk as he became known in the streets of Southwest started his gangster ways early on. He wasn't afraid to bust his guns and get his hands dirty.

"In 1974, I put my first fool in the dirt and in 1975 I started hustling." Wayne says. "In 76, I learned how to cheat with crooked dice, marked and cut cards. Older guys I never told I was cheating, used to take me all over to gamble cause they thought I was lucky." And the young Silk picked up on how the hustlers, players, dealers and street guys carried it. He molded himself in their image. "Silk was real smart and clever," says his close comrade Manny. "Slim was a good dude, more than fair. You just couldn't cross him, if you did he wouldn't have no understanding." That was just how he was. Wayne was real slick and no one could pinpoint him. How do you think he got the name Silk? He didn't hang out in spots like that, he'd just pop up. "If you knew Wayne like I do, it's no telling where you might run into him at in the city." Sop-Sop, another close comrade says. "Southwest would be his spot, but I would say he was international." It was in Silk's nature to keep people off balance and guessing so that they didn't quite know what to expect.

"I started robbing in 78. I started robbing banks. My little brother got killed in a bank by a pig in 79," Wayne says. At the time he was still attending Wilson High School, starring in baseball and playing other sports, but slowly slipping into the streets and adapting the gangster mentality. This would eventually lead him to jail. "I got locked up in 79 for shooting the hall monitor man in school but I didn't do it. The dude and his crew who did it blamed it on me because it was a riot, Southwest against Northwest, and I kicked it off by punishing this older joker from Northwest, but I didn't have a weapon." Wayne says. "Then I got put out of Wilson and I went to Randall and I beat the baseball team coach with a bat at practice and I got barred out of all D.C. public schools, so I went to Franklin GED school cause the judge ordered me to and I had to kill a fool for telling me he was going to take my chain."

The older dudes in the hood respected Wayne's gangster. They saw the makings of a thoroughbred in the youngster. "They knew I'd shoot anybody," he says on his growing reputation. "Police, killers, gorillas, etc. I also used to go on robberies with some hell of a gangsters but they always took the bullets out of my gun cause they said I was trigger happy." His name started ringing loudly on the block in the early 80's down in Southwest. He had a reputation as a young soldier with mad heart and skills, but to his friends he showed another side of him that the world would never know. "Wayne's a funny type of guy from the heart," his little cousin says. "He was real funny. I remember back in the 203 days we would all be around and he would be joking about anybody, what they had on, their girl, their family or whatever. He would have you dying laughing. He would play so much that if you didn't know him, really know him, you didn't know when he was serious." Wayne could play but when it was time to get serious, he turned deadly serious.

"They had this big crap game going on outside one day." Sop-Sop says. "A lot of well known hustlers and gamblers from other parts of the city was out there and Wayne and this other well respected dude got into it about a bet. Wayne shot him in his ass twice in front of everybody." Silk wasn't above getting his respect by gunsmoke when necessary. He would bust his gun at the slightest provocation. Stories like this abound about the man who became a legend and only add to his infamy and mythology. At the time though all his actions added to his reputation, which was growing by the day and leaving the streets wondering who this new wild and violent gangster was. "My brother hates arrogance and he ain't the one who speaks," Silk's little bro says. "He is silent as the wind but deadly as fire." And D.C. was *en fuego*.

"In 84, I killed a fool in front of the police, it was sort of like self-defense. I went down Youth Center One on that," Wayne says. And Sop-Sop remembers that too, "Some time after that, Wayne came in and went down Youth Center One where myself, Titus, Gator and many other good men were. Wayne established himself as a man among men." And in the streets a new drug called crack was introduced to the city and it took D.C. by storm. While Wayne was making city-wide contacts and solidifying his gangster at Lorton, the crack epidemic raged unabated, turning the Chocolate City into the Murder Capital.

Part 2- The Streets of D.C.

Washington D.C. will forever be known as the Murder Capital of the United States because of the drug violence during the crack era. In the late 80's, D.C. was a war zone in the areas of the city where drugs and crime had a stronghold. At that time there was really a murder almost everyday. Everybody knew somebody that had been murdered. It was nothing to turn on the news and see a body hanging out of a car with bullet holes in it. Real graphic stuff like that. The killers began to get younger and younger also. Another thing about that time was the fact that there wasn't just one or two dudes that were killers, at that time there were serious dudes that would hunt people down in all hoods, although there may have been only one or two killers in that one hood. "When coke was short, niggas ain't no picks in the streets," E says. Shit was chaotic and wild. It was like the Wild, Wild West in the streets of the nation's capital.

Many people may say that dudes that get money can't be on gunplay, but at that time in the city there were a lot of dudes that were getting a lot of paper that were still dropping bodies with their own hands. A lot of snake shit came into play as well. A lot of friends killed their so-called friends in the name of some paper during those times, letting money come between them. D.C. dudes were quick with their guns and they were known to kill in a minute without hesitation. Especially if they came across some out-of-towners trying to get money or some known suckers trying to get theirs. They were all fair game in the streets of D.C. But over all, in the late 80's, before dudes like Rayful Edmond went to jail, there was a lot of money for dudes to make if that's what they were about. The crack era was a brutal time but also a time where inner city hoodlums and thugs could come up rapidly and get theirs. And this was the environment Silk walked into when he came home from jail. It was a free for all and Silk was the wild card of all wild cards.

"Wayne's name started ringing on a serious tip around 88 when he came home from Lorton's Youth Center One," E says. After his time in prison, Silk had a different outlook on the streets. He'd been reading a lot inside and he came home with a game plan and made it work. He was always wild, with a violent side, but it just became more serious for him. His name started being recognized throughout the city from being around some known figures. His association with them brought attention to him because of who they were. Dudes coming home from the Youth Center from other sections of the city, that were known for being money getters or by any means type of guys, were his friends and comrades. Silk was moving in vicious circles and when things began to happen, it was either said that Silk did it or was behind it. And the streets were talking.

"The hood wasn't a place you'd want to get caught slipping when Wayne was around," Sop-Sop says. Because Wayne was known to make an example out of whoever crossed him. Silk was doing him- hustling, robbing, gunplay, sticking dudes up, extorting dudes- he found his niche and exploited it, playing his position to the hilt. But there were other more personal reasons why Silk chose the path he did. "When I came home my father was in critical condition after having two strokes," Wayne says. "I came home in late 87 and in a short time my father passed and I lost my mind and was on a death wish." Simply put, Wayne Perry didn't give a fuck. And this attitude, crossed with his intelligence, cleverness, cunning and desire to be recognized by the streets, was a deadly combination.

Part 3- Most Feared

"Wayne was so smooth with that murder shit that when he first started killing for money in the city niggas didn't even know who was knockin' them heads. Niggas was talking about it was a hit man in town from Detroit somewhere," a dude from the era says. And as Silk's name took on the eminence of his actions, he quickly became one of the most feared dudes in the city. "Some niggas used to try to feed slim to keep him off they ass." Manny says. "Rayful Edmond used to try to drop loads of shit down 203, but Wayne used to be like, 'Nah, I'm cool. I don't want nothing from you.' He wanted to make his own way. He had a game plan." It was said that when Wayne was on the streets, certain hustlers wouldn't even drive nice cars because they didn't want Wayne to think they were getting money. And weak dudes or those that were punks weren't supposed to have shit as far as Wayne was concerned. Eighty percent of the dudes that fucked with him back then did so out of fear. When he started taking money for hits nobody was safe. If the price was right and the joker wasn't in Wayne's circle he had no problem killing them. There are stories of Silk sleeping in the yards of dudes that had money on their heads until he could get them. "I don't play that across the street shit," Wayne says. "I walk right up and put seven in the head like it ain't shit." The fear that he put in the hearts of some people was like no other.

In every hood there's an individual whose supreme talent seems to be a penchant for murdering others for whatever reason. These individuals are elevated and upheld as heroes in their hoods and for good reason. "He went home in the late 80's and looked out for all the men he left behind," Sop-Sop says. "He did what he had to do to survive as a man in the streets." And those things included terrorizing the streets of D.C. with homicides, shootings and armed kidnappings. It was in the heavy drug trafficking areas of Drama City where Silk plied his trade and made his name. Silk was a master philosopher when it came to that street shit. He played the streets like a game of chess. He was more than feared. "People feared Silk because he was said to have a lot of humps in the ground. People didn't only fear that, they feared the fact that Silk got away with the shit he did." Manny says. His reputation itself put an end to any investigations or court cases against him. Sop-Sop explains it another way, "I don't think it was fear, but the possibility of what Wayne can manifest." The dude was unpredictable. He kept people off balance and witnesses in check. Nobody knew what to expect. Maybe not even Wayne himself. That's what made him so dangerous. In a world of ups and downs, betrayals and double-crosses he reigned king.

"He knew how to use fear and mind games real well." E says. "He was one man that had a large percentage of the masses shook. He didn't give a fuck what you thought about him as long as you didn't cross the line. There were a lot of dudes in the streets at that time that were head hitters, but some of them moved on the D.L., you didn't know they were killers unless you knew them. With Wayne it was a fear thing. Niggas knew he was about murder, it was no secret." Wayne once bumped into a dude that was like that down Lorton, the dude thought he was still like that on the streets, Wayne told the dude, "You ain't heard, I run the city."

He was feared because of the many reasons that set his name to ringing. His name was behind a lot of things that were going on throughout the District. "A lot of people couldn't understand how he was supposed to be behind so much shit and he was still moving around the city as if nothing was a problem." E says. When shit went down and the drama jumped off dudes were like, "It was Wayne Perry and them." He had a whole team of dudes that were very loyal to him. Wayne was the type of dude that if he came up on some kilo's, he showed love, breaking it down with all his dudes. He might hit 30 dudes off with a couple of ounces each just on G.P. Just to inspire that loyalty to that do or die attitude. His team would go all out for him. No questions asked. They were a bunch of youngsters, and in their eyes Silk was a god.

"On the real, I think Wayne's name started ringing because he was bussin' ass. He wasn't talking, it wasn't no playing when it came to putting that work in, plus he had some serious killers on his team." E says. Silk had a whole squad that he could sick on dudes in a minute. Wayne was the type of person that if dude had something and dude was weak or a sucker, then dude wasn't supposed to have it. It didn't matter what it was, Wayne was taking it and if dude didn't like it, fuck it. Wayne only respected men. If a dude was a rat, he wasn't supposed to breathe, let alone come out his hole. No matter how much money the rat had, spent or flashed or how hard he flossed, that shit meant nothing to Wayne. He was coming to get that. That bling-bling was his. Only integrity and heart counted to Silk. The whole, "he didn't tell on me thing," didn't fly with Wayne Perry. Dudes had to play their position. And if their position was to be up under him and do what the fuck he said, then so be it. That's how Silk played it. It was all or nothing with him. No half-stepping or in-betweens.

"One day me and Wayne went to pick up a bucket he had parked across town. He used the car to stash stuff in." Manny says. "Wayne popped the trunk and he had hand grenades, sticks of dynamite and a rack of guns, coke and some more shit. We had this other dude with us too. Wayne threw the dude the keys to the bucket and told him to drive the car back around Potomac Gardens. The dude was like, 'I can't drive all that shit back around the way.' Wayne pulled out his pistol and told the nigga, 'You better get your ass in that car and take it around the Gardens and if the police pull you over tell them it's my shit and if they take it I'm a kill your muthafuckin' ass.' The nigga got his ass in the car and did exactly what Wayne said. Silk ain't play no games." And dudes were wise not to fuck with him or try him in any way, because Wayne was quick to expose a dude and in vicious fashion. "One thing about Wayne, he went at whoever. If you was supposed to be like that and he had to see you he was gonna knock your head off. You would think he was some big 300 pound nigga, but when you see him he is this tall, skinny, funny nigga. Always joking and playing, but dangerous. Niggas didn't want to be on his shit list." Manny says.

There was no limit to the way Silk played either. He didn't care who you were supposed to be, he was still going to play with you. He would play with you even if you weren't trying to and if you got serious, he was cool with that too. A lot of times Wayne would try dudes he didn't like by playing with them. "One time, me, Wayne and two other dudes were in my Benz on the way to the mall. Wayne knew that one of the dudes with us wasn't who he thought he was in the streets. The dude was supposed to be a killer but Wayne could see through him. Wayne hated fake niggas. So Wayne starts playing with dude, trying to provoke him. When the dude gets fed up, he told Wayne to stop playing with him. Wayne said, 'Nigga fuck you, I play when I want to and if I wanted to I could fuck you. You's a bitch, you should be taking that dick.' The dude gets heated and tells Wayne can't no nigga fuck him. Wayne laughed at him and told him, 'I ain't no average nigga, I'm Silk and if you keep running your mouth I'm a leave your fake ass in this back seat with a hole in your head.' I tried to tell the dude to leave the shit alone because I saw where it was going, Wayne was going to end up smokin' the nigga. The dude wouldn't let it go, his pride was in it. Wayne ended up telling the dude they could fight if he had something he needed to get off his chest. When we got to the mall Wayne took off his jacket and slapped the shit out of dude, he tried to make the nigga fight him but the dude wouldn't fight. Wayne looked at us and said, 'I told y'all this nigga was a bitch.' Wayne then pulled out his pistol and makes the dude strip ass naked right in the parking lot, then he shot him in the ass and told him to get the fuck away from us. Everybody was laughing. Wayne exposed the nigga and it was all a big joke to Silk." A dude from back in the day relates.

Wayne was on that extortion time real hard too. "He put me on a nigga one time, he wanted me to lean on the nigga." Another one of Wayne's old partners in crime says. "I put the squeeze on the nigga, told him I wanted 50 grand. I worked the move about two or three times and broke down with Silk every time. At the same time Silk was playing things with the nigga, getting close to him, making him think they were cool. Then Silk acted like he found out I was squeezing the nigga and told the nigga that he would get me to leave him alone for 50 G's. From there he was milking the nigga for 50 G's anytime he wanted to and he would still hit me off. Silk worked that move so many times on different niggas too, even some niggas that was supposed to be like that. It was like taking candy from a baby for Silk." And when Silk's friend came home from jail he used his reputation to put him back on his feet.

"I remember when I first came home from Lorton and was in the halfway house," Manny says. "Wayne came to get me and told me to get in his CE and took me uptown. He asked me if I had money. I was just coming home, I was broke. I told him, no, so he said he was going to take me to get some money. We pull up in front of a well known spot that's owned by some dudes that supposed to be major in the city. Wayne looked at me and said, 'Go in there and tell such and such to send a bag of that money out here and don't make me come in there and get it either.' I thought Wayne was playing, he's a real funny dude, always playing, but he was dead serious. So I went in the spot and told the dude what Wayne said and with no problem the dude gave me a bag full of money. Wayne had niggas scared to death." He didn't stop at street figures when it came to his extortion game either. It's said that he went as far as extorting lawyers and Italians in Georgetown too. Silk was cool and calculating but he also fortified his bourgeoning reputation as the most feared man in D.C. with sporadic outbursts of violence that seemed to come out of nowhere with no rhyme or reason.

"I had a spot over Southwest on Orange Street. I had a few young dudes hustling for me," another dude from the era relates. "One day Silk came over there to holla at me and me and slim was sitting in the apartment talking shit and joking when my little man came in the spot and told me that a New York dude around the corner told him that he couldn't hustle until he was finished with his shit. Me and Wayne looked at each other and shook our heads. Wayne told shorty to go back outside and stand on the corner and sell his shit. Shorty acted like he was scared so I told him that if Silk said it was cool, then it was cool. The young dude went back outside and started pumping. As soon as the New York dude bent around the corner to say something to shorty, Wayne stepped out of the cut beside the building and hit his ass in the head with everything he had in the clip and stepped off with the hammer smoking. When the police and ambulance arrived, Wayne popped back up with a different set of clothes, just to see who was talking to the cops." It seemed Wayne did what he did just because he could. His aura of fear was impregnable.

Part 4- The Hook Up

As Wayne put the streets of the Chocolate City in a chokehold another young hustler from Harlem, with dubious credentials, called Alpo was setting up a cocaine pipeline on the east coast corridor from New York to Washington D.C. "Alpo was a go between for dudes from D.C. looking to cop in NY after Rayful went down." A dude from NY relates. The kid Alpo had the connect up top but what he was finding out was that dudes in D.C. didn't respect out of town hustlers and Alpo kept getting got or beat out of his money by the local gangsters. He was still getting his though, because the flow of coke was non-stop, but he needed something, or he needed someone if he truly wanted to lock the city down. After Rayful Edmond's conviction there was a vacuum to fill and Alpo wanted to be the man to fill it. He had serious visions of street dreams with himself as Lucky Luciano, he just needed his own Murder Inc., because the coke was there and the price was right. "I was giving it to them at a good price." Alpo said. "If someone in D.C. had them for 21 or 22 I was giving them up for 18 a kilo." Alpo knew D.C. dudes could be treacherous, so what he really needed was someone local, someone who got mad respect and props, to watch his back.

"I met Po in 89," Wayne says. "I was out to destroy him over a lie a girl told me he said. I didn't know him, he was scared to death, but he was with my close comrade Lil Pop, who asked me not to kill Po. The broad told me Alpo said he was putting a hit on me. When I ran into him I didn't know he was Po. I told Lil Pop I hear Po be with him and I'm trying to smash him so let me know who Po is. Pop said, 'Why?' I said he told this broad he was putting a hit on me. Pop said, 'That bitch lied, if Po said that I would have smashed him.' We were in the East Side Club, so then Pop said this is Po and Po begged me and said he never said that. So Pop got the girl for lying."

As a hustler in the city Alpo knew who Wayne Perry was. Everybody did. Most big hustlers like Alpo that were moving weight tried to avoid Silk, because everybody was aware that he robbed and extorted drug dealers. Alpo knew Silk's murder game was tight also. "Anyone that mentioned his name, mentioned murder in the same sentence," Alpo said. "Because he was about his work and didn't have no problem telling everybody, because if you tried to tell or testify he was getting at you." And as Wayne related above he and Alpo eventually met. But Alpo put a different spin on it. "Through Pop, a young wild 15-year-old coming out of Southeast D.C., killing anything moving I met the cat Wayne Perry, who at that time had the town locked on fear and was putting his murder game down." Alpo said. "The kid Wayne wound up going to jail for a murder and no one was trying to get him out. The people he thought were going to get him out and come up with the money never came up with it." And when this happened the schemer Alpo saw an opportunity. An opportunity to get the most feared man in D.C. on his team.

"The young kid Pop wound up stepping to me like, 'Yo my man in jail.' His bail was like 10 grand but I saw the bigger picture," Alpo said. "I knew if I get this kid out with the reputation he has, all that will come on my side I wound up giving up the whole ten and it was ten well worth it." Lil Pop got Wayne bailed out and that was that but Alpo played it smooth letting Silk come to him. "I never really stepped to him when I got him out. I just let it be known through my little man. He wound up reaching out to me through my little man." Alpo said. "Wayne knew what my little man was about and killers respected killers and we became real tight. The kid was a real good dude and he really respected that I got him out and he felt he owed me. One thing led to another and he handled the security aspect of it, if it was time to put the murder game down, because someone was getting disrespectful or if someone was trying to come at me, that's when he stepped in." But Silk's little brother tells a different story. "How Silk met Po is 65 percent lies. That didn't happen like that. Lil Pop didn't beg Wayne not to kill Po. And Pop didn't step to Po like that either. Wayne knew and met Lil Pop way before Alpo knew him. Wayne knew Po was a bitch. Alpo has spread a whole lot of lies about a lot of shit, but everybody know Po couldn't shit in peace if it wasn't for Silk."

With Wayne, Alpo had the muscle he needed and more to take over the drug trade in city. And don't get it fucked up Silk was way more then just some hired muscle. The dude was feared more for how his mind worked then any physical thing he could do although the gunplay did play a major part in the making of the man and legend. With Wayne Perry and his team of young killers acting like a South American black op's death squad on his side, Alpo became very powerful, very quickly. Alpo was moving 30 bricks of coke a day and Silk was eating like a king. Because of Silk, Alpo had a ghetto pass and could roam D.C. safely. He was worth more to Wayne alive than dead. The intimidation and fear factor that Silk brought along with Alpo's cocaine connection proved to be a lucrative and deadly combination that easily conquered the streets of D.C. But the two would end up doing a deadly dance where only one could be the victor.

"His name was really kicking for real in 89 and 90. Once he hooked up with Alpo he really took shit to another level," E says. But there were drawbacks to the fear Silk inspired too. "At first I got a lot of negative feedback, people were like 'we aren't really trying to mess with you like that because we hear you got the kid Wayne running with you.' Because a lot of dudes were scared of this dude." Alpo said and he was a little leery himself. "I had trust for him but I always said the less he knows about where my stashes are and where I'm keeping the money the better it is. I always said I'm worth more to him alive than dead because if he doesn't know where the money is or the stash is, why would he want to bring harm to me when I'm feeding him. That's how I became real strong in D.C." Riding Silk's coattails. Because Wayne wasn't a showtime gangster like Alpo, he was the real deal.

"If he wasn't Wayne or if Wayne ain't mean shit in the streets then niggas would have been able to do what they really wanted to do to Alpo." E says. "Not to say that there wasn't niggas that tried to get at Alpo anyway. At the time niggas was saying that he let Alpo use him and so on." But that was only because dudes saw the weak Alpo hiding behind the strong Silk. They wanted to get Alpo and rob him but their fear of Silk stayed their hand. For real dudes in the city were jealous and wanted to gank Alpo, but Wayne's presence made that impossible. Then there was the reverse angle to it too, because of Silk's rep in the streets. "There was a thing going around like if you got coke from Po, after you get the coke he puts the kid Wayne and them on you. But they was just doing that because they were scared of him and they were upset to see him out of jail." Alpo said.

Eventually though Alpo and Silk became thick as thieves. "Wayne and Alpo would have so much coke and money up in the apartment that a nigga could cuff two or three kilos and they never even knew it was gone. They used to have the steel suitcases full of money," a dude who ran with them says. "When we got on, we had it all. Wayne would give us bricks, cars, anything we wanted.

You name it." And Wayne took his protection duties serious. "I remember outside a basketball game where they were playing a five man game and Wayne was the fifth man, he never touched the ball though. He just ran up and down the court next to Alpo with his hand on his gun while Alpo dribbled the ball. Niggas was scared to d-up. It was crazy." And Silk would pop up driving the 560 Benz in Versace gear too. He had mad style. He didn't fuck around either. Anybody that owed Alpo money or was fucking with him was hit too.

"One time this big time nigga owed Alpo some money," one of Wayne's partners says. "Some say it was a million dollars or close to it, but the dude didn't want to pay Alpo, he was carrying Alpo like a ho. Silk figured that the money was free since Alpo wasn't doing shit about it. So Silk caught the nigga uptown and told him, 'Look here main man, the money you owe Po ain't Po's money no more, that's my money now and I need that. I want it by tomorrow.' I was with Silk the next day and we went to get the money. It was damn near a mil too." And Silk wasn't adverse to killing in Po's name either.

"Alpo had this one nigga on his back that had the streets scared to death," a dude who was down with the crew says. "This nigga was about his business, I got to give him that. He was known for snatching niggas, killing niggas and all that. Silk respected how the nigga got down in the streets, but business is business. Silk told Alpo he'd kill the nigga but the price had to be right. Alpo coughed up the money and Silk got down to business. Silk went on the move in a Benz. He spotted the nigga uptown getting out of his truck. Silk parked the Benz and eased out with his burner in hand, real smooth, not even rushing. It was broad daylight. Wayne had a tarn on his head. By the time the nigga looked up Wayne was putting slugs in his head. When he was done, Silk walked back to the car, looked at us and said, 'Lets go get something to eat.' Slim was a wild nigga, about his business for real. Murder was his hustle, it was nothing to him, he got high off it." And the streets of D.C. was where he practiced his trade.

"It was a known fact that slim was a serious thinker, he would use his mind to get you and blow your brains out." E says. "He was able to do shit in the city that most dudes would have to have a big crew to do." And in the dog-eat-dog world of Washington D.C.'s drug game Silk was the uber-predator among predators and Alpo recognized this. In the swirling chaos of Drama City's war-torn streets Alpo pulled Wayne in real close. "He was already there but that's when I said its time to bring him closer because he knew everybody that was about, that was conniving, killing people for this and that," Alpo said. "You couldn't say anything about me in front of my man Wayne, he was a part of me."

Part 5- The Double Cross

In the streets there's a code, if you're willing to do the crime then be willing to do the time. Basically, if you get caught by the police then keep your mouth shut. Some dudes hold true to the code others don't. Dudes like Wayne Perry embodied the code and he made sure people wouldn't talk by making threats, putting his intimidation game down and by gunplay. But what he couldn't see was the betrayal by his own dude, his so-called man whom he took in and treated like a brother. The one that he was building with and breaking bread with. Wayne thought Alpo was gangster like him, but in reality Alpo was a snake. The worst kind of snake. The kind that turns into a rat when things got tough. Alpo got picked up by the feds on November 6, 1991 for a variety of drug and murder charges. The feds put him in the violent D.C. jail where a lot of his enemies were laid up plotting on him. A lot of dudes wanted to put the press game down on Alpo in the city jail for various reasons but again Wayne reached in to protect Alpo getting his people to surround him and make sure no one fucked with him while he fought his case. If Wayne only had some foresight as to what would happen he would've put the hit on Alpo himself. He should have known. Even the *Washington Post* reported that when Alpo appeared in court after his 1991 arrest he, "Sniffed loudly as tears welled up in his eyes." But Wayne was loyal.

Alpo was chilling, taking it all in stride at first but when the government started laying out their case and talking numbers he got shook. "The government wasn't dealing with Alpo like well we are going to give you 10 years or we are going to give you 15 or even 20 years." He said. "No they wanted me for the death penalty and if they couldn't give me the death penalty they wanted to give me the rest of my natural life in jail. Them crackheads wanted me so they put the full court press on me. They said we're going to hit you with the death penalty. We got you for this murder, we got you for that murder, this is capital punishment, so I'm sitting there like, 'Yo, what the hell am I going to do.'" All that gangster shit on the street was cool, but when faced with the consequences of his actions Alpo couldn't deal with it. Looking at the death penalty or life wasn't kosher for Alpo. He wasn't built like that, even though he faked like he was. "Had it not played the way it did I'm sure Wayne would've ended up killing and robbing Alpo," the dude from NY relates. But Po had his own reasoning.

"Other crews before me were coming back with natural life and my lawyer was like you really need to make a decision." Po said. "I was trying to fight. I was going through the preliminaries to see what kind of evidence they had on me. I was really trying to see if I could fight these people. I'm talking to my lawyer and he said, 'Yo, you're ace in the hole is Wayne Perry, because they're asking about him.' And I said, 'We're not going there right now. Here is 80 grand and lets get this thing rolling.'" But as the pressure mounted Alpo's resolve broke and his true colors came out. "You see, the government didn't really want Po, they wanted Wayne," Silk's little bro says. And that was the truth of it.

"My lawyer came back at me like they are trying to make a deal, they want you, but they really want Wayne Perry," Alpo said. "If you got anything good on Wayne Perry they are willing to make a deal with you. I was the less of two evils. Me and Wayne were both evil, but they were like we can sleep with him but we can't do nothing with Wayne Perry." The feds must have known all along, Wayne Perry was unbreakable but Alpo was like clay in their hands. The wheels in Alpo's head were spinning, but it doesn't matter how you justify it, a snitch is still a snitch. Silk dropped bodies to keep Alpo alive and Alpo repaid him by telling the feds everything and helping them bury Silk. Still Alpo tried to justify his actions.

"Then they started bringing in the wife and talking about going to mess with mama dukes and the sisters and the nieces." Alpo said. "My lawyers was like look, your ace in the hole is Wayne. You really need to think about that and that wasn't until almost a year later that I decided to do that. My lawyer comes back at me like they are trying to make a deal, they want you but they really want Wayne Perry so I said hold on let's talk, what do you want to know? They had to prosecute one of us so I'd rather it was Wayne Perry than me." Alpo turned on his man to save himself. He sacrificed the straight up warrior and soldier who put his life on the line to save Alpo's plenty of times, because he couldn't face the consequences of his actions. "When Po said they were messing with his moms and sister, that's a damn lie," Silk's little brother says cutting to the truth.

And the truth was that Alpo, the alleged leader of the narcotics organization, entered the Witness Protection Program and snitched on the same man who was his bodyguard and protected him in the streets of D.C. In the Chocolate City the reverberations were immediate, and have echoed to this day. By breaking weak and snitching, Alpo doing what he called "doing Po," left a black eye on the drug game and on Washington D.C. "Many people were upset but I honestly believe that if Wayne knew Alpo was a snitch Wayne would have made sure that he didn't live to tell on anyone," Little Cousin says. "As a matter of fact, a lot of these known snitches wouldn't be safe if it was up to Wayne."

Part 6- The Case

The government used a multi-pronged effort to bring Wayne Perry down. First they arrested him on murder charges to keep him on ice. *Suspected Hitman Arrested In 91 Killing*, the *Washington Times* headline read on December 5, 1992. The paper reported that a man who police believed may have been a hitman in as many as six drug gang executions was arrested in Prince George County and charged with first-degree murder in one of the slayings. Perry, 29, was jailed in Maryland for several months in the county jail on other charges. He was arrested by members of the Safe Streets Task Force as he appeared in court to plead guilty to one count of selling a counterfeit substance to an officer and charged in the October 23, 1991 death of Garrett "Gary" Terrell, "in furtherance of a continual criminal enterprise," authorities said, and taken back to D.C.

The news release said Terrell, of the 5500 block of Fourth Street NW, was shot seven times and then dumped in Rock Creek Park near 16th Street and Sherrill Drive NW, where police later found his body. Officials said Perry ordered and participated in Terrell's murder after learning Terrell planned to rob Alpo of a 100-kilogram cocaine shipment. Sources identified Perry as the premier shooter and hitman for the gang that operated in the District, Virginia, Maryland and New York. The gang was reportedly the target of the theft planned by Terrell. "Gary was putting money together to cop six million worth of coke," E says. "He had to put two million up and owe four million. Alpo put up 1.5 million and Gary $500,000, but Silk got word that it was a set up so Gary had to go." But Silk's little brother says, "That shit about the 100 keys is a bunch of bullshit. Alpo told so many damn lies that it don't make sense." Perry was arrested after a lengthy investigation and meanwhile the feds got Alpo's facts straight for a superseding federal indictment that was ready to be handed down.

"Wayne didn't care about the police or none of that," E says. "Which is why the feds wanted him so bad." And armed with their super snitch Alpo, the feds came with a vengeance. *Three Indicted in Drug Gang Killings; U.S. Attorney Could Ask for Death Penalty for Alleged Hitman*, the *Washington Post* reported on March 6, 1993 four months after they first put Silk on ice for the murder keeping him off the streets so they could gather their witnesses without fear of reprisal from Silk. Federal prosecutors unsealed the indictment that charged three men had served as armed enforcers for a violent drug gang that was responsible for nine homicides in the Washington area from 1989 to 1991. The 27 count indictment charged the three men with committing murder in the furtherance of a continual criminal enterprise, conspiring to distribute crack cocaine, racketeering conspiracy, first degree murder, retaliating against a witness, kidnapping and robbery. U.S. Attorney Jay B. Stephens said in a prepared statement that the three defendants- Wayne Perry, Tyrone Price and Michael Jackson- were charged "with the executions of nine individuals as part of a coordinated campaign to protect and promote their drug organization."

The prosecutor's office in Washington D.C. had recently become more aggressive in using sophisticated criminal laws such as the racketeering statute and continuing criminal enterprise statute against Washington D.C. drug gangs. Prosecutors said that the Perry indictment was an evolutionary step in the effort. According to the indictments the three defendants worked for Martinez and were paid for the killings either in drugs or cash. Over the life of the alleged drug conspiracy Martinez shipped more than 600 kilos of cocaine into Washington. The case was one of the first to focus on a specialized subset of a drug gang, in this instance on the three alleged gunmen. "These defendants allegedly served as hitmen to eliminate witnesses, assassinate rival drug dealers and murder disloyal gang members. The organization used these defendants as paid executioners to establish their drug organization in Washington and to eliminate those who threatened its operations." U.S. Attorney Stephens said.

From 1989 to 1991 the indictment alleged Perry was involved in eight of the groups nine alleged homicides, one of the killings described in the indictment was the July 17, 1990 shooting of Michael "Fray" Salters, a notorious Washington drug dealer who was himself the subject of a five year investigation by the D.C. Police and the FBI. Salters died the indictment alleged because Perry and Martinez learned of his plans to kill Martinez. According to the indictment, Martinez and Perry paid Jackson $9,000 cash, a half-kilo of cocaine and a 9mm handgun to kill Salters. "The indictment said Wayne and Po paid Michael Jackson nine grand to hit Fray. Bullshit." Silk's little brother says. "Po made all that shit up. Po said Fray had a clean up list of names so he could get back in pocket. Fray was already rich. And plus everybody knows Silk don't pay hits. That was all a lie in that indictment. And Michael Jackson is a fucking snake. He played Silk so false." Still Wayne had more to say about the Fray murder.

"As far as the Fray thing, I'm going to tell you about it. I wouldn't if it could get someone in trouble." Wayne says. "But dig, that was a cruddy snake move. And his trusted friends got him, not me. They put it out there that I did it. Yes, I was after Fray, because he put a hit on me. He said he had to get me out of the way so he could extort Alpo. Alpo was scared of Fray but I wasn't and Alpo felt okay as long as he had me. So I end up finding out about the hit on me and I got at those in Fray's crew who took the hit and let him know that he was next. But I couldn't track him down. So those snakes that used to be down at that shop on Georgia Avenue who were close to Fray but were scared of him tried to play both sides. So Alpo and them set it up for Fray's close buddy to hit him and then tell all Fray's people that I did cause he was close to me too, but he is a snake and has no loyalty. He even told the feds that he heard they got Fray. The dude is a snake. All the time he was the one that did it and the dudes at the shop was in on it."

In addition the indictment charged that Perry was responsible for seven other homicides, including the killing of three women in 1990 and 1991 who had been cooperating with authorities investigating the Martinez organization. Among the six persons Perry was accused of killing in the District were Evelyn Carter who was shot in the head as she left a concert at Constitution Hall in July 1991. Prosecutors said that Miss Carter and another woman, Yolanda Burley, were killed because they were cooperating with the police investigating Perry and his cohorts. Other killings were supposedly to eliminate rival drug dealers or disloyal gang members.

"When we killed this big drug dealer, Michael Fray, in D.C. that was such a big deal that this hooker started running her mouth about a situation she really didn't know anything about," Alpo said. "My man, Wayne, got upset at that. He said she has to go, she's talking too much. He killed her after a Keith Sweat concert at this place called Constitution Hall. That's just two blocks away from the White House and he just left her there." The hooker Alpo was talking about was Evelyn Carter. But Wayne found out different later. "Evelyn heard the whole lie about me killing Fray at Fray's funeral where all the dudes and the dude that got Fray were saying I did it," Wayne says. "At the time I don't know all of this and the dude who did it was my man at the time. The dude knew Evelyn heard him at Fray's funeral so he hurried up and came to me and told me she was at the funeral telling people I killed Fray. The dude knew I would believe him and ask no questions and just do what I did best, which I did. And that's my only regret. May she rest in peace. If I would have let her talk she would have told me the truth. But I wouldn't have listened because I stand for loyalty and my loyalty was with that dude. That was my man. But he was a snake." And the man Silk's talking about was his co-defendant, Michael Jackson. The feds still hadn't showed their whole hand yet though.

The indictment indicated that the case was based on the cooperation of the former leader of the gang, Alberto Martinez, also known as Alpo. Law enforcement sources familiar with the case said Martinez pleaded guilty to ordering multiple murders and received an undetermined sentence in return for his cooperation. All three defendants pleaded not guilty in an arraignment before U.S. District Court Judge Thomas Hogan. The judge, who said he would insist that all defense lawyers in the case have substantial murder trial experience, did not schedule a trail date.

The case was one of three pending in federal court in the District in which U.S. Attorney Stephens had the option of seeking the death penalty. Stephens declined to say whether he would ask for the death penalty in any of the cases. Not like it mattered too much because any case that he didn't seek the death penalty in would result in a mandatory life sentence without parole. So Silk's chances didn't look good. Defense lawyers familiar with the case said that it would be unwise for Stephens to choose these three defendants for the city's first death penalty case in more than three decades. Because the case against Perry 29, Price 38 and Jackson 33 depended on Martinez's testimony. The defense lawyers said it would prove very difficult for a jury to decide that some members of a drug gang should be executed while the confessed leader received an undetermined sentence in prison due to his cooperation against his alleged underlings. But the U.S. Attorney's office was adamant in going for the death penalty. "The reign of death which this indictment alleges vividly illustrates the kind of violence that has plagued this city as a result of narcotics trafficking," U.S. Attorney Stephens said, and he decided to hold Wayne Perry responsible for all the ills of the city.

Part 7- The Death Penalty

Execution Sought in District; First Death Case Brought Since 1971, the *Washington Post* headline read on June 9, 1993. The paper reported that Perry's case was the first death penalty case brought in D.C. since 1971. The last execution was in 1957, when Robert Carter was electrocuted for killing a police officer. In their efforts to get the death penalty approved by Attorney General Janet Reno, prosecutors filed a list of aggravating factors stating that Wayne Perry was responsible for killings for hire, torture, kidnappings and retaliation against witnesses. Federal prosecutors announced they would ask a D.C. jury to use a federal death penalty statute to convict and sentence Wayne Perry, an accused eight-time killer for the Martinez organization. Assistant U.S. Attorneys Jackson Thomas and John Dominguez informed U.S. District Court Judge Thomas Hogan that they intended to seek the death penalty for Perry. U.S. Attorney Stephens held Perry up as an example of one of the most brutal residents of the city, claiming Perry was a prime defendant to face the death penalty. According to federal law enforcement agencies the decision to seek the death penalty for Perry was approved by Attorney General Janet Reno after a review by lawyers in the Justice Department's criminal division. In the courtroom there was silence for a few moments after AUSA Jackson Thomas told Judge Hogan and Perry that the federal government would ask for the death penalty. Then in an unprecedented move AUSA Thomas handed a copy of the death notice to Perry in open court as Robert Levin, Perry's attorney stood and vigorously objected. "There is no need for them to touch my client." He said. "That was a grade B movie cheap trick." And the prosecutor's theatrics were far from over. Perry smiled broadly at friends during the court hearing despite having just heard the grim news.

Perry and his co-defendants pleaded not guilty and prosecutors did not explain why they were seeking the death penalty against Perry and not the others. Perry's wife, Twala McClain was visibly upset at the courthouse. She said it was unfair for Wayne to be singled out for the death penalty. McClain said the announcement was a surprise after the U.S. Attorney's Office had decided against seeking the death penalty in two other unrelated cases involving drug-related murder charges. "All I can do is hope and pray that things turn out for the best," McClain said. Outside the courtroom Perry's other defense lawyer Christopher Daum said the decision would have far reaching implications in the way the case was tried. "I'm not anxious to let Wayne be convicted, let alone executed," he said. He said the trial, set for September 1st would contain, "A lot of surprises," including a parade of government witnesses who had struck plea bargains with prosecutors including Albert, "Alpo" Martinez, a convicted drug kingpin who was under federal witness protection and was lined up to testify against Perry, who allegedly served as his bodyguard and chief enforcer.

"I was facing the death penalty," Wayne says. "And believe me Alpo did everything in his power to get me executed by the feds." But in the city there was a lot of outcry over the government's tactics. Several District leaders citing the results of an initiative the year before expressed concern about the prosecutor's decision. "It involves a District of Columbia crime and the voters of this city sent a very strong message of opposition to capital punishment." D.C. councilmember Jim Nathanson said. The city was clearly against the death penalty for Wayne Perry. D.C. voters had overwhelmingly rejected instituting a local death penalty the year before. The announcement that the federal government was seeking it caused an uproar in the District, where 67 percent of voters in the referendum rejected a law that would have reinstated the death penalty. "The people of this city said they don't want to be killers," councilmember David Clarke said. While federal prosecutors chose Perry as the District's worst-case scenario to use the federal death statute, Mr. Clarke said sentencing him to death went against the majority of votes cast in the congressionally mandated referendum. "If he is guilty of doing all the things he is charged with then I think he should get the maximum punishment. And the voters of the District have said that should be life in prison," Mr. Clarke said.

Vada Manager, the mayor's spokesman said the mayor supported the sentiments expressed by D.C. voters when they rejected the initiative by a 2 to 1 ratio. She said Mayor Sharon Pratt Kelly's sentiments stood with residents, who rejected the death penalty. "But these kind of prosecutor decisions are out of our less-than-sovereign status," Vada Manager said. Perry was to be tried under federal law in U.S. District Court. A 1987 federal statute provided for execution of defendants convicted of killing in furtherance of a drug conspiracy. Capital trials were the only federal trials in which jurors made the sentencing decisions. In all other cases the judge imposed the sentence. This is why there was so much outcry. If the voters already shot the death penalty down, then why would the federal government expect jurors from the city to sentence Wayne Perry to the death penalty. It smacked of prosecutor grandstanding. "It was no doubt that Silk was going to stand up like a 'G' when it came time to face the music," E says. And as the government maneuvered to put Wayne Perry to death for his alleged crimes and the allegations of government stooge and snitch Alpo, the street legend and most feared man in D.C. took it all in stride. The politicking went on in the courtroom and in the papers for another six months with several delays and much fanfare. Finally the dust cleared and it was time to see what was what.

Death Penalty Trial Probable for DC Drug Case Defendant, the *Washington Times* headline read on February 21, 1994. It was to be the first death penalty case brought to trial in the city in more than two decades. Since that June when the U.S. Attorneys announced it would seek a federal death sentence for Perry, defense attorneys repeatedly challenged the decision in court. But U.S. District Judge Hogan rejected their legal arguments, meaning Perry's lawyers failed to block federal prosecutors in the case. Perry was preparing to go on trial for his life. "As it stands now we're preparing for a death penalty trial," Robert Morin, one of Perry's new defense lawyers said. Morin and fellow defense lawyer Henry Asbill, both with extensive experience in capital cases, were appointed to replace Perry's former attorneys after prosecutors announced the death penalty decision in June. It was to be the first death penalty case brought in the District since 1971.

Part 8- Guilty Plea

But all the fanfare and grandstanding was for nothing because when it came down to it there was no trial and no death penalty. Call it a government bluff to get the newspaper headlines, but that's all it turned out to be. *Killer Cops Plea, Gets Life Sentence in Five Murders*, the *Washington Times* headline read on April 1, 1994. A District man federal prosecutors had said they would seek the death penalty against for numerous drug-related homicides pleaded guilty in U.S. District Court on May 31, 1994 and was immediately sentenced to five life terms in prison to be run consecutively without parole, the paper reported. Wayne Perry was scheduled to stand trial the next week, but he pleaded guilty to five counts of murder and furthering a continuing criminal enterprise instead of going to trail and facing execution, Kevin Olson, a spokesperson for the U.S. Attorney's Office said. Immediately after entering his plea, Judge Hogan sentenced him. Perry pleaded guilty to, "Murder in the furtherance of a continuing criminal enterprise," for the killings of Domenico Benson, who was shot as he shook Alpo's hand because he allegedly slapped Alpo's wife in a previous altercation with her, Evelyn Carter, Yolanda Burley, Alveta Hopkins and Garrett Terrell. "With a plea like this we can guarantee the outcome," AUSA Dominguez said, who together with AUSA Thomas signed the plea bargain agreement.

Perry pleaded guilty to five counts of his lengthy indictment in exchange for having all the remaining counts dropped, a promise that federal prosecutors would not pursue those counts at a later date and that the death sentence would not be imposed during sentencing. The Justice Department also agreed to recommend to the Prince George County State's Attorney office that it not prosecute Perry for the murder of David "Duke" Short who was murdered on December 26,1989. "I'm a very loyal man," Wayne says. "I don't fear nothing and no one but God. The fear of weaker guys put me in prison. Alpo made false statements and told countless lies that got me five consecutive life sentences. Make no mistake about it, Alpo is a spineless coward, a rat of the highest order."

Despite smiles and encouragement to his common-law wife, Twala Mc-Clain and laughs he shared with defense attorneys, Perry was concerned his plea bargain agreement not have the appearance of cooperation with prosecutors against the codefendants in the murder racketeering case. The judge acknowledged for the record Perry was not trying to implicate others with his plea. Before the proceedings Perry looked back to his wife and said, "Be strong." She smiled back at him. "I'll always be there for him," his wife said after sentencing. "He was good to me."

U.S. Attorney Eric Holder said that lawyers for Perry approached him to re-open negotiations on a plea agreement 10 days before the trial. "They told us there were a number of changed circumstances. In light of the changed circumstances and an offer to plea to five counts of murder we thought it appropriate to accept the plea." Holder said. "This was the best decision for everyone concerned," Henry Asbill, one of Perry's lawyers said. "The guilty plea obviously involved sensitive and personal things. Eric Holder is to be commended for making the difficult decision of depoliticizing the death penalty and withdrawing the death notice." Tyrone Price, Perry's co-defendant, plead guilty a week later. Tyrone Price admitted to killing Garrett Terrell in October 1991 and Alveta Hopkins in September 1990. Ms. Hopkins had testified against Price in a D.C. Superior Court case.

"I maintain that this criminal justice system is corrupt and that these so-called African American men are its prey." Wayne says. "If we black people of this society will open up our eyes we can make this society a better place for us. But our own kind keeps aiding and assisting the problem instead of fighting the problem." And Velma Porter, whose son Rich Porter was murdered by Alpo up in Harlem had this to say about the situation involving Alpo snitching on Silk. "When Alpo admitted to snitching on his most prize confident in D.C., Wayne Perry, that must have ripped Wayne's soul apart more than any sentence that could have been imposed. Its said that Wayne Perry was so hurt during his indictment he didn't even try to deny the accusations because he couldn't believe that the very man he tried to keep alive at all costs was trying to kill him via a lengthy prison sentence."

And for all the speculation about Silk and his guilty plea it all comes down to one factor, death before dishonor. Silk lived by the code and when he could take all the weight on his shoulders he saw no reason to share the burden. That's just how the street legend was cut. But let him tell it. "I didn't cop out because of the death penalty," Wayne says. "I live to die. I copped out to make sure others didn't get life. I took the bull by the horns to save others. That's the kind of man I am." And so the legend lives on. In March of 1994, at 32-years-old, Wayne Perry's run in the streets was over.

Part 9- The Legend

"Wayne was known for being a dangerous motherfucker. A nigga that didn't care who you was supposed to be. He also knew how important it was to have a rep. He got a lot done in the streets because of who he was," E says. In the streets his rep was legendary, and since that time he has become a mythical figure, a gunslinger-type and go-hard soldier from the crack era. "When

I was young niggas used to talk about Wayne like he was Billy the Kid or something, a lot of things that legends are made of are bigger than the truth, a little bit added here and a little bit added there. Niggas that feared him made him larger than life. If you heard about him you wouldn't want to get to know him. But if you were a man you could deal with him." E says.

"Those in the game know that I am a man that believes in death before dishonor as well as kill or be killed," Wayne says and unlike most he really means what he says. "There was no other like slim, he took the murder game to another level." Manny says and the accolades Silk has received from his peers, those locked down in the belly of the beast, are far reaching and numerous. They know his values, they recognize his credentials and they respect his gangster. They appreciate his worth and realize the true merit of his legend. "Coming from Southwest 203 and being able to move about the city and get money, protect a sucker like Alpo that most robbers chased around until Wayne gave him a pass and all the gunplay and shit Wayne got away with made him a legend." Little Cousin says. "I consider him a legend because he moved about the Murder Capital during its most dangerous years, doing most of the things people claimed he did." A larger than life persona whose stature dwarfed the times he was present for on the streets.

"If you was to pick the top five niggas out of D.C. when it comes to the murder game, Wayne would be number one and number two. Silk knew how to get away with murder. He was a nigga that could kill with no mask. Nobody was going to tell, they knew what he would do if somebody was telling. Silk ain't have no picks," Manny says. And that's real. Dude was vicious. "Even if I knew it would cause me life in the pen I would have put at least seven shells in a head that deserved it," Wayne says and he did. Ain't no fronting about it. He's not some actor or rapper rapping about it. He's real life, he lived the life. A real live gangster. "He wanted to be the baddest nigga that ever did it and when it comes down to what he did, he was the baddest nigga that ever did it. Point blank, you can't get around that. Slim has been gone for over 15 years now and he is still talked about and will continue to be spoken of." Manny says.

And Wayne doesn't support the hip-hop industry glorifying dudes like Alpo either. "As for the DVD on the dude, I care less," Wayne says. "I know fools out there sell their soul due to the love of money. So they have no morals. They'll glamorize a rat just for the sake of a dollar. Alpo ain't never been a man. He always was a coward. Just like Rayful. And fools will accept them for the sake of money. That's why I have no respect for a lot of rappers and NY dudes as well as dudes from D.C. and all over. Jadikiss said, 'The game is getting scary, everybody talking about Alpo, what about Wayne Perry?' Jada said fools are giving props to snitches and forgetting about the stand up warriors. I respect that. Now fools talk like 50 Cent is street when he hot as fish grease. I will never understand how people praise and romanticize snitches, rats and sellouts." Silk doesn't have to worry about that, his legend is intact.

"Wayne was one of the best who ever put D.C. in a chokehold," Sop-Sop says. "He was a good, well respected man of honor. He was well respected by myself and by other men like me. Wayne used to come down Lorton with the Southwest basketball team and leave us money, shoes, clothes, whatever he had to give. He always made sure we was alright." Silk's loyalty and the way he looked out for his homies was well known. He was one of the few who talked the talk, walked the walk and backed it all up. If Silk said it, it was as good as gold. His word was steel. Dude was not faking it. "I didn't fall down from heaven, but I surely came up from hell and if I'm ever offered to betray the life I lived I would rather spend the rest of my life in jail," Wayne says.

"To me, Wayne's legacy as far as street legends go, is that he was one of the most notorious killers in the city. He is a nigga that will always be remembered, always be loved and hated, but more important he will always be the first street nigga that the feds wanted off D.C. streets so bad that they were going for the death penalty on slim," E says. "Dudes that fuck with him speak highly about him. Those that know him remember how funny slim was, slim was a wild nigga. Niggas remember how he used to put that work in." Now that's gangster. And the streets have mythologized the man. Still Wayne is fucked up by the state of the drug game, "What has the game come to? When has it been right to praise or accept rats, liars and traitors? Never. Even the government that prosecuted me, as hypocritical, oppressive and corrupt as it is, despises those that defect or betray, for they reject and punish their own traitors for treason." Wayne says. "Rats have tainted the game. You can't trust guys in the game because when the heat comes down they're selling out."

But Silk's legend will forever be remembered as that of a gunslinger straight out of the Wild West or more accurately straight out of Drama City, the nation's capital. He came up under a hail of bullets with his gunplay on one million, and left with the shots still ringing. A dude from the era remembered it best. "Silk done saved my life more than once," the dude says. "One time I was up the Met rapping to this bad-ass little broad and her man came out of nowhere talking a rack of shit so me and him ended up getting into it inside the club. He had like four or five dudes with him. The dude told me that we could take it outside so I'm like cool, but I gotta get to my car to get my pistol and these niggas right on my back. As soon as I stepped outside who do I see? Silk and a few other men down from the west. Silk was like, 'What's up slim?' I told him that the niggas was on my back and without talking Silk pulled his shit out and opened fire on them niggas. Silk aired the joint out." Just like a gunslinger of old, shoot first, ask questions later. Billy the Kid doesn't have anything on Wayne Perry.

Part 10- In Retrospect

"Wayne Perry is probably the realest nigga that I have known or come in contact with," Manny says of the street legend now serving five life sentences locked down at ADX Florence, the feds supermax. Even from there his name reverberates in the streets. And Silk has spoken out about the publicity dudes like Alpo have received in street publications, DVD's and documentaries. "Cowards like Alpo are not to be looked up to as honorable," Wayne says. "He betrayed the game in many ways. No rat or betrayer can ever be honorable. I am a victim of circumstances as well as a scapegoat for a rat, snitch, liar, fuck boy who had no guts, morals, principles or compassion for anyone other than himself. I was Alpos sacrifice, me and others. He used us to save his own ass from a 35 year sentence." Because in reality that's probably all Alpo was facing. All the life sentence and death penalty stuff Alpo alluded to was just a justification for why he snitched. It wasn't true. In Silk's opinion a dude like Alpo deserves no glory, no recognition and no respect. Any snitch in

Wayne's book deserves death. "I would die a thousand deaths before I ever compromised my principles as a man." Wayne says. "As I think back, I always knew Alpo was weak and capable of everything displayed. I had my reasons for not putting him in the dirt. I should have put the barrel in his mouth." That was Silk's biggest mistake, not hitting dude in the head before he told.

"My reason for pleading out loud is to further expose and apprise you of two cold blooded bitches and snitches named Alberto Martinez aka Alpo and Jerome Kerney." Wayne says. "Why do I further apprise you of this rat Alpo? Because he has been getting praised and respected as if he's an honorable man that has principles. My question to all those who have been praising and glamorizing this coward and bitch is this, how can you consciously and intently give a known rat, liar and coward, that would sell out his own flesh and blood in order to salvage himself, a forum to speak and voice his opinion as if he was an honorable and principled man?" And Wayne has a valid point and he long ago realized his downfall. "My biggest mistake was that I trusted a half-rat, half-snake and I'm a victim to his master plan." He says.

"There are niggas that call Wayne dumb because he protected Alpo and Alpo sold him out," E says. "But overall, like him or not, niggas know slim was about his business on them bricks. I say that because for all the shit he was doing in the streets, niggas ain't get at him. Nobody killed him and we all know he was getting his man when it came time to grab the guns." Silk's stature on the bricks is legendary and his loyalty to the code of the streets is unquestioned. Dudes know what's up with Silk and some like to talk that shit but they know they never could've ate in his presence. "Niggas that talk shit about Silk now that he's been gone 15 years wouldn't dare jump their ass out there. One thing about Wayne, he went at whoever," Manny says.

Whether on the set or in the pen, Silk's known to get his. He doesn't and never has fucked around. He lets others talk and stays true to himself and stays humble about his exploits and status in the streets and in gangster lore. "I really don't speak about my past and haven't spoken about my past in a long time," Wayne says. "Because even though I speak facts and the truth, one could easily mistake the truth for arrogance. I hate arrogance." And the streets recognize and honor Silk for the man he is.

A coward dies a thousand times, a soldier only dies but once and in reality, Wayne Perry would die a thousand deaths before he would accept kissing ass and rolling over. But being the soldier he is he only has to die once with his reputation and integrity intact. "I refuse to kiss ass or compromise," Wayne says. "It's death before dishonor with me. I ain't going for nothing." It's always been death before dishonor with Silk and when he says death before dishonor, he means it and will die for it, it's what he stands for.

Wayne Perry was a stand up guy to the fullest. He stood up and received five life sentences. He played the game and took the heat when it came and didn't try to pass the blame like so many showtime gangsters do today. To him a rat is the worst thing a dude could ever be. "I will say that Silk was one of the most ruthless niggas to ever play the game in D.C. or any other city." E concludes. "There was a lot of mean niggas to come out of D.C. on that gunplay tip, but Wayne, during his run, was at the top of the list when it came to the murder game."

Chapter 3

Anthony Jones

Born and raised in the mean streets of Baltimore, a city famous for its culture of drugs and murder, Anthony "AJ" Jones embarked on a reign of terror that the city had never seen before and has never seen since. In the violent world of Bodymore's inner city drug gangs, at the young age of 18, Anthony Jones reigned king. Holding court in East Baltimore's gritty neighborhoods and holding fast to his thuglife ideals of "get mine or be mine."

The most feared drug dealer and gangster in Charm City, AJ allegedly ordered murders from his prison cell. He was a boss in every sense of the word, from the streets of his hood to the federal penitentiaries. His reputation of being willing to kill anyone who stood in his way was demonstrated by the fact that AJ reputedly had his own brother killed because he believed that he was snitching on him. AJ played the game the way it was supposed to be played, as long generations of B-More hustlers had before him, but with his own vicious twist. He will forever be remembered in B-More as the legend that he is.

Part 1- East Baltimore

The 1700 block of East Oliver Street could be any ordinary Baltimore venue on a hot asphalt day, neat little rowhouses with windows agape, neighbors on their stoops watching life go by, children splashing one another with water guns. But then there were other sidewalk details not uncommon in an impoverished stretch of the city such as that, the sound of random gunfire at sunset that forced residents to cower in their kitchens. It was a puzzling atmosphere in which the likes of Anthony Ayeni Jones rose to become one of the most vicious drug lords in the city's history.

The son of two highly intelligent, doctorate-holding Nigerian immigrants, Jones was given up at an early age by the well-to-do couple from Africa. A series of homes with relatives followed, including one where his new brother and mother were killed in his formative years. "His mother is actually real blood kin to my mother who was killed along with my brother. The person who adopted us is our blood great aunt." Darnell "Mookie" Jones, AJ's brother says. "She adopted me, Anthony and my lil' brother named Tugg who was killed in 1993. That was the person who raised us all our entire life. We always lived with members of our own family." But Anthony's upbringing in a neighborhood beset by poverty, rampant drug use and violence contributed to the person he became. In East Baltimore, drug dealers damaged the community severely, crippling it with crack, heroin and cocaine. Drug dealers were a way of life where AJ grew up. He saw them and the destruction they caused daily from his earliest years. They sold drugs with impunity and for every dealer locked up three more young men jumped up to take their place. That was the way it worked in Baltimore.

Good cops, bad cops, drug lords and snitches roamed the streets of East Baltimore. It was just like *The Wire* portrayed. In the hard luck neighborhoods, drug dealers sat on the front steps and sold out the front door. The Baltimore police worked hand-in-hand with the informants and undercovers trying to unearth that next hood star and money-getting hustler who had the game on lock. B-More is a black man's world. The blacks are politicians, cops and administrators. They are the wealthy, the poor, the gangbanging and the bourgeois. *The Wire* depicts the violent world of Baltimore's inner city drug gangs, but Anthony Jones was real life, in East B-More the code of the streets was in full effect. Because with AJ and his crew it was death before dishonor. This world of drugs, violence and street culture is what AJ rose out of. Just like Tupac, he came from the gutter. To survive, people in AJ's world knew they had to rely on themselves and their own set of rules. Some call it the street code and Anthony Jones lived by it. He was the embodiment of the code. In the streets of East Baltimore he was admired for getting his props by any means necessary. He accomplished this with violence, by confronting authority, by having mad heart, by having nerves of steel, and by really doing it his way and not conforming to societal norms. He was an innovator as well as an organizer.

"Anthony has a smart head on his body." Ruth Jones, the great aunt who adopted him said. "I wanted him to go to college." And in a different world AJ might have. He was a good student in math and reading in high school. In some respects he was seen as a positive role model urging youngsters to stay in school, even as he felt the pull of the streets. "Anthony was about the best child I ever had." Ruth said. "I'm 71-years-old and I don't have no right to tell a lie. Anthony is a good child. He had respect for me, and he didn't do nothing in front of me. Anything they go and do, they do on their own. All I know is I love him. He's still my child." A child who grew into a monumental street legend.

In economically and socially deprived areas there's a tendency to look for people who become successful in any business, even an illicit one. Youngsters need someone to look up to. With a lack of role models and a lot of single mothers, kids in the ghettos usually turn to one of their own. These role models are chosen as leaders because they control a segment of their surroundings. They control a piece of the violent drug markets which dominate their worlds. It's a completely different set of values and one that Anthony Jones mastered and seized upon brutally.

Part 2- Coming of Age

The complicated dance between the law and Anthony Jones began when he was in his teens. Officer Edward Bochniak and Sergeant John Sieracki- part of a team of drug investigators known as the Zone Rangers for their zealous pursuit of dealers-learned in 1990 that a gang that recruited neighborhood youngsters was using the rowhouse where Jones lived to stash guns and drugs. The gang's main business took place a block away on the Boulevard.

"The whole crew was young boys back around 90-91, except for Darty." says Kid, an East Baltimore hustler now doing time in the feds. "Back then they had some guys called the Schoolhouse Boys, they blew up the Boulevard, then Ant and them came up." The Boulevard, which was actually Monford Avenue and Biddle Street, consisted of old rowhouses. "Nobody lived on the block," Kid says. "There's a bar on one corner and a Chinese store on the other. There's a school right there and a laundry mat too."

The Schoolhouse Boys was a gang led by Nathaniel Dawson Jr., a native of

New York, who held a firm grip on the turf for years, defending it with deadly force when the need arose. Local residents were hired as managers, sellers and lookouts. It was here that the young AJ first earned his stripes as a drug dealer while still in his early teens. First working for Dawson learning the ropes, then later on his own, opening up spots on East Federal Street and Rutland. AJ developed a reputation with police as polite when confronted with authority but brazen and violent on the street. "AJ was a vicious dude," Kid says. "Even back then. They were into a lot of robbing and killing. That's what his crew was into. All of them used to ride dirt bikes. Like YZ80's and shit. Little Net, AJ's man, was the baddest. He was like a dirt bike specialist. He'd be doing tricks, one handed wheelies with the peace sign, throwing it up." The whole crew was wild and mobile, young and dangerous, on dirt bikes, with guns and drugs for sale.

"I met Anthony through my homeboy Bryant from Warrick," Sweat says. "They used to ride them dirt bikes. I always thought he was Bryant's connect because AJ looked like an African. I figured he had the heroin hook up. A lot of them Nigerians in the city do. He used to observe a lot of shit. He was real quiet. Me, Anthony and Little Net got tight. I liked him as a person. I remember one day I was Westside on 1400 block of Fulton Avenue. I seen them all coming up on dirt bikes, Little Net, Bryant, Anthony came over and hollered at me. They had blue scarves on, asking me if I was hanging out. They would put me up on shit. Ant showed a lot of love." From his two-story rowhouse at Rutland and Oliver Streets, AJ built a small but loyal core of heavily armed and ruthless associates all in their teens. At the age of 17, when most teenagers are looking for an adult to buy them beer, AJ got an older cousin to buy him weaponry. Guns became his M.O., his signature feature was laser aim sight systems, which projected a red dot on its target. Being the innovator he was, AJ also flipped the script and sold cocaine in heroin city.

"Anthony loved everything about being a drug dealer," said a law enforcement source who investigated Jones for years. "He took the job to heart. He played the game real hard." And as he was coming of age he also developed a reputation as a stone cold killer and stick-up kid. He would rob people from around the way at will. "Most of the dudes they robbed were older, more established hustlers," Kid says. "Anthony had the long trench coat with guns down each side," Sweat adds. "Ant was cool. If you was on his team it was good. We used to go over there and holler at them." And as AJ's name started ringing bells, the Zone Ranger investigators slowly built their case, arrest by arrest, struggling to develop informants and leads that would get them enough evidence to search Jones' house. Then the unexpected happened, a shooting invited them in. In Jones' bedroom, 14-year-old Tezara Horsey died on June 21, 1991 from a bullet to the head, suffered as she chatted with him, police reported.

According to Darnell "Mookie" Jones, AJ's brother, the first time the police became aware of the crew was with that event. Mookie, 13 at the time, was playing with a gun and it accidentally shot and killed his girlfriend who died immediately. "It was an accidental shooting because I was playing with a gun and it skipped chambers and shot her in the head," Mookie says. "Anthony was upset with me because he had told me numerous times on numerous occasions about playing with guns." The police went to the house and took him into custody. And while they were there they claimed to have observed numerous plastic bags and balloon material that they believed were cocaine kilo wrappings. "They killed the girl in the basement at their house," Sweat says. Word on the street conflicted with Mookies' account though, rumor had it that the girl was cheating on AJ. "What really got him on was when his brother took the charge for the girl that got killed at his house," Kid confirms. "They said the gun fell. Everybody thought AJ was gonna go to jail but his little brother Mookie took the charge." But Mookie sets the record straight, "The rumor that the police planted, that Anthony murdered her and got me to take the charge wasn't true. I was the person who was locked up for the murder of Tezara Horsey, which was not an actual murder." The shooting, tragic as it was, had another unfortunate twist. The plastic kilo wrappings the police found gave them probable cause and led to a warrant. AJ wouldn't be free for long. His little venture into crime was out in the open and so started his long descent into the criminal justice machinery. But AJ battled them admirably.

Detectives found several guns- a Glock, two Berettas and two Mac 10's. All the guns had infrared laser lights attached to them, something usually only seen in hitman movies. The .40 caliber Glock matched ballistics for the weapon used to seriously wound a young man named Lee Lane and put a bullet in the foot of one of Jones' suspected drug runners, 16 year-old Roosevelt Hurt. There were bullets and shotgun shells, drug paraphernalia and 25 grand in cash, leading to multiple drug and weapon related charges against AJ. It was a dreary October evening in 1991 when police arrived and arrested the 17-year-old Jones on conspiracy charges. His arrest was headline news in the city as police swept the neighborhood, proclaiming an end to AJ's teenage crew.

The police arrested 15 youths connected to the drug operation, some as young as 11. Police said AJ and his youthful cohorts were linked to 20 shootings. Jones and the 15 juveniles were charged with numerous conspiracy, drug and weapon counts. Police reported that AJ could spend a century behind bars. To the Eastern District cops from the Zone Ranger squad, who posted pictures of AJ on their walls, and conducted the investigations, and to the neighbors who feared what police called a ruthless gang of dealers, only halfway through their teens, AJ's arrest that night was a huge victory.

"He was young, he had guns and he had a lot of young people involved with him." Baltimore Police Major Alvin Winkler, who was commander of the Eastern District during the height of the 1991 Jones' investigation said. But AJ's notoriety was just starting to build. "He didn't really catch his reputation until he came home on that million dollar bail," Kid says alluding to the big arrest. And neighborhood residents were pleased with Jones' arrest. "You want to know if the neighborhood is pleased?" Evelyn Hinton, a neighbor said. "Yes. It was a long time coming. Now if they can keep them from going through the revolving door, we'll be all right." But despite the high hopes of police and neighborhood residents, that the kid kingpin would be put away for a century, he served exactly 363 days.

The charges from June and October boiled down in a plea bargaining process and a relatively stiff sentence turned into parole. AJ pleaded guilty to conspiracy to distribute drugs and with no adult record, Baltimore Circuit Judge Ellen M. Heller sentenced him to 10 years with 5 suspended. But AJ appeared an ideal candidate for the state's new boot camp program because he was still a teenager. AJ was sent to the military-style boot camp where he marched his way to parole within a year. All his co-defendants took suspended sentences after pleading guilty, so the whole crew was shortly back out on the street. Eastern District Police were shocked, to say the least.

"We thought we had a strong case. When the federal government didn't prosecute we were very upset about it. It was a slap in the face," Major Winkler said. City police said Jones' cousin, Shelia Kelly, bought eight guns for her underage cousin, two of which were found in AJ's house. The case went to the ATF who investigated and forwarded it for prosecution. But federal prosecutors declined to proceed, starting AJ's remarkable run of slipping through the cracks of the justice system and his rise to infamy in Baltimore's underworld.

Part 3- Notoriety

The story of Anthony Jones begins one block south of the old Rutland Elementary school, in the 1700 block of East Oliver Street where there lies a long history of pain and violence. Ten year old Tauris Johnson died on this block on November 4, 1993, the innocent victim of a gun battle between two drug dealers. A key witness to the shooting was executed three months later. In the streets of drug and murder-torn East Baltimore this was nothing new. The gangsters who plied their trade in the streets inspired fear and respect. And those qualities were bought at the barrel of a gun. When AJ came home from boot camp his crew coalesced around him.

"All of them were at boot camp- Baby Dan, Ant, Shugg- then he came home and they started going crazy like 93. Darty, Anthony Green. They shot Fat Kev and robbed him, they robbed Rosalyn's mother. They weren't hustling. They were robbing people. They were catching licks the whole time. This was when they were hitting people. Down in VA too." Kid says. AJ was trying to make up for lost time. To get back what he had before. As he built up his cash flow and product from the robberies, he opened up more drug spots, but he changed up his operation.

AJ became wise to police tactics, shifting his operation from house to house. Part of playing the game meant learning the methods of police and the mistakes of other dealers. AJ was adept at thwarting officer's attempts to monitor his business and this time he recognized most of the detectives who set sights on him. After the shooting at his house in 91 he moved the tools of his trade out of the house. He surrounded himself with workers young enough to flow through the juvenile system quickly, with less chance of harsh punishment. He changed telephones and pagers like shoes. He was on point. A young ruthless businessman trying to come up.

"He got real dangerous in like 93, 94. Since then his name has been ringing, ringing loud. Shit started getting crazy. He had strips, big strips. He had them locked. They were gangsta, taking niggas out. Selling them vials. Lots of them." Sweat says. And the robberies continued. "The niggas was doing so much stuff. AJ had control of those dudes. They were robbing dudes they weren't all right with. Wearing the masks and shit. They got that shit from *Point Break*. Ronald Reagan and George Bush masks in the hood, that shit was crazy. They would kick dudes doors down and shit like that." Kid says. But AJ had some close calls too, with both his life and the law.

"In 93, the girl's father, that his brother took the beef over, was a bartender at Sinclair Inn. He shot AJ in the back. AJ grabbed a chair and jumped right through the window to get away. That was the first time he got shot." Kid says. And his arrests piled up, but AJ had help from a corrupt cop who was on the druglord's payroll and who made cases against AJ disappear. "He was the new era. He had police on his team," Sweat says. AJ had learned the stakes of the game and decided that he would up the ante by getting a five-O in his pocket. AJ also kept his crew in check and took care of them. "He took care of people in his organization. In many ways he was a good manager. He expanded his marketplace and thrived." An investigator said. As the four corner hustlers in East Baltimore did their thing under AJ's leadership, the drug game started popping, gaining the crew admiration and respect in the hood. They handled all problems with that vicious gunsmoke. Nobody in AJ's crew was afraid to bust his gun. They thought they were in the Wild, Wild West, but they were in East Baltimore. Things progressed from bad to worse.

"You can't use your living room and sometimes your kitchen because they start shooting at night," a resident complained. But AJ didn't care he was dispensing ghetto justice, living and dieing by the gun. As the money came in he allowed himself some fancy touches- a gold Gucci watch, a black Blazer out-fitted with a Nintendo game, a television and CD player. In his bedroom, dur-ing one raid, police found leather coats and 150 pair of sweat socks. In general though, he kept the fruits of his alleged one million-a-year business out of sight. And he kept his crew thirsty too, so they'd be more willing and ready to kill at his command. "Most of his dudes were thirsty, they weren't getting no bread. They had like 5-10 grand." Kid says. AJ didn't buy his crew's loyalty, he inspired it with words and deeds and the overall magnitude of his personal-ity. His influence was magnetic.

Part 4- Locking It down

The local pastor, Reverend Anthony Johnson of Mount Hebron Baptist Church described Jones as "a real nice young man," one on one. And he tried to get AJ to join his church. "He told me that he would attend," the Reverend said. "But he never did." And how could he? AJ was too busy in the streets getting shit locked down. It's not easy being a druglord and it's not easy to put your 'G' down in the streets of Bodymore. "B-More is a hustlers paradise," Sweat says. "But you've got to be able to hold your own or you'll get took off." And AJ was working both angles. He was an equal opportunity gangster. Holding his own and taking other people off. Court papers say Jones, "was dis-tributing large quantities of cocaine and heroin in Baltimore City." But they didn't know about his extracurricular robbing activities. His status as a druglord grew though, due to his management skills in matters of fear and de-struction. AJ wasn't shy about putting in work or busting his gun and neither was his crew. "He had a reputation as a gangster. He had a whole crew of dudes that did what he said." Kid says and the reputed baby 'G', because re-member he was not even 20-years-old yet, was a definite force to be reckoned with on multiple levels. AJ was like pure chaos on the streets. A triple shot of speedball right into the vein. "They was laying their murder game down. They didn't fuck around. It wasn't an ego thing. It was just business," Sweat says. "They were on the block at Ellsworth getting that 28 grand a day. AJ was on a bunch of streets. He was basically trying to take over the whole joint."

And AJ put the city on notice, fuck with me or my crew and face swift and deadly retribution. The kid wasn't selling death, he was dealing it in spades. "He's one of the most violent drug dealers in the history of Baltimore City, without a doubt," said Zone Ranger Detective Ed Bochniak, who investigated Jones' organization in the early 1990's. "He was unbelievable, and I was messing with him when he was 17. Even then, he was a scary guy." And AJ's reputation was well deserved. "Dudes were getting leery of shorty. They was known for robbing dudes. Every week it seemed like they were doing something. They chased a dude into the barbershop and shot him. They shot another dude in the parking lot. AJ always had like 10 dudes around him." Kid says. "He wasn't playing. He was serious."

Gang violence escalated in 1994 when AJ was arrested in the slaying of Keith "Shugg" Westmoreland, who was shot in a Gay Street rowhouse over a drug debt, police reported. AJ spent a month behind bars before prosecutors dropped charges. There were no witnesses. "The mask move that the media made so much about was Shugg, they used to be all together, but they fell out over a girl named Sarah. That was 94. That was the second time Ant had shot Shugg too. He got him one time before that." Kid says. In December 1994, police charged a 17-year-old member of Jones' crew with killing two people in a drug related robbery in a Streeper Street house. Those charges were also dropped, no witnesses. It would become a recurring theme.

"He created total devastation in that neighborhood." Major Winkler said. "This fellow should never have been let out of jail." The cases against AJ and his crew were weak though, and with witnesses scared to testify against AJ or his people, a culture of terror spread across East Baltimore. Cross AJ and you die. Testify against him and you die. Invade his territory and you die. That's was just how it was. The kid was playing for keeps. That was just the way the youngster carried it.

Part 5- The Beef

AJ was locking shit down but not everyone bowed down. Dudes were still willing to get theirs, AJ's reputation or not. AJ was still flesh and blood, no matter how menacing he was. Elway Williams was an East Baltimore dealer with a $15,000 a day heroin ring that prosecutors said competed against Jones.

Instead of sharing the market, AJ and Elway decided to battle it out, turning East Baltimore into a killing zone. The beef which started out as a death for death retribution type-thing, quickly spiraled out of control, turning into a murderous web between the warring drug organizations, where victory or death became the only options. "You had love from both sides," Sweat says. "But that shit turned into a snowball flip. The beef started over some foolishness. Both Anthony and Elway had egos. Anthony was quiet, but vicious and Elway thought he was Al Capone. He was a Bumpy Johnson wanna-be type nigga. And he didn't think Anthony had it in him, but he found out." Elway would lock horns with AJ in a battle to the death. May the victor win all the spoils and be crowned the king of East Baltimore.

"It was always a twist to that." Sweat says. "Who was gonna be the king of East Baltimore? They was playing for keeps. They was going back and forth. It was some jealous type shit. They were trying to get each other." And in this environment of fear and suspicion, bravado and one-upmanship, retribution and death were swift. "The streets make you. They say who the boss is. Both Elway and Ant's ego's were bigger than their pride." Sweat concludes. Assistant United States Attorney Christine Manuelian said that the Jones and Williams groups frequently battled on city streets. "There are a number of murders that have been allegedly linked to both organizations," she said. In East Baltimore the bullets were flying. It wasn't Beirut, but it was close. The deadly dance was played out with Mac 10's, mini Uzi's and sawed off shotguns.

Describing the duel of drug kingpins that created a climate of kill or be killed, AJ's rival, the heroin dealer Elway testified that he was in a race against time to assassinate his nemesis who was allegedly intent on killing him. "He was out to assassinate all of us. We had to fix the problem and the problem was Anthony Jones. We had to continue to search to assassinate him. It was either they kill us or we kill them." Elway testified after becoming a prosecution snitch. He testified that no show of strength- he frequently had armed bodyguards protecting him- seemed to be able to ward off Jones' attempts to assassinate him. AJ was on a mission. And he was trying to win at all costs. It was like 50 Cent said, get rich or die trying.

"It was all dudes from East Baltimore," Kid says of the beef. It started in early 95 when Baby Dan and AJ formed an alliance against Elway. AJ killed Elway's partner and his former running mate Anthony Green first. On October 3, 1995, AJ was shot in the arm. "The second time he was shot was when Elway put the hit on him." Kid says. And Sweat goes into more detail, "Anthony told me, he said he came out some house and somebody tried to assassinate him. His man was there with the car to pick him up and when the shots started busting off and Anthony got hit, he jumped on the back of the car to get away. While he was in John Hopkins Hospital they got his man Little Net. This was the breaking point. Elway was the one he was beefing with and the whole thing with this was when Tupac killed Little Net for Elway and didn't get AJ too, he basically signed his own death warrant."

Raymund "Tupac" Harrison admitted to the killing on October 5th, 1995 of Deshane "Little Net" Carter, Jones' right hand man, who was gunned down on East Madison Street. Tupac said it was done to avenge the slaying earlier that year of Anthony Green, Elway's partner. Harrison said during his guilty plea that Little Net was thought by Elway to have been the trigger man in the Green killing. After AJ was shot up and Little Net killed, Elway was profiling like he was the king of East Baltimore. "He was at 32nd Street Plaza, when we got over there, Elway's sitting at the bar. He tells the bartender all drinks on me. I noticed he was celebrating because they killed shorty. I was wondering what was running through Anthony's mind. When Elway left, his sky blue 735 BMW pulled up front of the club. Tupac opened the door for him like he was a don." Sweat says. But Elway slept on AJ, who recovered, planned and had his revenge six months later.

AJ coerced three teenage members of Elway's crew to cross their boss and kill him so that AJ wouldn't kill them. On February 26, 1996, the double cross went down. The three dudes opened fire on Elway and his bodyguard while they were sitting in the car with him. From the back seat they put a bullet in the bodyguard's head and then started firing on Elway who was in a car adjacent to them on a dark portion of Wilcox and Biddle Streets in East Baltimore. Derrick Rivers, the bodyguard was fatally shot in the back of the head. Elway said the three men were Alan "Wali" Chapman, Warren "Red Dog" Hill and Mark "Keedy" Coles. He said they turned against him in favor of AJ. "I could smell the gunfire," Elway said remembering how he jumped out of the car wounded and ran into the cold night down the dimly lit street. "I heard footsteps behind me and six, seven, eight gunshots. I was hit two or three times in the chest and back." Elway ran to a home on nearby Valley Street, knocked on the door and collapsed after a woman let him inside. He spent nearly three weeks recuperating at a medical center where Jones was alleged to have made the next attempt to get him.

"This what they did," Sweat says. "That's how they brought them down. Double crossing. Anthony told me when the dudes came to make the deal, 'You want to make it right? You want to kill Elway?' He was gonna use them to kill Elway and then kill them. He was on the double cross. You got to like his style. He was vicious. Much love to that nigga. I almost got caught up in that bullshit. When Elway got to beefin' with Anthony, Elway got in a bind, he was fucked up. I gave him a couple of bricks. I didn't want to get in the mix. He called me, we breaking shit down at the stash, he was like where you at? The day he called me he was with those little kids, the ones who shot him. I never got with them, that was the day the double cross was in. They pumped three or four bullets through the window to kill him. I could have been caught up in that foolishness. We lost a lot of good people. It was going both ways. You didn't know who was who. People were taking money for hits."

And AJ took it a step further. He wanted Elway dead, so he turned to his corrupt cop to kidnap Elway from his hospital bed. AJ offered the cop 5 grand for info on Elway's whereabouts and offered 10 grand to the cop to arrest Elway and turn him over to his crew. He even attempted to get one of his crew to sneak into the hospital with a hypodermic needle full of Drano to inject into Elway's veins. AJ was gangster for real. Court papers filed in U.S. District Court accused AJ of conspiring to have his rival, Elway Williams, kidnapped from his hospital bed by having him falsely arrested and turned over to Mr. Jones. But the cop didn't do it and Elway, 29, was arrested and charged with selling heroin. At a later bail hearing U.S. Magistrate Paul M. Rosenburg said about Mr. Jones, "One can only assume that the kidnapping was for the purpose of an execution or to inflict substantial harm to the individual." And before it was all over, AJ probably regretted that the hospital bed kidnap move didn't go down, because Elway would turn into a snitch and the star witness against him.

Part 6- Slipping Through the System

Suspect Symbolizes Police Frustrations; Repeated Arrests on an Array of Charges Doesn't Yield Conviction, the *Baltimore Sun* headline read on May 19, 1996. The suspect they were talking about was Anthony Jones, who had repeatedly been arrested by police on a variety of charges such as destruction of property, discharging a firearm, battery, using a deadly weapon with intent to injure, murder, drug loitering, handgun violations and assault by threat. A series of nine arrests, none prosecuted, including a handgun charge in 1993, where a police officer saw Jones pulling a gun from his waistband and throwing it into a backyard, an October 1995 charge that he assaulted his girlfriend, who declined to pursue the charges in court and another gun arrest for having a handgun loaded with 14 cop killer bullets. Police hoped to stop the revolving door that sped AJ from jail and back to freedom, time after time, but they just couldn't make any charges stick.

"It was difficult to put away someone like AJ," a prosecutor said. Law enforcement often lost out to shaky evidence and big money legal talent, witness intimidation and smarts that successful drug dealers had at their disposal. "It is more difficult to pin down a kingpin because of the way they run their business. They shield themselves. They put other people to do the dirty work," the prosecutor said. But AJ's lawyers offered another view. Paul Polansky said his client had, repeatedly been hit with "ridiculously bad charges." He said the 1994 murder charge resulted from police finding a gun in his brother's bedroom. "There is a reason these cases were dropped- they were bad arrests." He said.

A review of Jones' many court files and interviews with police, lawyers and federal agents showed that they could not cross a crucial hurdle- proving AJ guilty. The man police labeled as a brazen druglord, avoided hard time. The best chance authorities had for putting Jones away for a long time, evidence linking him to illegal guns used in shootings from his 91 arrests, died when federal prosecutors did not file charges. Officials blamed each other and refused to release case files of the closed investigation. But it seemed there was something more in play. Prosecutors just couldn't figure it out. But it all would come to light.

On February 19, 1996, police officer and DEA agents arrested Jones again on gun charges. Jones gave the undercover officer two grand "in exchange for an understanding that the officer either not testify or alter his testimony regarding the handgun arrest." The mystery was further resolved when Baltimore City Police Officer Erick McCrary, a seven-year veteran "offered himself as the contact person for Anthony Jones." During all this AJ was released on bail, angering the head of the Baltimore DEA office who publicly labeled Jones "a well known drug trafficker." Two months later on March 4, 1996 Officer McCrary was charged with bribery in the alleged scheme to protect Jones, the convicted drug dealer who court papers said recruited children for his violent, million dollar cocaine operation. The officer resigned after federal drug enforcement agents and city police arrested him at his Northwest Baltimore home.

"AJ was beating a lot of gun charges," Kid says. "Shorty was strong. He had police working for him. They was expunging them joints. He had someone on the inside working the computers. Shorty was serious, I'm telling you. They'd just erase the charge. He was getting knocked with a gun and boom the charge was gone. He got the police to try and get 20 grand out of an impounded car too." AJ was moving on multiple fronts, playing the game, but taking it to new levels at the same time. Court papers offered a rare glimpse of how even violent drug dealers could be protected and helped by those sworn to bring them to justice. The six-page affidavit filed in U.S. District Court in Baltimore charged that Jones used McCrary as a conduit to offer five grand to the officer who arrested Jones in February to alter his testimony or not show up in court. McCrary also tried to recover $21,000 of Jones' money hidden in a compartment in a seized car.

At a news conference, U.S. Attorney Lynna Battaglia and Baltimore Police Commissioner Thomas C. Frazier said they were ashamed to have had a city police officer suspected of being linked to such a violent organization. "This is a case I think that outrages all of us," Mr. Frazier said. "A police officer was working with Anthony Jones' drug organization and offered another Baltimore City police officer a $5,000 bribe to change his testimony in a gun charge." Prosecutors claimed that McCrary was a middleman between Jones and other officers.

"This kind of stuff makes me sick to my stomach." said Officer Gary McLhinney, president of the police union. "We have officers risking their lives and cases like this are a slap in the face for all the men and women trying to do their jobs." Police charged that McCrary had become associated with Jones and became close enough to have secret pager codes and each others home numbers locked in their pagers. Police officials declined to comment on how far back the connection between McCrary and Jones might go. Said one investigator, "Look at everything he has been able to get away with. You have to wonder." As the police officer was held without bail his former comrades hunted Jones, then 22. Jones parole for his 92 drug charge was about to end.

On April 4, 1996, AJ surrendered to police and was ordered held without bail also, on two gun possession charges resulting from the February arrest and a previous arrest in 1993. At the bail hearing in U.S. District Court, officials outlined a slew of gun charges that previously had been dropped by city prosecutors, raising concerns by the police. At the hearing, officials read AJ's lengthy arrest record, which included 10 arrests since 1990 on gun, drug and assault charges. The 1994 murder charge on Keith Westmoreland was brought up also. All the charges, except the conspiracy charge for 91 and 93 and 96 gun charges he faced had been previously dropped. Officials also said at the hearing that Mr. Jones' alleged drug organization was again under investigation.

Police Commissioner Frazier said investigators believed Jones' organization "was responsible for over a dozen murders and shootings in the city." He also said that he made it a priority not to drop gun charges. "Those are cases we want to keep in the system. The fact that gun cases didn't stay in the system was a concern to me." He said. Jones now faced federal charges of being a felon in possession of a handgun, bribery and witness tampering. "When you paint the defendant as a monster, nobody seems to care what the evidence is." Jones' lawyer said and he was right. The feds were effectively putting AJ on ice to get him off the street and out of circulation. In November 96, AJ was convicted for criminal possession of a loaded gun as a prior felon and was sentenced to 37 months and sent to FCI Allenwood low, a federal prison in Pennsylvania. While he was serving his time, Baltimore Detectives and DEA agents were securing physical evidence- guns, narcotics and vehicles with stash boxes and questioning key players in what was known by government officials as the Anthony Jones Drug Ring. But the feds found it a tough task, as the crew was more afraid of AJ than they were of the law.

Part 7- Most Feared

"It wasn't so much respect. Niggas feared Anthony." Sweat says. "He took chances. He murdered muthafuckas with no conscious. He did what he needed to do." And he left a trail of bodies in East Baltimore even as he sat in a jail cell. Anyone suspected of cooperating or talking to police was marked for death. AJ wasn't taking any chances. On February 16, 1996, a man who testified before a federal grand jury was shot repeatedly and disabled at a Chinese carryout on North Gay Street by Jones' henchmen. On May 13, another police informant, Octavian Henry was fatally shot nine times in the head by a hitman who reported back to Jones' lieutenants that he delivered, "nine to the dome." On May 19, one of AJ's alleged former street dealers was executed around the corner from where Jones used to live. On May 23, another witness who testified before the grand jury investigating AJ's powerful drug gang was killed, found shot in the head in his dining room.

"AJ started that stop snitching shit. He was brutal, killing dudes suspected of cooperating, even his own brother." Sweat says. In order to build their case, Assistant U.S. Attorney Jaime Bennett subpoenaed Jones' brother, John Jones, a father of three. John testified before a federal grand jury about his knowledge of a recent drug seizure and a gun he once saw Anthony carrying. When John spoke to Anthony from prison he told his brother that he told the grand jury nothing incriminating, but he did mention the fact that Anthony carried a gun. Seven weeks after John testified at the grand jury he was dead. Shot three times in the head and once in the back of the neck, severing his spinal cord at his East Baltimore home. After that dudes stopped talking about AJ. But the streets were buzzing.

"Anthony Jones felt that if he ordered the killing of his own brother, it would send message that he would go to any length to silence cooperators," AUSA Robert Harding said. "This was all part of a war, a war about how Anthony Jones wanted to be the most feared and most powerful drug dealer in Baltimore." AUSA Harding continued, describing Jones' group as one of the most murderous in city history. "In the pursuit of these goals, many people died." One crew member told AUSA Bennett, "I'm not talking. You'll get me killed." The stop snitching code was in full effect, but would it last?

"The name Anthony Jones holds a lot of weight. It means a lot. He's a trendsetter not only in Baltimore but in all the ghettos across the country," Sweat says. "When dudes speak on Ant, they speak on a lot of the violence and his methods of dealing with things." Brutal methods that sought to insure that nobody was left alive to testify against him. AJ wanted to be feared, he wanted to be seen. He loved the attention and fear he inspired. He wanted people in the hood talking about him and his exploits. He was a merciless ghetto star that thought he was invincible. But his outsized reputation was in contrast with his appearance.

"He's a slim dude, like 5-foot-10. One of his eyes is crossed. Ant was real low key, quiet, he cool. He laid back. He ain't no outburst type nigga. You wouldn't even know it was him," Sweat says. Kid confirms his appearance. "AJ was a skinny dude, 150 pounds, dark skin, one of his eyes was messed up, he had cross eyes. He was Nigerian." And he had a vicious streak like no one else. Believed by authorities to be one of the most heavily armed dealers, the man police so desperately wanted to make an example out of became instead a symbol of their limits and frustrations. Imprisoned by the feds, AJ was flexing his muscles, flaunting his power and exercising his authority by reaching out from his prison cell and touching people.

"He got two dozen murders. He wasn't doing all that stuff. He might know about it. Dudes were paying him to hit people." Kid says. "Black Jerry and Mookie, they were his mans. AJ was just a nigga that controlled dude's minds. He was on some real shit. Them niggas would do whatever he said." AJ used the prison telephones at FCI Allenwood to order associates outside prison to murder the witnesses and his brother who he thought was testifying against him. He ordered the slaying of several witnesses and even their mothers, prosecutors alleged. "It was the criminal justice system that failed," the Reverend Anthony Johnson from Jones local parish said. "What we have to ask is how an Anthony Jones is able to manipulate the system the way he did."

Prison authorities at Allenwood, at the request of the federal investigators, had taped all of Jones' conversations on the prison telephones since his incarceration, but after listening to them the words meant nothing to them. "That nergy jergy got to get wergy tergy," AJ said over the prison monitored phone to Jerry "Black Jerry" Williams, his man. The code translated gave an execution order against John Jones, prosecutors said. And this code recorded on the prison phone system would come back to haunt AJ. Black Jerry would get 17-year-olds Timothy "Denasty" Simms and Hilton "Dinkles" Thomas to kill AJ's brother on February 26, 1996, paying them three grand each. In East Baltimore life was cheap, very cheap indeed.

Anthony became numb to the violence he inflicted in his quest to become the most feared, prosecutors said. He set fire to a man, sent a lieutenant into a hospital in an attempt to kill another by using a hypodermic needle filled with Drano and killed at the slightest provocation. In short, AJ became the all powerful don the prosecutors made him out to be. "He remind you of the nigga Charles Manson," Sweat says. "He used his mind to make people do things."

Part 8- The Case

In December 1996, a sealed indictment was handed down. Seventeen of AJ's underlings were named in a lengthy indictment charging murder, racketeering, narcotics distribution, kidnapping and firearm violations. Seven of those defendants pled guilty, many in secret negotiations so that Jones wouldn't immediately know who was cooperating with the government, AUSA Bennett said. The remaining 10 defendants chose to go to trial, maintaining their innocence and claiming that those who pleaded guilty were selling their testimony to the government in exchange for lesser sentences. At least four who pleaded guilty were expected to testify for the prosecution, AUSA Bennett said. Among those testifying was Elway Williams, Jones' archrival, who AJ had unsuccessfully tried to assassinate. Elway teamed up with Baby Dan to snitch on Jones and his crew. A reversal of the previous team up of AJ and Baby Dan to kill Elway. The prosecution couldn't build their case until both Daniel "Baby Dan" Ross and Elway Williams, who were both facing life sentences on conspiracy and racketeering charges signed on and agreed to plead guilty and become witnesses against AJ.

"It was a three way joint, the beef- guns, drugs and murder. Mike and them had the drugs, Ant and them had the guns and murder. It was probably the biggest case in Baltimore." Kid says. Basically, what the feds did was round up everyone in East Baltimore who was involved in the AJ/Elway war and then anybody else who was selling drugs in the area and put them all in one indictment like it was one group. But it wasn't. There was AJ's crew, Elway's crew and Michael Cheek's crew. Then the feds starting offering up deals, seeing who they could flip. The ultimate target was Anthony Jones. "You would see dude one day, the next they'd be gone. Everybody was getting grabbed." Kid says. With their snatch and grab routine the feds played the dealers off each other. Relying on their fear of AJ and his penchant for deadly retribution, the feds probably made it seem like their deals were the only options available, and many dudes took them.

Prosecutors said that the members of the gang sold millions of dollars worth of cocaine they called "Space Jam." They alleged the crew carted millions of dollars worth of cocaine in secret compartments in cars. Prosecutors also said that Darnell "Mookie" Jones was ordered by his brother AJ to carry out contract killings of informants and their mothers. AUSA Bennett maintained that Mookie was responsible for the 1994 slaying of rival drug dealer, Keith "Shugg" Westmoreland, who was shot by two men wearing the masks of U.S. presidents. He also allegedly killed Octavian Henry, who was shot repeatedly in an ally across from Jones' home, prosecutors said. Henry was thought to have been cooperating with police. The case offered a rare first hand account of life inside Baltimore's drug-ridden killing zones.

Claiming "murder was the hallmark of the operation," federal prosecutors began the trial of 10 alleged members of the ruthless East Baltimore organization that had been linked to more than a dozen killings and had sold hundred of pounds of cocaine and heroin in October 1997. The Anthony Jones

Gang had a history of violence so severe that authorities feared for the lives of witnesses, some of whom had been targeted for execution on orders that came from the jail cell of the organization's kingpin, prosecutors said. The prosecution was so afraid of Jones' ability to reach beyond the walls of prison to commit murder that they had jurors travel to the federal building in police escorted vans with tinted glass. The vans would pick up jurors each morning at alternating street locations to insure their safety. Even the prosecution team walked with caution. They were forbidden to take public transportation or use public parking lots. They entered the federal building from an underground garage. The defendants were watched over by 15 armed U.S. Marshals at all times. Jones trial was severed as prosecutors elected to try him in January.

Several former members of the ring testified including the corrupt cop. Baby Dan, one of the gang members, who pleaded guilty in secret arrangement with the feds, was the first of more than 100 witnesses, who gave a glimpse of what the organization was like on the inside. Baby Dan told how he met Anthony Jones eight years before near an East Baltimore alley where, "I saw him and an associate engaged in a shooting." Baby Dan, 25, testified that Jones and the associate shot a drug addict called Snake. AJ came to Baby Dan's home a few days later and asked him whether police had questioned him about the shooting. "I told him, no, no one had come by. And besides I hadn't seen anything." Baby Dan said. After the show of trust, "We became cool. We became good associates," Baby Dan recalled. Eventually AJ got Baby Dan to set up shop near Durham and Larvale streets. "Anthony had a shop across the street where he was selling coke." Baby Dan testified. "He had a lot of guys working for him. But after a while he wanted to use my runners, selling dime bags of heroin. I didn't mind."

But Baby Dan almost didn't make it to testify. One day before the Anthony Jones Drug Gang trial was to begin Baby Dan stepped out of the shower at Charles County Detention Center in Maryland, to see AJ. Deathly afraid for his life, Baby Dan began to speak apprehensively to AJ. He didn't know whether or not AJ knew he was testifying against him and the crew. Luckily for Baby Dan, AJ didn't know and he began speaking openly to him about the

Shugg murder. According to Baby Dan AJ told him, "I know they ain't got no witnesses because we were wearing masks when it happened."

According to Mookie, "We had numerous guys testify against us. Guys came from New York to testify against us, Derrick Hailstock, a high member of the Preacher crew came out of the Witness Protection Program to testify against us. He testified about events involving our crew and the Preacher's crew that supposedly happened in NY and Baltimore." Elway was a key witness in the two-month trial of nine of Jones' drug lieutenants also. He gave vivid details of the war between him and AJ verifying all the casualties. Prosecutors portrayed AJ's crew as a vicious group that obeyed orders to kill without question. In the world of East Baltimore, AJ's word was law.

The trial, in U.S. District Court in Baltimore saw dramatic testimony by gang members who assisted in murders. Defense attorneys labeled the government's case as fiction created by about a half-dozen admitted killers, who took the stand in the trial as key prosecution witnesses. Stanly Needleman, attorney for one of the defendants told the jury that prosecutors resorted to testimony "from sociopaths and abominations." Quoting from Shakespeare's *Macbeth*, Needleman said the accusers couldn't be trusted. "All of our yesterdays have lighted fools the way to dusty death. It is a tale told by an idiot full of sound and fury signifying nothing," he read from the famous play. In his words Needleman said those that testified, including New York drug dealer Derek Hailstock- who admitted his role in nine contract killings- were, "just telling a tale of sound and fury. In the government's quest for victory at any cost, they have resurrected these fools."

AUSA Harding maintained that the witnesses were truthful on the stand and took great risks to testify against Jones' crew, which normally took deadly revenge against snitches. "They were given the maximum incentive to tell the truth," AUSA Harding said. "The plea agreements were structured so that they would lose all their incentives if they did not tell the truth." But defense lawyer Stanley Needleman wasn't satisfied. "The government says that sometimes you must stoop down and make deals. But sometimes when you stoop down, you can't stand up straight again," he said alluding to the age old maxim that says be wary when you make deals with the devil.

The two month trial was not without its incidents. During a short break in the federal murder and racketeering trial, Darnell Jones allegedly told Baby Dan that he planned to kill his family, the witness testified. "I'm going to kill your family," Mookie allegedly mumbled to Baby Dan. But Mookie fired back about the whole case, "Ninety percent of what the media and government claimed was lies." He said. "There was no physical evidence against us in the case. We were found guilty because of cooperating co-defendants who testified that we told them we did it. The government said we confessed to these murders to our friends, so we were found guilty." Prosecutors portrayed Jones as a ruthless plotter whose gang was responsible for more than a dozen murders, one of which he committed wearing a Ronald Reagan mask. Most of the other killings were arranged through contracts in the East Baltimore drug underworld. About the trial and case Black Jerry says, "Those are alleged crimes, most of them altered, fabricated and coached stories by some rats who were scared to fight for their lives."

Sweat says, "I went to the trial, Little Vic and Boonie were clowning, playing football at the table with a little paper football flicking it through their fingers like goalposts. I'm fucked up with Elway because he gets down too. You would never think he did that shit. Elway terrible." AUSA Harding in his closing argument said Anthony Jones ruled his narcotics ring with an iron hand. He was known to despise informants and arranged to have several suspected rats terminated. AUSA Harding portrayed the men on trial as ruthless followers of Jones, who would devise twisted murder plots to satisfy his orders for revenge. "But there was a fatal paradox in this organization." AUSA Harding told the jury. "They had to let people know about the shootings and now it has come back to haunt them."

Three days before Christmas the jurors reached the verdict. The defendants who were fitted with electronic stun belts, didn't move a muscle as the jury found all nine men guilty. "It was a sad day for Baltimore," Sweat says. "They made history off this shit. They were the first people to wear stun belts in the court." But it wasn't over, AJ was up next.

The city and community was filled with fear and tension as the young druglord came to trial. "He needs to be put away forever. Make it a safe place for kids to live in," Delores Shield, a neighbor said from her rowhouse across the street from where AJ lived. And AJ's lawyer was in fine form. "They've got him being Al Capone," Paul Polansky said. "He's been charged with many, many things that he's not guilty of. There's nothing clandestine happening here. Cases weren't prosecuted because once they were looked at there was no case." His firm had represented Jones and other alleged crew members for years but the federal indictment and trial looked to be the last straw. It didn't appear that AJ could get out of this one. The feds came out with all guns blazing. They had hundreds of hours of tapes recorded on prison telephones that AJ used to communicate with his people while incarcerated. The only thing was the words AJ used didn't make sense. It was some kind of code and AUSA Bennett set out to crack it. She spent hundreds of hours unscrambling the taped conversations.

"My major concern was- 'Who is in danger and what can we do to protect them?'" AUSA Bennett, who began analyzing the language of the tapes, recalled. "We had a witness killed. There's nothing that focuses a prosecutor's attention more than that." She found her time dominated by the Jones' tapes. She listened to the druglord's fast talk at home, in the office, and even on her car's cassette player. "When I was home I would listen to the tapes after I finished my domestic chores. When I was in my office I listened to them on a portable boom box." The words and sentences she heard befuddled her.

"If yergy don't dergy tergy, tell mergy to get them two nergies little dergy and werwergy, you know what I'm sergying." AJ said on the prison phone at FCI Allenwood in February 1997. "That nergy jergy gotta get wergy tergy." It sounded like nonsense to AUSA Bennett but it was a death sentence. After listening to the tapes extensively and exhaustively, it wasn't long before Ms. Bennett saw how the "fergy-dergy" language worked. Jones, she realized, was taking the first letter of a word and simply replacing the rest of the letters with "ergy." The language was a derivation of pig Latin and street slang from around the neighborhood where Jones grew up in the 1700 block of East Oliver Street in East Baltimore. The roots of coded communication in AJ's violent drug world apparently began as slang on the street and gradually evolved into secret language, cryptic symbols and bizarre telephone banter.

Jones used cunning to devise a language he hoped would stump the authorities who had tracked him so fervently for seven years. But he didn't count on the overzealous relentlessness of Assistant U.S. Attorney Jaime Bennett, who became AJ's nemesis much more so then the rival drug dealer Elway ever could be.

Wenzell "Moo" Hinton, one of Jones' top lieutenants who cooperated with prosecutors, described how the language worked during trial testimony. "Maybe you could say, 'Good morning, my friend,' Gergy mergy mergy fergy." But even knowing the rules of the language didn't afford federal agents with any deep insight into Jones' taped conversations. A word in the language could have any number of meanings, "mergy" could mean morning or my as in Hinton's example, so the receiver of the order had to have a clue as to what Jones meant. The "mergy dergy" message above, that was repeatedly played at AJ's trial as proof of his guilt, read according to prosecutors, "If you don't do it, tell Moo to get them two niggas Little Dink and Woo Woo, you know what I'm saying. That nigga John gotta get whacked tonight." AJ allegedly implied in the code, giving the order for a death sentence to be carried out against his brother John who had testified at the grand jury.

That message and others issued in code to his loyal lieutenants became the main thrust behind prosecutor's attempts to put Jones to death for running the most murderous drug gang in Baltimore history. Jones, prosecutors told the jury, stopped at nothing to kill, even if it meant dreaming up a whole new language. "It's like nothing we'd ever heard before," said AUSA Bennett. "Once we had the code, it opened the door for us into a very chilling world Anthony Jones had created." Prosecutors said the death penalty was the only way to guarantee that AJ's cryptic orders would stop. Jones was going to be the first to face a possible death penalty for a federal crime in Maryland.

Perhaps most remarkable about the coded communication system was the ability of Jones underlings to understand their leaders intentions with so many words possible from mergy and dergy. The handful of lieutenants who spoke the code relied on a keen sense of AJ's mind and intentions. Jones himself pointed to the ambiguity of the language when he testified in his own defense, saying that prosecutors couldn't know what he was thinking when he spoke in code and therefore couldn't translate it. "Its just slang we use in the neighborhood." Jones told AUSA Harding. "Going back and listening to it later doesn't work. I'd have to know what was on my mind at the time. What you have transcribed is wrong. You can't know what I'm saying in mergy, dergy, wergy."

But Assistant U.S. Attorney Bennett's breakthroughs in the language were confirmed by her snitches. She pieced together strings of sentences aided by the fact that Jones spoke partly in English during the conversations. That enabled Bennett to get a sense of what he was saying. "It would be a little bit of English interspersed with mergy," Bennett said. The translations were labor intensive. Over the course of her work she reconstructed the sentences, running them by her snitches for confirmation that they said what she wanted them to say. In the end she had translated 22 hours of mergy-dergy conversations and with all that, the feds had a solid case against AJ. No matter what the coded conversations meant, the prosecutor would spin it to her angle. "As it took shape you started to see Anthony Jones with his hair down in his own words. It was very creepy." She said.

"Tergy deyergy to gergy them nergys like you know what I m saying thergy dergys a pergy." AJ told Black Jerry in another recorded phone call from FCI Allenwood. The translation according to the feds, "Tell Di to give them niggas like you know what I'm saying thirty dollars a piece." The order relates to the payment of $3,000 each to Little Dinkle and Woo Woo, the two 17-year-old hitmen who killed the federal witness John Jones in 1996. Prosecutors said the young assassins followed AJ's coded instructions to the letter even knocking on the door, "Knergy of the dergy," as the druglord put it, before barging in to do the killing.

The jury convicted AJ of running an elaborate drug organization responsible for more than a dozen murders. They begin deliberations on whether Jones should become the first person ever executed for a federal crime in Maryland. "You must ask yourself how we as a society are to deal with an individual, such as Anthony Jones, who is completely committed to a life of crime, who has killed for highly personal reasons of control and pride, who has manipulated the system and who stands before you completely free of even a shred of remorse," AUSA Bennett said in her opening statements to the death penalty phase of his two month trial. Prosecutors gave a vivid description of the 25-year-old AJ, convicted of murder in aid of racketeering, federal witness retaliation and drug dealing, as a youth so ruthless that he ordered the murder of a bit player, they say, for simply selling cheaper grade cocaine in similar green-tinted crack vials.

Jones' lawyer though fought for his client. "I'm asking for compassion," William C. Brennon Jr. said. "We are not here today on the mean streets of East Baltimore. We are in a civilized courtroom where the hallmarks are justice and fairness. Justice, fairness and morality do not need the death of Anthony Jones." And the jury bought it. They refused to give AJ the death penalty. When jurors opted not to sentence Jones to death, they cited among their reasons, that he had a difficult youth and his accomplices were all spared the death penalty. AJ was ready to deal with it like a soldier though as Sweat relates, "Ant's a thorough dude. When we was in the courthouse and he was going for the death penalty he was really humble. I asked him 'Why they got your suit hanging up over there?' And they got him in the white pullover joint. The officer overheard me and said, 'We got his suit hanging up because we don't want him to kill himself. We want to kill him.' Ant didn't respond to that. He wasn't upset about his case. He was real low key. Like the case was nothing."

Part 9- The Convictions

The U.S. District Court jury in Baltimore returned guilty verdicts against all nine men accused of murder, kidnapping and drug charges for their participation in the alleged Anthony Jones Drug Ring, which prosecutors said was one of the city's most violent drug gangs ever. The verdicts came more than seven years after the first killing noted in the case and six years after the first search warrant was issued. The trial took two months. Deliberations by the jury of six men and six women took ten and half hours over three days. Eight other defendants in the case pleaded guilty and cooperated with the feds, testifying against their co-defendants. Dressed in plaid flannel shirts or sweat shirts, the nine defendants smiled as they filed in to hear the verdicts. They scanned the heavily guarded courtroom for familiar faces. They showed no re-action as the 23 verdicts on six counts were read. No reaction was heard from anyone in the courtroom. The defendants did not smile as they filed out in handcuffs.

"It is hard not to be pleased when all defendants are convicted." AUSA Bennett said. "The jury was excellent. I certainly hope it makes an impact in the community." In her closing arguments, Bennett told jurors the prosecu-tion, "would like to offer you witnesses of unimpeachable character. But these defendants don't associate with priests and nuns. They associate with other killers." Using such witnesses was necessary, "where defendants' actions are cloaked in secrecy," she said. Bennett said the defense witnesses had more to gain by lying than the government's witnesses did. "They are just rolling the dice for a more favorable outcome." She said.

AJ's brother, who was described in court proceedings as a hitman for the organization was sentenced to life in prison for killing Keith "Shugg" West-moreland, who was shot a dozen times by executioners wearing masks of U.S. presidents. Darnell "Mookie" Jones became the first of nine. Black Jerry Williams, convicted of murder in aid of racketeering and drug conspiracy for his role in the crew was sentenced to 2 lives. Alan Vincent Chapman, Warren Devon Hill, Allen Jett, Victor Underwood, Rodney Montgomery and Anto-nio Depaul Marshall were also all sentenced to life for their roles in AJ's crew. Each was convicted of conspiracy to kidnap and murder, murder in aid of racketeering, attempted murder in aid of racketeering and conspiracy to dis-tribute narcotics. Eight of the nine were sentenced to life. John Levi Benton, found guilty of conspiracy to kidnap and murder received the maximum ten years. Dinkles Thomas and Denasty Simms got life also for killing the federal witness John Jones, AJ's foster brother. "The message should be clear that the federal government will use all of its resources and all of its powers to see to it that an attack on a federal witness will be vindicated," AUSA Harding said.

On June 5th, 1998, The *Baltimore Sun* headline read, *Prosecutors Say Jones Must Die To Stop The Killing.* The feds pulled out all the stops to kill AJ. The life of the convicted killer and druglord was put into the hands of the federal jury after prosecutors described him as "a killing machine," who deserved to be put to death. His $30,000 a day East Baltimore drug ring was linked to multiple homicides in the city. He was convicted of ordering the killing of his own brother from a prison telephone. In the fed's eyes, "AJ was the worst of the worst, deserving to reap what he sowed." A vicious criminal not fit for life.

"Anthony Jones is a killing machine that must be put to death to stop killing." AUSA Harding said. "There is no one in the same category as Anthony Jones. He is no ordinary criminal. He has killed ruthlessly and has left in his wake many shattered lives. He is a man who kills, and kills and kills again." But the jury didn't quench the prosecutor's bloodlust. AJ was spared the death penalty because his jury recognized that he was more a product of his environment. The mean streets of East Baltimore, home to drug addicts, prostitutes, drug dealers, stick-up kids, thugs, pimps, and killers. Jones, as he had throughout his two-month trial, showed no emotion as the sentencing verdicts were read in a packed courtroom in Baltimore's U.S. District Court. A short time earlier he had chatted with his lawyers about basketball star Michael Jordan. "It comes down to an issue of relative culpability. Other participants in the crime will not be executed, so why should Anthony Jones?" His lawyer argued. The jury of nine women and three men, which convicted Jones on May 27 on charges of murder in aid of racketeering, federal witness retaliation and drug dealing, deliberated two and half hours in the death phase of the case before deciding against execution. "We're relieved that our client will not be put to death," Harry J. Trainor Junior, one of Jones' lawyers said outside the courtroom. "The death penalty would not have been a deterrent in this case. In fact, it may have even turned him into a martyr." For prosecutors, the decision was a disappointment. But many pointed to the overall success of the federal investigation, which gutted the once powerful drug crew.

Part 10- The Aftermath

"Anthony is the king. Nobody knows what he thinks now but he stood up," Sweat says. "They gonna remember him for standing up. He took them shits like a champ. He took what was his and kept it moving. He played the game to the end." Jones was never the city's biggest drug dealer, but in many ways his case epitomizes the frustration police faced daily in Baltimore's war against drugs. To the police he was a monster capable of endless chaos but to the hood he was a hero, a mythical figure like Robin Hood, a certified street legend. In reality though, he wasn't Robin Hood, he was just another youngster from the hood.

"He was a good person, he never done anything wrong. He didn't have a fair trial. They have no idea how the ghetto is," 23-year-old Alicia Adams said. This type of sentiment was nothing new in America where people have always looked up to notorious criminals. Even as AJ was spared the death penalty in federal court, many neighbors on the block where he once sold drugs held fast to their admiration for one of their own, portraying AJ in stark contrast to the murderous descriptions given in court. To hear his family and friends tell it, AJ was a good guy who treated children to ice cream and helped friends pay for college tuition and books. "He'd say, 'Don't use drugs, don't sell them,' not to play with guns," said 20-year-old Natasha Harvey. "He was a positive role model to everyone who knew him." But the feds contend that even a killer knows how to lay on the charm, spread goodwill and install loyalty among his crew and neighbors. Still AJ was a two sided coin. "If you knew him personally, then you would know he was a nice person. He wasn't what they portrayed him to be, a killer." 24-year-old and lifelong friend Brian Brooks said. But in prison he's viewed differently.

"Without a doubt he was one of the baddest to do it in Baltimore," Kid says. "Shorty was young. He was a powerful dude. They were getting at jokers. But they definitely had some beefs they didn't do. Other people started wearing the masks too and it attracted attention to them." Prosecutors said the Anthony Jones gang killed at least eight people, set fire to a man, disposed of a body in a trash barrel, corrupted a police officer, threatened federal witnesses and their families and infected several East Baltimore neighborhoods with drugs. AUSA Bennett called the case "one of the most shocking and horrible case I've encountered." Anthony's alleged ability to reach outside of prison walls to run his drug organization and order murderous revenge slayings was sighted by the Federal Bureau of Prisons as one of the major reasons that they have restricted all federal prisoners to 300 minutes a month and increased the monitoring of all prisoner phone calls. The *Washington Post* headline- *Behind Bars, Its Dial-A-Crime-* that detailed AJ's actions, garnered national attention in the media in 1999 and further spread AJ's legacy of gangland killings.

There were even indications that Jones and his violent henchmen were still using code to communicate with each other and arrange contract murder. In June 88, federal agents intercepted a remarkably elaborate coded letter, so intricate that the symbols in it resembled hieroglyphics, sent from Maryland's Supermax prison by AJ's chief enforcer, Black Jerry. "I miss my militant comrades," it read. "I send my salute and thug love. That cat Cory Henry, he got to go." Cory Henry was a former member of the Jones gang who testified against the crew in court. The other snitches on the case were Daniel "Baby Dan" Ross, Michael Cheeks, Mark "Keedy" Cole, Elway Williams, Wenzell "Moo" Hinton, Dartagnaan "Darty" Norton, Derrick "Dee" Hailstock, Thomas Bogier and Alphonso "Fonzo" Harper. "All these dudes are rats and will testify against their own mothers." Mookie said from prison.

"There has never in my life been a time that I have ever contemplated the thought of snitching. There has been many times before my current circumstance that my life and freedom has been on the line in a court of law and the only recourse for me was and still is to fight to the best of my abilities with all the resources I may have- win, lose or draw." Mookie said. "Our course is an eye for an eye. Many of us are innocent of the crimes that we have been found guilty of. We need more people to start questioning the authenticity of these rat's stories and their motivations for telling. To all my codefendants that took on these devils head on with me we lost the battle but in war we will find victory."

After all these years Anthony Jones, the king of Baltimore, is still silent. Denied access to the mail, phones and visits he sits at ADX Florence, the federal supermax, under the tightest of security in permanent lockdown by court order. He sits in silence, cut off from the rest of the world seemingly forever. But in the real world his legend lives on.

AJ, as he is known in Baltimore, has the honor and respect of his homies, and those that live by the code of the streets, recognize him for what he is, a street legend of mythical proportions. When they talk of the baddest from

Bodymore aka Charm City AJ's name is always the first to come up. And what's remarkable is that he did it all at such a young age. The kid was gangsta from the jump. Starting his drug empire at age 16. "I love him for holding fast," Sweat says. "He stood up like a man." His example should be honored by all. Because if you're bold enough to be in the game, then you should be bold enough to carry the weight when it comes down. And it will come down. This isn't a rap song, AJ's story is real life.

"My feelings about my brother AJ's situation is unexplainable," Mookie said. "These devils have sentenced him to a life of solitude simply because he is a young unbreakable man. There is no criminal that I can recall in the history of the supposedly civilized America that has been sentenced to a life of no human contact from the outside world including no mail or phone calls and the judge made it perfectly clear no exceptions would be made." And to date, over ten years later no exceptions have been made. But still his legend has grown and AJ has been recognized as a true and real gangster for all the ages.

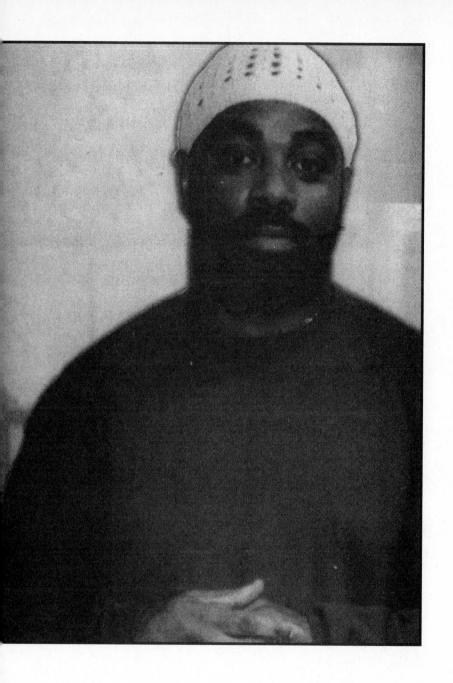

Aaron Jones

Anthony Jones

George Rivera 2000
USP Beaumont

George "Boy George" Rivera

George "Boy George" Rivera

Kenneth "Supreme" McGriff

Kenneth "Supreme" McGriff

Kenneth "Supreme" McGriff

Kenneth "Supreme" McGriff

Kenneth "Supreme" McGriff

Peter "Pistol Pete" Rollack

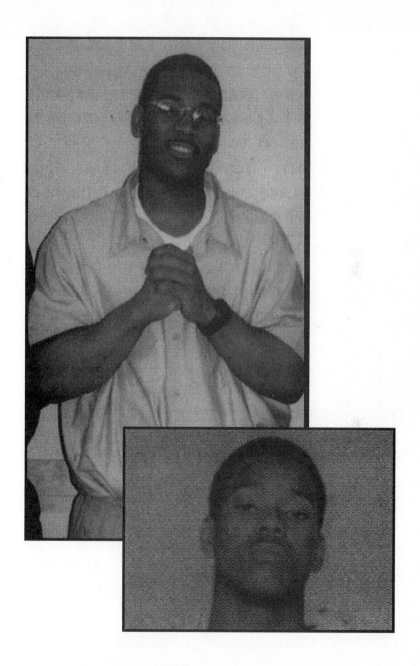

Peter "Pistol Pete" Rollack

Wayne "Silk" Perry

Wayne "Silk" Perry

Wayne "Silk" Perry

Chapter 4

Aaron Jones

AARON JONES

It was said that Aaron Jones was obsessed with the popular film *The Godfather* and crafted his persona in the mold of Marion Brando's character Don Vito Corleone. In Philadelphia he was both admired and feared but the respect he commanded was paramount. The alleged founder and street boss of the Junior Black Mafia (JBM), he locked the city of Philly down. His organization was one of the most feared in the history of black organized crime in Philadelphia. Taking its cue from its violent predecessor, the Black Mafia. It's said the JBM controlled a significant portion of the local cocaine trade and its members didn't hesitate to use violence to eliminate the competition and keep its members in line. Their motto was "Get down or lay down" and Aaron Jones epitomized that ideal as his crew set the city of brotherly love on fire with some un-brotherly violence. If you crossed the JBM back in the day than you crossed one of the most notorious crews to ever come out of Philly. As their legend has grown, Aaron Jones, their leader has taken on a mythical aura as one of the top black American gangsters ever. His name and JBM's rings loudly, living on in the hoods of Philly and in the streets across the nation. As they say real recognizes real and Aaron Jones was as real as they get.

Part 1- Origins

Aaron Jones was brought up in West Philadelphia. One of 13 children, Aaron was raised by Church going parents. Like any ghetto, the streets of West Philly that Aaron grew up in were hardly ideal. Abandoned cars, thrown away forty ounce bottles, discarded needles and dirty trash-strewn lots marked the ills that plagued his neighborhood. But it wasn't all bad. "It's basically rowhouses in West Philly," says Ock, a Philly native. "But it's somewhat a middle class area. They got nice size blocks out West Philly, but there's projects too like Bartram Village, Middlecreek, Westpark and Markoe Street." Aaron rose above his surroundings though. He graduated from West Catholic High

School in 1979 and went on to Temple University. "Aaron used to make steaks at 57th Street at a restaurant," a hustler from the era remembers. But the lessons he learned early on in life in the streets of West Philly stuck with him. By societies standards his life was supposed to turn out much different than it did. But like Aaron said, "It's so easy to get pulled into the streets." And in the streets of West Philly temptation was readily available.

From 1968 to 1984 organized crime flourished in many of the city's African American neighborhoods under the average Philadelphian's radar. The so-called Muslim mob or Black Mafia controlled most of the narcotics trade in Philadelphia from their base at the notorious corner of 20th and Carpenter Street. In the corridors of Southwestern Philly these gangsters held sway. Violence led to more violence and only the most ruthless ruled. The men that had the neighborhoods locked down were the hood stars that youngsters like Aaron looked up to. "The Black Mafia ran the heroin trade in the city. They were ruthless and ultra violent. They ruled major sections of the city." A dude from the era remembers. Legend has it that the Black Mafia was a group of locals that were holding up crap games, extorting drug dealers and numbers runners, along with other illegitimate businesses in the city. As BET's *American Gangster* showed, they were nothing to play with. Vicious to an extreme, they killed indiscriminately.

In 1970, the Black Mafia and the black Muslims had a beef over the underworld's illicit businesses in Philly, this sparked a rash of violence. To abort an all out war, Robert "Nudie" Mims, founder of the Black Mafia, joined the Nation of Islam and became an enforcer for the Fruit of Islam, cementing an alliance between the two groups which combined them into one organization, forming a powerful crew. The Black Mafia was responsible for numerous murders and 60 percent of the heroin sold in the city, law enforcement officials said. But their real crime was the impact they had on the younger generation and in particular Aaron Jones.

At a furniture store called Vanguards, Black Mafia members like Aaron Jones' older brother Eddie would have meetings. The neighborhood youngsters noticed the expensive cars and nice clothes the gangsters had. "All the guys who went into that store drove fancy Cadillac's and Lincolns." James

Cole, another founding member of JBM said. "They were doing it to death, with Benzes, sharp clothes and money." The older Black Mafia members laid out the rules of the game for youngsters like Aaron and James. "They gave us insights on the street code," James said. "They was very hard on rats. They said never sell your soul to the devil. Being at my young age I questioned as to what was the devil. They said the white man. They said if you sell your soul to the devil and be a rat, you are the lowest form of life. Until this day I never forgot what they told me." The young aspiring gangsters would hang out on 21st and Norris Street, 23rd and PAL. They would make money in West Philly running errands for the O.G.'s and party at a bar called Neets in North Philly. Under the Black Mafia these youngsters came of age. Their impression of what was important formed at an early age. The lure of the streets proved an all too easy temptation. Especially for Aaron Jones.

"The streets are very alluring and seductive." Aaron said. "They pull you in with things like fast money, jewelry and slick rides. Especially when you see a nigga pull up dressed all fly with a dime piece on his hip, man you're like 'That's going to be me in a minute.'" But the youngsters had to pay their dues first. There wasn't anything given away in the game for free. Before you could talk about it, you had to be about it, especially in the streets of West Philly. James Cole remembers shining all the players' shoes and running errands for them when he was young and James also remembers the first time he met the man who would become a street legend. "I met Aaron through a friend of mine named Aquil." James said. "I had a girlfriend who lived on 52nd and Spruce Street. Aquil and I used to hang out there because it was easier to get to the strip. Aquil brought Aaron around my girl's house to meet me. After me and Aaron started talking, I found out that I knew his brother Eddie Jones as being one of the same guys we used to run errands for when I was younger. I told Aaron that me and Kermit Brown would go over to New Jersey with his brother to clean up his farm for their annual picnic every summer. I also knew his older brother Ike who owned a cleaners at 52nd and Cedar Avenue. We hit it off good. I introduced Aaron as one of the boys and Aaron and Niam and them hit if off very easy. I told them to look out for him if he needed them." James Cole not only introduced Aaron to a lot of the dudes that would form his future crew but he also became a sort of advisor and most importantly a connect for the future kingpin.

By the 1980's most of the Black Mafia were either dead or in jail. With their imprisonment police sources say that their sons, nephews, cousins and younger brothers formed a new organization called the Junior Black Mafia. The JBM started as a handful of cocaine dealers in the city's Germantown section and continued to grow, filling the vacuum in the narcotics trade created by the Black Mafia's demise. The JBM grew from a small crew in 1985 to a well-organized drug team that controlled most of Philly's drug trade. In their late teens and early twenties they numbered about twenty at first and each member had his own small drug organization in one of six sections of the city- North, South, Southwest, West Philly, Mount Airy and Germantown. Each of the leaders had to put up about $1,000 to become a member of JBM and was required to pay $1,000 weekly into a JBM pool that would invest in legitimate business. The group was active in West Oak Lane, North Central Philly and many other parts of the city growing from a handful of men in Germantown to a huge many-tentacled organization that cornered the drug trade in the whole city. They were young and on the hustle, street smart and well connected and they knew there was a gaping hole in Philly's drug business.

"The JBM was an operation of young black men from Philly. The origin of JBM stems from the Black Mafia." A local from the era remembers. Through remnants of the seminal Black Mafia the JBM continued to orchestrate criminal conspiracies and engage in a variety of illegal acts including predatory crimes such as robbery, extortion, contracted acts of murder and violence, the police reported. From prison Black Mafia founder Robert "Nudie" Mims acted as a mentor to the younger generation playing a significant role, authorities said. From prison, Nudie had a phone link to the street and as he served 2 life sentences for murder, he acted as advisor. But in reality, the few ties between the new group and the original crew were sporadic and fleeting, not at all the lineage and mentoring suggested by the choice of the name Junior Black Mafia.

"At first Aaron was selling dime bags of crack on the corner of 52nd and

Walton Avenue." James Cole said. "I told him there was a better way to hustle than being on the street corner in the cold. Aaron came up through the ranks. People don't know this. People don't remember Aaron used to be a driver for Norristown Sam, he used to be a driver and an errand guy. Aaron paid his dues." And Aaron agreed, "The game is to be sold not told, is something I heard a lot growing up. Truth be told you had to have someone's blessing from the first to be introduced to the game. You paid up down the line." And Aaron was blessed from the first, with a loyal crew and a solid connect for coke.

Following James Cole's lead Aaron started dealings half-kilos from a stash on Fayette Street in the Mount Airy section in 1986. As he gained means he started to build a crew around him. "The more you come up, the more them dime pieces are noticing you and coming at you in all directions." Aaron said of his rise to infamy. "Before you know it, you're knee deep in the game." Selling bricks, running a crew and dealing with all the trappings of being a hood star. Certified, no doubt. A lot of the original JBM members came from the section of West Philly known as the Black Bottom. They congregated around 36th and Market and 40th and Market, the strip for all the bars, clubs and stores in the neighborhood. The young men were friends. They lived in the same neighborhoods, attended the same schools and had close family ties. Newspapers reported that at least eight men founded the JBM in 1985. They were identified as brothers James and Hayward Cole who were referred to as the big bosses who were rarely seen in Philly. In reality the Cole brothers were the ones with the cocaine connections. James had a West Philly security firm and specialized in debugging phones, cars and houses, tracing telephone calls and spent much of his time traveling the country promoting his security firm and making drug connections. Rick Jones was allegedly right under the Coles in the JBM hierarchy. He was known as one of the wealthiest JBM dealers. Aaron Jones was the street boss who ran things in Philly. Leonard "Bazil" Patterson was the enforcer. Benjamin "Bennie" Goff, Tracy Mason and Mark "Goldie" Casey were all identified as high ranking operatives. An early law enforcement memo called these founding members, The Warlords of Crack.

"The JBM was started in West Philly and then expanded to other parts of the city. When they first started they started from within, then they went into other areas of Philadelphia," Derrick Williams, another dude that got down with the crew said. Ock reiterates this origin, "It started in West Philly and they branched out to Germantown and Southwest Philly. All of them used to be out West Philly, 47th and Wylusing. Sister Clara Muhammad had the school. Everybody came out of that mass. You had some following the teachings of the Nation, some following Sunni, but everybody was Muslim. You'd see everyone out there. On Fridays during Juma prayer with their gators, jewelry and cars. That was their thing. The JBM, the way they went about things, was adapted from the Black Mafia. Basically all of them were Muslim. The way JBM was moving, using tactics, it all came from the oldheads." A hustler out of that era agrees, "Everybody coming with their car shining for Jumah. Their mink coats, their girls, their gators. Everybody was eating in the basement of Sister Clara Muhammad talking business." It started out local, but the JBM soon took over most of Philadelphia. They held sway in almost all sections by putting their press game down.

Police cite a meeting in LA in late 85 or early 86 and several subsequent meetings in Philly as the points where the JBM began to take shape. Attending the LA meeting were James Cole, his brother Hayward Cole, Mark Casey, Tracy Mason and Aaron Jones. This was where they solidified the connect that allowed the kilos of cocaine to flow into Philly unfiltered. A network that would soon turn violent, of loosely affiliated black drug organizations that cooperated in buying and selling 150 kilos a week, was cemented. Back in Philly they were joined by at least five other men and then more as their plan came together. The founders divided Philly into six sections and set out to contact every freelance drug organization in each section to bring them into the fold. The hierarchy was fluid with key players moving in all six sections of the city. The organization was structured so that a supervisor and a second in command from each different section sat on a commission similar to the Italian Mob's tribunals. If a dealer was arrested, bail was posted immediately and one of several lawyers on retainer provided counsel.

"It was wild. Back then they were selling $5 caps, $5 crack vials when crack hit Philly around 85 or 86." Ock says. "Rick Jones had a deli joint, Pulaski Town in Germantown. Rick was older than Aaron. He had the connect too." And Aaron was the street dude, putting work out, recruiting and making things pop. "Aaron had a good relationship with all of us. He actually relocated and was staying in the area I was from and Germantown eventually became headquarters." Derrick Williams said. "We would go over there and have parties and chill out." And as the money came in, Aaron wanted to do something special for the crew. To signify who they were and what they were about. "The letters JBM formed when I moved from Philly to LA," James Cole said. "I received a call and the caller stated Aaron and his crew are wearing diamond initial rings with the letters JBM. I thanked the caller and called Aaron. I asked Aaron if they were wearing rings with the name JBM. He said yes. I asked him what it stood for, he said 'Just Blowing Money.'" But Ock from Philly disagrees, "Dudes add their twist to it. I always understood that it meant Junior Black Mafia. They had the money, the drugs, they were JBM. They were moving like the old Black Mafia but were youngsters under them." But another hustler from the era remembers it differently still, "In 1987, I started hearing about JBM. They had these rings with JBM on them. Originally JBM was for James, Bazil and Mooch. They used to say Just Blowing Money. They were the oldheads. They had rules like you couldn't fuck with the bosses' wife. That was JBM."

As many as six JBM diamond rings were custom made by jeweler Barry Sable of Sable Diamonds on Jeweler's Row on Samson near 7th. "Did I make the rings, yes," said Sable. "Did I know what they were for? No. It's not my business to ask anybody what the initials stand for. Anybody could come in here and I'd custom make a ring for them." Asked at the time what JBM meant, ranking JBM member Leonard "Bazil" Patterson told police, "Just Burn Money." His ring, which was seized by Philadelphia police, consisted of

29 small diamonds that formed the initials JBM. And Derrick Williams had this to say about the rings, "Aaron would buy the ring and he would give it to you. It wasn't like a fee. You didn't have to shoot anybody as was reported, and he would give you your ring as confirmation you was now a member of the JBM." And to dudes in the inner city, having a JBM ring was like being a made man. Older brothers let their siblings wear their rings and dudes let their girl-friends hold them. They were a status symbol of the inner city elite, the Junior Black Mafia, as the crew finally became known as. Members wore the rings as symbols of their affiliation with the group.

The flashiness of the rings and Aaron's lifestyle was what brought him to the attention of the police. Law enforcement claim it was the expensive cars that JBM members drove that caught the attention of the police in 1987. It was Sergeant Steve Arch and other 14th District police officers who noticed the expensive European cars with JBM tags being driven by young black men in Germantown in the spring of 1987. They drove Jeeps, BMW's and Mercedes-Benz's and they all seemed to be headed for A-Tech, an auto detailing shop on Wayne Avenue near Washington Lane in Germantown owned by Benjamin "Bennie" Goff that was used as a JBM meeting place. The youngsters were styling and profiling, flashing their newfound wealth and trying to shine in the hood. "Frog had a white Volvo wagon with a burgundy ragtop and he had JBM on his license plate," a Philly hustler says. "Everybody had the four door wagons. All of them had Volvos. Aaron got a gold Volvo coupe, a Bertone, that was hot. He also had a convertible Saab with a Gucci interior." The attention grabbing automobiles were like a beacon to the police, that and all the bodies that started dropping.

Part 2- Body Count

"Your ultimate goal is to make a better life for you and your family," Aaron said, but in the game it's like Biggie said, *"Mo' Money, Mo' Problems,"* and the only way to handle the type of problems that resulted in the streets was with that gun smoke. As the stakes got higher Aaron changed. "Aaron was a loyal dude," James Cole said. "He wasn't like that from the beginning. Everybody thinks I made Aaron Jones a monster because I hooked him up. That really isn't true. Aaron changed because he got tired of dudes taking him for a sucker because he was successful at a young age." And success bred jealousy. "The Muslims were pressing him," the Philly hustler says. "He was arrogant at first. The Muslims told him you got part of the city, you gotta take care of the brothers. He didn't want to kick down." Aaron dealt in fear and he created that fear with blazing guns.

It wasn't until the guns began firing and bodies began to drop that the JBM began making newspaper headlines. An OCU intelligence report critiqued the gang in 1988: "The JBM is a group of young black males deeply involved in drug trafficking in the Philadelphia area, these members are flashy in their style and flaunt their profits, driving expensive cars mainly Mercedes and BMW's, which are completely customized with gold trim, black windows, etc. They wear brightly colored jogging suits along with expensive jewelry." West Philly, Southwest, Mount Airy, Germantown- the JBM had the city on lock. "AJ called the shots," the Philly hustler says. "He was running the streets. Everybody was working for Aaron Jones."

Get down or lay down- simply put- join them or be killed was JBM's motto according to police. By 1989 the government associated 25 murders with the JBM. It was rumored that many of the alleged victims of the JBM were rival dealers and anyone who played with their money. The rumors about their violent tactics said, if you skimmed off the top, if you tried to become independent, if you threatened their businesses in any way, you were dealt with. The JBM was so feared that survivors of alleged assassination attempts refused to testify against their shooters. "From what I understood, basically they had so much coke that they were making people buy from them," Ock says. "If dudes didn't buy from them, they were getting rid of them. It was like, 'Buy from us or we'll take your block.' Dudes weren't trying to give up their blocks." And the ensuing confrontations ended in bursts of gunfire. "They would come at dudes, try to beat the price, if dude was like 'No, I'm cool', they'd try to muscle the block. When that happened everybody in Philly was saying that Get down or lay down shit. That's when all the killing started," Ock says.

Aaron Jones and JBM had a surefire marketing plan, buy our coke or else.

With the California hookup through James Cole, Aaron flooded Philly with cocaine. And the market wasn't open. Aaron didn't believe in free enterprise. "Aaron knew how to organize his supply." The Philly hustler says. "He was a visionary; he really tried to run his organization like he was Scarface." Aaron believed in his enterprise and only his enterprise. He wanted a monopoly. He wanted to insure that he was the only supplier. "Unconsciously you know the risks and what is at stake but you tune them out," Aaron said. "You get caught up in the raptures of the streets. On the way you begin to encounter more and more obstacles, things you didn't anticipate so you try to deal with them." And in dealing with them Aaron dealt with death. Harsh, cruel, and ruthlessly. "They were on that syrup bad," the Philly hustler says. "They had the water bottle dispenser full of syrup. Their homicides were sloppy because they were high."

Many of the victims of the JBM's "Shoot first, ask questions later" mentality were rival dealers, feuding members of competing JBM factions or associates skimming profit. But others were innocent victims, including a 45-year-old Montgomery County man gunned down while he dined at a West Oak Lane Tavern on August 10, 1989 and 6-year-old Ralph Brooks who was paralyzed in a JBM related shooting in the summer of 88 in South Philly. Much of the violence involved smaller independent dealers trying to prevent the JBM from encroaching on their turf or JBM affiliated dealers trying to go solo. Dealers suspected of skimming profits such as JBM lieutenant Reginald Rittenburg were killed. Rittenburg was said to be pocketing $1,500 from every kilo of cocaine he was moving in his Mount Airy neighborhood. JBM dealers who wanted to become independent such as Albert Ragan who broke away to avoid the street tax, were gunned down also. These murders soon begat retaliation murders. After Ragan was killed in West Philly on March 26, 1988, two more West Philly dealers were killed in retaliation- Dennis Caldwell went down on April 2 and Brock White on April 9.

The police said that the JBM was a criminal organization that ruled through violent intimidation and whose individual members were targets of violence. Shootings sponsored by the JBM furthered their goal of eliminating all competition. The continuous acts of violence strengthened their control over the drug market. The gang dealt primarily in cocaine and worked loosely with remaining factions of the Black Mafia and the Scarfo crime family. Police conducting surveillance in February 1988 observed a leading JBM figure meeting with an Italian mobster inside the LCN clubhouse at 16th Street and Oregon Avenue. Sources also said that younger members of the Scarfo family like Joey Merlino, were working with the JBM to commandeer various drug territories throughout the city and Southern New Jersey. "We were really friendly with those guys," a mobster from Joey Merlino's crew says. "Aaron and Joey were good friends."

According to the 1989 Pennsylvania Crime Commission report, "JBM members and young LCN associates such as Joseph Merlino continue to associate and work together in the distribution of cocaine." The report said that Tracy Mason and Benjamin "Bennie" Goff were the key intermediaries. Mason visited the Italian Mob's clubhouse in South Philly regularly and warmly embraced Merlino like a long term friend, law enforcement officials said. JBM members even attended the federal racketeering trial of reputed Mob boss Nicodemo "Little Nicky" Scarfo in U.S. District Court in November 1988.

To control the various markets the JBM had different squad leaders who were in charge of distribution for different areas of Philly. "Philly was crazy back then. If you came through the streets you'd think it was Marshall Law. Nobody on the streets at night. It was just that fucking dangerous. Niggas was killing each other. Young cats were dying. It was crazy," a local from the era remembers. There were hits and attempted hits all over the city, some in broad daylight and one in the City Hall courtyard. The JBM was tripping, they were out of control. "If you mess up their money or mess with the product they'd kill you. This was like Al Capone stuff. Somebody was watching the Godfather too much. These young guys were crazy, walking into courtrooms with guns. Niggas was tripping," The Philly hustler says.

"The JBM laid them boys down." Ock says. "You just heard about the killing. The JBM was jumping out on dudes. Four, five carloads. It would be Aaron and them. They'd catch dudes out at one of the clubs or bars. With the JBM it was on, on sight with them. They were real heavy on the baby Uzi's,

357's, .38 snubs. Basically, Uzi's, pumps and revolvers. Revolvers weren't leaving any casings. So that was good. Remember Philly is a big city, but everything is connected. It takes 10-15 minutes to get to every neighborhood." And this let Aaron and his crew wreak havoc and keep tabs on the whole city. A moments notice and they were there, rolling en masse. The ultra-violent JBM was known for their Get down or lay down motto and they followed through on their pledge all too often. "He's the one that got all those bodies." Ock says of Aaron Jones. "He was vicious."

At least 25 people were killed during the JBM's most violent years between 1987 and 1989. They pressured independents to give up their street corners so that they could control the citywide narcotics trade. Bloody ambushes left several dead as part of a turf war over the lucrative 46th and Parrish drug corner of West Philadelphia. "It's JBM guys battling in different areas of the city to see who's going to control things. Everybody's got guns. Big guns." A law enforcement official said. And reports of drug dealers opening fire at each other in broad daylight, frightening children, parents and onlookers was regular, as the bodies dropped fast and furious due to internal disputes for getting funny with the money. "They were beefing within their own clique," the Philly hustler says. Aaron Jones didn't play, he was serious about his money.

"I used to get a lot of calls during the days of the Get down or lay down time," James Cole said. "Brothers would call and say, 'Aaron has fucked up the city. He's gonna take everybody down. We can't hustle because the feds are all over the place.' Maybe I should have done a little more preaching, but Aaron Jones was his own man. I guess when you go from syrup to champagne that is the result. At the time, all of the brothers who he was introduced to by me were basically in jail. Aaron was left with his own domain. Left to make authority decisions by himself." And with no guidance, Aaron followed his own advice to the best of his ability. Caught in the raptures of the game, he was deep in a pool of blood, in the brutal and murder-stained streets of Philly. "You begin to adapt to the mentality of the streets," Aaron said. "You're beginning to rationalize every move instead of seeing it from what it is. You rationalize and rationalize. Sometimes you may turn to whatever you use to get your buzz to help you on the way. It is hard to change that mentality once you're in." And by adapting to the kill or be killed mentality in the dog-eat-dog world of the streets, Aaron rose to the top. But it was a violent rise with no foresight of the consequences.

"I remember a guy killed in a bar," Ock says of all the murders that plagued Philly during the JBM's reign. "This was up my end too. They sent one JBM guy in to talk to dude and while he had dude's attention, they came in from the back and shot him at The Place bar. Another incident was when they killed this dude and his body ended up burnt up in his car at Richards Island projects in North Philly. They dumped his body with the car and made it seem like they killed him down there. Another time they took and tied a dude down to a tree at Huntington Park and killed him." JBM's reign of terror was public and brutal. Every murder was made to set an example for the next man. It was Get down or lay down for real. Aaron Jones and the JBM weren't faking.

Part 3- The Taskforce

"Drugs became my business and in 1987 I got down with the JBM. I was with them until I was arrested in 1989." Derrick Williams said. "Mark 'Goldie' Casey hooked me up with Aaron Jones and that's how I got down with them. They were based in West Philly because that's where everybody was at. But they were spread out everywhere. That comes from knowing different people in different areas." And as they spread out and the violence got thick they showed up prominently on the police radar. So prominently that a local task force was formed to bring them down.

"It's going to be quite a job to take them down," a law enforcement official said at the time and that was because the JBM had been in existence for four years before police developed an overall strategy against them. But the members were easy to identify, they wore expensive clothes and frequented fine restaurants and trendy clubs. BMW's and four-wheel drive vehicles were their favored modes of transportation and many of the vehicles were mono-grammed with the initials JBM.

"These are mostly young guys. And these are signs of their immaturity. Normally you don't go around flashing things of value without any means of support," a police investigator tracking them said. "They're entrepreneurs and they believe in demonstrating the trappings of their success. That's why we're seeing the jewelry and the cars. Its awareness and status in the neighborhoods. They take the position that it's no use being successful if no one knows about it. In one BMW we seized the stereo system alone was worth $10,000."

Philadelphia District Attorney Ronald Castille set up a special unit to target drug kingpins for prosecution. His main target was Aaron Jones and the JBM. The task force, local and state police along with federal agencies launched an attack on the JBM with the same approach that brought down the mob run by Nicodemos "Little Nicky" Scarfo. The task force started what would become a five year investigation. Through their snitches they determined that the JBM had been in business two years, quietly amassing millions. The government spent thousands of man hours and hundreds of thousands to investigate the JBM.

The investigation started according to Derrick Williams, "From different shootings and crimes that we didn't even go to court for and then we had the rings, we had the cars with JBM on the back of them. It was all foolish when I look back at it. Arrogance always comes in, money can be a curse or it can be a blessing." The JBM was implicated in a 100 kilo delivery at Miami Mall along with the numerous shootings and murders. According to court records, on July 11, 1989 Aaron Jones gave orders to wipe out a corner of all rival gang members. JBM enforcer Christopher Laster and four other gunmen sprayed bullets at about six men standing at the intersection. Willie Bowmen, 23, was killed in the shooting at 24th and Moore in South Philly. The police claimed he was an innocent bystander. This only added fuel to the fire and the March 1989 shootout at City Hall with Craig Haynes, leader of a rival gang brought the fire to a fury. As did the mistaken identity death of Donald Branch which resulted from Haynes effort to kill JBM leader Aaron Jones. "They was beefing with Craig Haynes," the Philly hustler says. "Craig Haynes didn't get down, but it was really about a broad. Craig was fucking with this broad and AJ smacked the shit out of her at Studio 57 because she wouldn't get with him. And this was after Craig fucked Aaron's girl. The basis of a lot of their beefs was women. It went back to that whole you don't fuck the bosses' wife thing. Craig Haynes had to come down to South Philly to get a crew to come against Aaron and them." The Craig Haynes/JBM beef was vicious but produced no winners because the murders brought a lot of heat to both organizations.

"You feel you can be slicker, smarter, do a little bit of things differently than the last man did that you seen fall." Aaron said, but his downfall was all but foreseen. As he was making plans with his money and product, other people were making plans for him, namely D.A. Castille's task force. And their plan had Aaron ending up in jail. "Everybody has a plan, so don't fool yourself to think your plan is smarter that the next mans." Aaron said. Still at the time the JBM was all the rage and all the young boys wanted to get down. The JBM was a club where only selected members could enter. And like the most elite clubs, everybody was trying to get in. Crew members had a license to kill. They wore bulletproof vests and carried guns. Members greeted each other with hugs and called each other family. They were recognized on the street and catered to by the inner city populace. The word in the street was that, "JBM got West Philly sewed up." They were the princes of the criminal underworld and Aaron Jones was its king. And his kingdom consisted of not only West Philly but most of Philadelphia.

The task force found out that the JBM had established at least 45 loosely affiliated cocaine franchises that fed the city's insatiable appetite with an awesome 100 to 150 kilos of high-quality cocaine a week- much of it in the form of crack. There were as many as 40 ranking leaders, 300 active associates who did their bidding and thousands of smaller players such as crack cooks, lookouts and couriers. "They're going around grandstanding with their rings on, with their medallions around their neck," one police source said.

"It was heavy in 89. Everybody had the Lincoln LSC or the 190 Benz," Ock says. "Jarrods was a real popular hangout for them. It was topside in the Mount Airy section of Philly." It was here that Aaron allegedly had the meeting where he discussed the fact that James Cole was withdrawing from the organization but that Jones would be taking over Cole's California cocaine connect, Earl "Mustafa" Stewart also known as Unc, who began supplying cocaine to the JBM in early 1988. "James Cole was playing a dangerous game supplying both Craig Haynes and Aaron Jones at the same time." The Philly hustler says. "He ain't no street dude. He stayed out of the beefs. He was the connect. James had his whole house bugged. He was JBM's main connect." But with all the drama James Cole decided it was time to bounce. "When I left Philadelphia and moved to California, Aaron began to be around brothers where his authority making decisions came into play." James Cole said. And this switch was not without problems. "AJ let too many people know about the connect," the Philly hustler says. "Unc was the connect. Gump (Joseph Cobb) was trying to cut into Unc over Aaron. They had some in-house beefs over that. That shit was crazy. And Unc was gonna cut AJ off at one point because he got in too much drama. There were too many bodies." And Cole's departure was precipitated by information Aaron got from his brother-in-law who was an FBI agent.

"When Aaron first told me he had his brother-in-law in his pocket I was a little skeptical. But as Aaron began to give me certain information about investigations, I really believed he had the agent in his pocket. Especially when he told me about the DEA looking into my activities. I really knew he had the agent in his pocket." James Cole said. "I got a call from Aaron. He said he needed to see me because it was very important. I never met Aaron in the city. So I told him to meet me at the Sands Casino in Atlantic City. Aaron explained to me that his brother-in-law, which was the FBI agent, had told him that the DEA was investigating me for drug trafficking. He said the DEA believed I was a high scale cocaine dealer. I knew that was coming. I thanked him for the info." And Cole split the scene after that to lay low in Cali. But as more and more JBM crimes surfaced the FBI agent couldn't hold back the information on Aaron's drug activities without implicating himself as a go between. Aaron's brother-in-law decided to give information about Aaron to the DEA agents handling the JBM investigation without Aaron's knowledge.

"He was the main dude in Philly at that time," Ock says. "All the other dudes were under him. Getting stuff through him, reporting all problems to him. He was the boss." And as the investigation mounted, the disguised telephone trucks and Gas Works vans full of feds would be all up on the block watching the drug activity and taking photos, doing their surveillance and the like. The undercovers driving boxed off Grand Furys, the narc cars, making buy and busts, picking off the lower level street guys and trying to flip them to help build the case against the big man, Aaron Jones. So many agencies were on to them that they'd be falling over each other watching the JBM. A host of law enforcement agencies- the FBI, the Philadelphia Police Narcotic Unit, the State Police, the U.S. Organized Crime Strike Force and the Pennsylvania Crime Commission were conducting investigations. The multi-agency shotgun approach worked as over 30 ranking members were arrested in 88 and 89. A drug raid on December 1, 1988 netted six JBM members including founding member Tracy Mason in which police confiscated 90 grand, two pounds of coke, a .357 Magnum and two cars. But most of the arrests amounted to nothing and the JBM members were quickly returned to the street.

"Philly is mostly blacks and the cops are mainly white," Ock says. "They harass you, some might be worse than others but some will take your drugs and keep them, hold you and question you. It all depends." And these volatile race relations created a vibrant dynamic. As Aaron Jones and the JBM's profile rose in the streets and in law enforcement circles the papers picked up on the story and turned it into a daily running drama with subplots and everything. The JBM was a tabloid sensation and their story was unfolding live in Philadelphia's papers. The media hype had begun.

Part 4- Media Hype

According to the Philadelphia Crime Commission, Aaron Jones and his associates built the JBM into a violent multi-million dollar drug organization that controlled all of Philadelphia between 1985 and 1991. It was alleged that the JBM was comprised of 50 members and had up to 300 associates that were responsible for the sale of up to 300 kilos of cocaine generating almost 30 million dollars a month. The JBM assets included plenty of money, mansions, luxury cars, furs, jewelry and weapons. Between 1985 and 1991, the organization infiltrated or obtained a financial interest in more than 33 businesses to launder money and provide legitimate fronts for their operations. They were linked to businesses such as video stores, delicatessens, detail shops, security firms, car washes, barbershops and restaurants. Law enforcement viewed members of the JBM as young, well connected, street smart hustlers with a no-nonsense approach to their business. And the media, well they fell in love with the notion of the JBM and ran headline after headline on them, seemingly connecting them to every crime in the city.

"I was not looked at as a man but as public enemy number one, a monster because of all the saturation of propaganda," Aaron Jones said. It got so bad that every murder case that was unresolved during this period of time was put on the JBM to further substantiate the JBM profile of drugs and violence. Stories were told and embellished upon to the point that the truths of events were no longer identifiable. The papers reported that JBM leaders who were in their early 20's wore diamond encrusted JBM initial rings, drove flashy late model foreign cars and ordered rivals, feuding members or associates skimming profits- Get down or lay down, cooperate or be killed. "That's some media shit, it was never really like that. That was some paparazzi shit, it sounds good as a slogan, but that really wasn't true. You meet somebody, you have some coke and 99 percent of the coke out there was on consignment. If you give them a good price they will accept it." Derrick Williams explained.

"The motto Get down or lay down is the police motto coming from suckas on the street. No one went around telling people that or giving this ultimatum," Aaron said. But the newspapers and law enforcement officials ran with it. They maintained that the JBM threatened drug dealers in Philadelphia to "Get down or lay down." Weapons were JBM's tools of the trade, the police contended. "Members of the JBM would and did carry semi-automatic handguns and other firearms in order to protect themselves and their drug businesses and to threaten and inflict violence upon rival drug dealers," court records indicate. The motto was used to headline many stories done on Aaron Jones and the JBM by the media and it was used by the prosecution to further substantiate their claim of unchecked violence.

The JBM was so adept at intimidating witnesses that survivors of assassination attempts refused to testify against their assailants who usually carried high-powered, semi-automatic weapons. Authorities said JBM operatives also tried to buy even more powerful weapons including hand grenades. Fancy cars, furs, jewelry, new homes and legitimate businesses made for a comfortable life, providing of course, the drug money continued to flow. And the flow of JBM financed cocaine turned into a flood. Law enforcement officials contended that the cocaine network established by the JBM began with the Colombians and included members of the Scarfo Mob family. They sold cocaine out of fortified house with armor-plated doors and windows. Drug deals were conducted through mail slots. Besides drugs they were also linked to extortions and gambling, Fred Martins, executive director of the Pennsylvania Crime Commission said. Martins also confirmed that JBM members were connected to "certain key people"- relatives of Scarfo's crime family. And in the city they put their press game down.

"From what I understood dudes were submitting to their commands. Whatever they said went. If they felt dude was a problem he'd end up dead." Ock says. The cars, the jewelry, the fly girls- JBM had it all. And the extreme violence that occurred was necessary to control their business. This was a given from the street point of view, but everybody knows how the media can flip the script and portray all the ills of society on the latest bad boy in town. America loves its heroes and it loves its anti-heroes even more. "The authorities used to name every drug murder in the city a JBM murder. One thing about the streets, every body knows everybody. They knew the so-called JBM murders were some hype." James Cole said. But hype can make a man or break him. And the monster the media made Aaron out to be was far from the truth.

"He was like medium size build, he wasn't all that big. If you was to see him you wouldn't even think it was him." Ock says. "He was an average looking dude but his name carried a whole bunch of weight." In the city it was all JBM and Aaron Jones. Every time something went down it was Aaron and them that did it as far as the streets were concerned. There was only one gang in town and that gang was the JBM. They were all over the city and their names were ringing. The media focused in on Aaron Jones as the leader but Ock saw it differently, "Ultimately you would think Aaron was the leader but it might have been Rick Jones too because he was around since the jump and he was behind the scenes. Aaron was riding around, his name popping up, he was too much in the limelight. He was the face of JBM. The enforcer. The street boss." Ock says. And his whole click feared him.

"Around 89, it was real heavy. They had different corners, crack houses, people in the bars. In Philly everybody is on the corners outside. They'd set up abandoned houses as crack spots, have people on the block, watching for police, collecting money, giving out bundles," says Ock describing the scene. And JBM was flossing too, with that platinum bling-bling. "Belmont Plateau in West Philly on Sundays was the popular spot. Everybody got their girls, their cars, music. Everybody drinking Forties- Old English, Saint Ides and Philly blunts or EZ Wider. They thought Top papers had the pork in it." Ock relates. Anybody and everybody living in Philly was talking about Aaron Jones and the JBM during the mid-eighties and early nineties. If they weren't talking about them, they weren't down. Everyone had their own version of things and most made it up as they went along but everyone agreed "that they were not to be fucked with." The JBM had Philly on lock.

The newspaper headlines were crazy- *Inside the JBM's Rise to Power, Brash Youngsters Rule Over Drug Trade, 25 Murders Linked to the JBM.* The JBM's cocaine empire rivaled the defunct Black Mafia's in scope and violence. What took the Black Mafia decades to build though the JBM conquered in a matter of years. "There were anywhere from 25-40 JBM guys," Ock says. "That's how deep they were. That's just the people who were in position. They had countless people under them. Dudes were associated with the JBM but they weren't official members. They were just putting in work." And as the media reports continued no one was ready for what hit next. It seemed straight out of a movie. The Shower Posse/Junior Black Mafia war.

The Shower Posse was a notorious east coast organization of trigger happy Jamaicans who were known for shooting first with wild blasts from Uzi's and asking questions later. They had dominated the drug trade from Kingston to Miami to New York and eventually started branching out to other parts of the country as they brought more of their people in from Jamaica. They were rumored to have a Wild West attitude with no regard for human life. If someone was in their way they let out a shower of bullets, hence the name. They were also on point with their murder game and had a cadre of vicious Jamaican nationals who were stone cold killers.

The Shower Posse had a stronghold in Southwest Philadelphia and the JBM wasn't having it. One of their goals was to take back the territory controlled by the Jamaican drug dealers. "Initially when I heard, I was apprehensive," Willie Byrd, special agent for the Philadelphia Crime Commission said. "I thought some of it might just be street talk. But then we started to get the same thing from other informants and from other agencies and I knew there had been some conflicts between blacks and Jamaicans. I was aware of competition between the two groups. Some of the reports made sense."

The Shower Posse may have met its match with the brutal and pragmatic JBM. The headlines in Philly said the JBM was balling out of control, definitely putting their thing down. But like all champions a challenger was put forth, to fight JBM for the street crown of Philly. It was like Ali vs. Frazier, Hopkins vs. De La Hoya. What was big news before, turned into real big news with the entrance of the Shower Posse, who were encroaching on the home team's territory with a murder spree of their own. But was the war more hype than reality?

In March 1988, a man appeared on a television documentary, his face obscured, and claimed to be one of the city's top four drug dealers. The man threatened to kill his rival Jamaican drug dealers. "We're going to start exterminating them. I'm telling them we're corning. Not maybe, might or we're thinking about it, we're coming. Just think when, where or how, who's going to be first." The man flashed his JBM ring and identified himself as the leader of the Junior Black Mafia. "The name Junior Black Mafia came about when a fellow, unknown to anyone, went on national television and stated his group was formed to rid the City of Philadelphia of a group of Jamaican drug dealers known as the Shower Posse. He claimed his group was more heavily armed than the Shower Posse. He declared war on the Shower Posse. He stated he was a group called the Junior Black Mafia," James Cole said. "I called Aaron and asked him did one of his boys go on television claiming that he was the Junior Black Mafia. I asked him was it him. He asked me if I believed in the Easter Bunny, I laughed and understood." Still the television appearance sparked a war, real or not.

"I'm familiar when the Shower Posse was in that era too." Ock says. "Shower Posse was the Jamaican dudes. They were moving too. They didn't believe in nobody owing them five dollars. They'd ride around in the Volvo's with those baby Uzi's- spray your whole family." And that's how the war went, death for death on the streets of Philly. Here's what Tony Black who led the Philly branch of the Shower Posse said of the JBM situation, "The JBM were some clowns. Some of the guys that hustled with me had a beef with them after they left me and went on their own. I think one of the guys killed one of their leaders." But in reality was the whole war concocted by the government to get the two groups to kill each other while police watched on the sidelines?

"Aaron said he saw the interview and didn't know whom it was because the viewer had his face scrubbed out." James Cole said. "He told me he didn't understand how the dude got a JBM ring. Aaron knew the Philadelphia police took Lenny 'Bazil' Patterson's ring when he was stopped in his car with Simon in Mount Airy. We never knew who it was until recently we put it together." James Cole explained. "Through court documents we later found out that the ring Bazil had when he was stopped by the Philadelphia police, was turned over to the DEA. How someone got that same exact ring to go on television is unknown. But with the help of somebody in the government they started a war." The guy on the tape turned out to be a drug dealer named Michael "Blood" Youngblood who was a known DEA informant with ties to the original Black Mafia, that later became an aide to a Philadelphia city councilwoman.

"Years later my co-defendant Joseph Cobb sent me an article his sister got off the Internet. In the article was a story about the city of Philadelphia's councilwoman's aide." Cole said. "From the article we learned that a guy went on national television and claimed he wanted to kill the Shower Posse. The article stated he was a longtime federal informant who did anything and everything that the federal authorities asked of him. Youngblood could not have staged that event without the help of someone in law enforcement. He would have been locked from the door."

In March 1990, the Pennsylvania Crime Commission issued a report that an organization called the Junior Black Mafia had been formed to take control of Philadelphia's drug traffic. It also gave details on the alleged Shower

Posse/JBM war for the streets of Philly. But in truth, much of what was reported was the invention of one man, Youngblood and his DEA handlers who were trying to throw some shit into the game by causing frictions between the crews. Divide and conquer were the feds tactics. "I read or heard that the Shower Posse had said something that the JBM was a crew of clowns or something of that nature but listen to this, the Jamaican Shower Posse had several members flip. Now, who is the crew of clowns?" Derrick Williams said. It's rumored in the streets that even the leader of the Shower Posse flipped, but that's another story.

With the feds orchestrating events, the so-called war had some casualties, but it didn't take off like the feds wanted. It was all just some media hype in reality. But still there were some consequences. "I was in FCI Otisville in New York when a member of the Shower Posse who caught a case in Southwest Philly approached me." James Cole said. "He wanted to know why Aaron went on national television and declared war on them. I told him how could a member of the mafia go on a television station and claim he wants to kill other human beings. I told him Aaron couldn't do that. It was somebody with authority. He said that event caused a couple of his buddies to be shot. I told him I believed him because I read the 1990 Crime Commission report on the JBM and The Shower Posse drug war. The Crime Commission tried to say it was for control over drug turf in Southwest Philly. But he told me it wasn't like that. He said they didn't know who was who and some innocent people got shot because they were under the impression that everybody black in the drug trade was JBM members."

Part 5- In Jail

In 1989 Jones, then 27 and the JBM boss, was prosecuted by the Philadelphia D.A.'s office for shooting Richard Issacs, a drug dealer from West Oak Lane. The February 21, 1989 shooting resulted when the alleged independent drug dealer Issacs refused to Get down or lay down. Issacs who was shot 10 times in the arm, hip, chest and face was paralyzed from the waist down due to the incident. When the case went to trial an alleged JBM member was arrested for possession of a handgun while in the courtroom, where the government witness Issacs was set to testify against Aaron Jones from his wheel chair, where he was now confined. But with the inevitable prospect of death for testifying against Aaron, Issacs recanted his testimony and Aaron went free. The frightened witness refused to testify against Aaron, stunning the D.A.'s office and putting all their plans in a twist. The intimidation game put down by Aaron and his people shocked the justice system but not for long.

Another grand jury was hastily convened and Aaron was again indicted but not before a rival seeking to kill him mistakenly shot to death an innocent man in a West Oak Lane tavern after learning Aaron was free, further infuriating prosecutors. In August 1989, Aaron was rearrested on charges of conspiring to murder, aggravated assault, simple assault, reckless endangerment, possessing an instrument of crime and violating the uniform firearms act. The prosecutors weren't playing and Aaron was held on a five million dollar bond. The story was that the wheelchair bound Richard Issacs had fell out of favor with the JBM street boss and this led to his shooting and confinement to a wheelchair. Death threats stopped Issacs from testifying the first time but when Aaron was rearrested and the witness testified at a preliminary hearing, a Sheriff's deputy stood between Issacs and Jones to prevent eye contact. In the second trial in May 1990, despite Issacs' testimony, Aaron was acquitted of the shooting.

While being held on that case Aaron had an incident at the jail that led him to be charged in November 1989 with another aggravated assault case, along with reckless endangerment, conspiracy and possession of an instrument of crime in the stabbing of a fellow inmate in the prison yard at Philadelphia Industrial Correctional Center. The D.A.'s office was determined not to let Aaron back out on the street so they slammed him with the prison yard stabbing, holding him as the DEA slowly put together their federal indictment of the whole JBM crew. *Reputed JBM Boss Sentenced*, read *The Philadelphia Inquirer* headline on February 15, 1991. The paper reported that Philadelphia Common Court Judge John W. Herron sentenced Aaron Jones, alleged boss of the JBM to the maximum 10 to 20 years in prison for the 1989 prison yard stabbing. An extraordinary amount of time for a prison stabbing but with the federal indictment looming there was no way that the authorities were going to let Aaron loose again. They had learned from their mistakes. With witnesses refusing and scared to testify against Aaron and his fellow JBM members holding fast to the code of the streets, authorities had to get Aaron however they could. And with Aaron knowing he faced serious prison time he converted to Muslim. "When he caught the body he went to take the Shahadah," the Philly hustler says. "He wanted to become Muslim before he went upstate." Because as Aaron well knew the Muslims ran the prisons and if he had beefs from the street he would need strong allies in prison.

"The unexpected will come up and bite you in the middle of your plan," Aaron said and he never expected to be convicted of the prison stabbing, but Aaron being the man that he was, rolled with the punches. And the punches were just starting. The 10-20 year sentence was the jab, now the uppercut and knockout punches were being readied. Aaron was taking the governments best, but he was in danger of getting knocked out the box, completely. A JBM gunman, Christopher Anderson told the feds that Aaron and one of his top lieutenants Samuel "Black Sam" Brown had ordered and planned a 1990 execution style slaying of food store owner Bruce Kennedy. At the time of the Kennedy shooting Jones and Brown were being held for the Issacs shooting. *Alleged JBM Chief Charged in Execution-Style Slaying, The Philadelphia Inquirer* read on September 20, 1991. It was reported that reputed JBM leader Aaron Jones, 29, faced new charges that he ordered the execution of former JBM member Bruce Kennedy inside a West Philadelphia food market. But the story would get deeper as the federal indictment came down, that was the uppercut that rocked Jones. And the state's D.A. was going for the death penalty against Aaron for the Kennedy murder. Can you say knockout?

Part 6- The Feds

"As time went on so many young brothers started to compromise their principles and that deteriorated the level of thoroughness amongst brothers. There was a self-serving mentality that transcended down to later generations that bred a lot of those rats," Aaron said. And as the notorious JBM case was handed down the rats started coming out of the gutters. "Twenty-six of us got indicted but there was more." Derrick Williams said. "Fourteen of us was already in state jail and the other twelve had to be picked up." And the feds were in full effect, snatching JBM members and associates off the streets. "The connect got caught and he told the feds he could get them the JBM and we were already hot. We were in all the newspapers in Philly." Derrick Williams said. Law enforcement started receiving good intelligence on the gang not long after it was founded and the federal strike force was assigned to investigate the JBM in 1989. Investigations discovered the group put several hundred kilos of cocaine, especially in the form of crack, on the street a month. The JBM murdered several dozen people, including rivals, witnesses, innocent bystanders, and their own confederates. Most of the gang's members who survived the numerous internecine battles were arrested in 1990 and 1991, and the remaining infrastructure was decimated in March of 1992, when twenty-six defendants went on trial for operating a continuing criminal enterprise known as the JBM.

On October 2, 1991, a grand jury in the United States District Court for the Eastern District of Pennsylvania returned a thirty-two count indictment charging Bryan "Moochie" Thornton, Aaron Jones, Bernard "Qadir" Fields and twenty-three others with conspiracy to distribute cocaine, crack cocaine and heroin between late 1985 and September 1991. The indictment alleged that all defendants were members of a criminal organization known as the Junior Black Mafia ("The JBM"), which sold and distributed for resale large amounts of cocaine and heroin in the Philadelphia area. The indictment further alleged that Thornton, Jones and Fields were, at various times, the principle leaders of the JBM. The district court ordered the trial of these three defendants to be severed from the remaining defendants and then denied motions by Thornton and Jones for separate trials.

In this case, all three defendants were charged with participation in a single overarching drug conspiracy beginning in late 1985 and ending in September 1991. Most of the evidence presented at the trial concerned drug transactions that occurred while all three defendants were active participants in the JBM. The feds even went so far as to empanel an anonymous jury. In its motion the government argued that the defendants' history of extreme violence, the press coverage surrounding the JBM's activities and the murder charges brought in state court against Thornton and Jones could cause the jury to be apprehensive about its physical safety. The government also asserted that members of the JBM had intimidated witnesses on four prior occasions. In granting the motion the district court stated that, "In light of the news media coverage of persons and events purportedly associated with the so-called Junior Black Mafia the court finds that sufficient potential for jury apprehension for their own safety exists to justify use of an anonymous jury to ease such tensions." The feds were going all out in their attempt to break the JBM's hold on the Philly drug trade. With the wide sweeping indictment and conspiracy laws, the feds figured that they had their man. As in Aaron Jones. To the feds, Aaron was the key. The feds wanted everybody to flip on Aaron Jones but it wasn't happening. "I remember when they asked our lawyers was anybody cooperating and each lawyer stood up and said we weren't." Derrick Williams said. "Once you get that indictment you are essentially by yourself, it's you and that indictment. They start to send you all over the state to keep you separated. They sent us all over the place and we were facing life. Most members were charged with 841, which is a conspiracy to sell five kilograms of cocaine or more with three or more individuals, which carries a 10 to life sentence. And Aaron, Bryan Thornton and James Cole received the 848 which carries a life sentence." But even facing life, all 26 of Aaron's co-defendants stayed true to the game.

"Aaron was a very level headed guy who was very loyal," James Cole said and the way the crew stuck together showed this, but it didn't mean there weren't any snitches. There were plenty of those- William Mead, Chris Anderson, Rodney "Frog" Carson, Earl "Mustafa" Stewart, Stacy Rucker- the list went on. With all the core JBM members off the street the fear of retribution was alleviated and dudes started signing on with the feds. The prosecution relied heavily on the testimony of former JBM members and associates. Earl "Mustafa" Stewart, the California coke connection, testified that he delivered approximately 554 kilos of cocaine to the JBM beginning in early 1988. He told the court how he was paid with garbage bags filled with money. Numerous accounts of lower members flashing the JBM rings that Jones gave out were given. In the city the diamond encrusted rings bearing the initials JBM were a sign of gangster royalty. But in the end they led to an indictment. It was a free for all and the prosecution was dead serious. They weren't playing. But they didn't get the whole crew. James Cole was a fugitive, as was crew member Eric Pearson.

"When we first got indicted the feds thought I was in Atlanta, Georgia," James Cole said. "The day the indictment came out I got a beep from a guy. He told me the FBI just left his house looking for Skip Jackson. It was something about a JBM indictment. He said watch yourself. I was in West Philly at the time laying low. My sixth sense started working. Always follow your first thought. I turned the radio to KYM, the all news station. I heard the indictment being announced. They said they got the top three leaders of the alleged JBM. I refused to turn myself in. I wanted to see if they were really sharp and could catch me. After my co-defendant's trial I went out to Cali. The feds couldn't find me."

At the fifteen-day jury trial that followed, the government introduced a substantial amount of evidence in support of its charges against the three accused leaders- Jones, Thornton and Fields. Including the cooperation of ten cooperating witnesses who were members of, or who had direct dealings with the JBM, more than sixty wiretapped or consensually recorded conversations concerning members of the JBM, physical evidence, including documents, photographs, drugs, weapons and drug-related paraphernalia. This evidence demonstrated (1) the founding of the JBM by Aaron Jones and James Cole; (2) the numerous sources from which the defendants purchased and then distributed over 1,000 kilos of cocaine and lesser amounts of heroin during the period of time alleged in the indictment; (3) the administration of the JBM by Jones, Thornton and Fields; (4) the division of the organization into squads which controlled the distribution of drugs in various sections of Philadelphia; and (5) the violent tactics used by the members of the JBM to expand the organization territory and to gain greater control of the drug-trafficking business in Philadelphia.

"It was a straight bullshit case," James Cole said and the case was not without controversy. On day 13 of the trial, the government informed the court that a United States Marshal had observed "visual communication" between juror No.3 and defendant Fields consisting of smiles, nods of assent and other nonverbal interaction. Juror No. 3 was removed. There was also a big deal made of the DEA paying its informants. During the trial the DEA detailed payments made to two cooperating witnesses, Dwight Sutton and Darrell Jamison, who the defense contended were professional snitches. The government produced witness agreements, including immunity agreements and information documenting payments to several cooperating witnesses. The defense cried foul but the court contended, "The testimony by Sutton and Jamison was not critical to the government's case but was rather cumulative in view of the testimony by the other government witnesses, the wiretaps and consensually recorded conversations and the physical evidence utilized at trail."

Several other witnesses other than Sutton testified that Jones wore a "JBM" ring and gave orders to other members of the organization. Recorded conversations revealed his role within the JBM and the court referred to the testimony of numerous other government witnesses and to physical and documentary evidence demonstrating Jones involvement with the JBM, his leadership of the organization and his participation in numerous drug transactions. "Aaron Jones was the top man," the Philly hustler says. "He had Bernard Fields transporting two to three million dollars at a time for him. Fields wasn't no street dude but Aaron trusted him. Aaron would send him with the money." Federal prosecutor Joel M. Friedman, in his closing arguments to the jury at the trial, said the gangs three leaders- Aaron Jones, Bryan Thornton and Bernard Fields were responsible for the distribution of millions of dollars worth of cocaine in Philadelphia, along with countless JBM related shootings and murders. Defense attorneys criticized evidence, contending the government's case was weak. But the evidence proved to be enough.

The jury found the defendants guilty of conspiracy to distribute and to possess with intent to distribute cocaine and heroin, possession with intent to distribute and distribution of a controlled substance. Thornton and Jones were convicted of participating in a continual criminal enterprise and Fields was convicted of using a firearm during a drug trafficking offense and possession of a firearm after having been previously convicted of a felony. The case was a resounding success for the prosecution. "First they knocked Aaron," Derrick Williams said. "Then they broke the rest down in crews of eight."

The court ordered the remaining defendants to be tried in two separate trials. In the second trial seven defendants including squad leader Reginald Reaves, advisor Leroy "Skip" Jackson and enforcers James "Squeezie" Price and Joseph "Gump" Cobb began what would be a sixteen-day jury trial. Again, the government introduced a substantial amount of evidence in support of its charges against the defendants including the testimony of eight cooperating witnesses who were members or who had direct dealings with the JBM. The evidence was similar to that introduced in the Jones trial and demonstrated that (1) Reginal Reaves was a squad leader; (2) Anthony "TL" Long was a member of Mark "Goldie" Casey's squad; (3) Price worked as a courier and enforcer for Jones; (4) Reginald Reaves brother Darrell Reaves was his right hand man; (5) Jackson dealt in drugs, facilitated the JBM's meetings and advised the JBM in general, and Jones in particular; (6) Cobb facilitated drug purchases for the JBM and acted as a courier and enforcer; (7) Michael Williams was associated with members of the JBM and sold drugs. From time to time, there was a shift in their various roles and responsibilities. The jury found all the defendants guilty of conspiracy to distribute and to possess with the intent to distribute cocaine and heroin. The remaining nine defendants who were to be tried in a third trial all plead guilty pursuant to plea bargains as did five others.

The three trials of 25 members of the conspiracy who had been jointly indicted showed that the defendants shared various roles like couriers, enforcers and dealers. They were all active participants in furthering the JBM's organizational reach and scope in the streets of Philadelphia. Rodney "Frog" Carson, one of the government's main witnesses testified extensively. Defense attorneys argued that the only people who seemed to be able to corroborate Carson's testimony, "were dead people."

Part 7- Convictions

Leader of JBM Gets Life, The Philadelphia Inquirer declared on September 16, 1992. Aaron Jones was sentenced to life in prison on charges of conspiring to distribute 100 million dollars worth of cocaine in Philadelphia between 1985 and 1991. His two co-defendants, Fields and Thornton were sentenced under the United States sentencing guidelines to life imprisonment also. The U.S. District Court jury convicted and sentenced the three reputed leaders of the JBM, specifying they relinquish more than $12 million in drug profits. Defendants Price, Cobb, Jackson, Darrell Reaves and Long were each sentenced to 360 months imprisonment. Williams was sentenced to 292 months. Reginald Reaves and Mark Casey were sentenced to life. Other members in the conspiracy like Derrick Williams pled guilty and received sentences of 10 years and up.

"There's no pension plan for players in the game." Aaron said. "One or two might fall through the cracks but the hard truth is you will either come in or go under." Aaron seemed resigned to his fate. But by holding true he became a legend. "I take solace in the fact that all the comrades I broke bread with remained true," Aaron said, saluting his co-defendants. "Aaron was good at picking his crew," Derrick Williams said. "The reason I say he was good at choosing members is because he had 26 co-defendants and not one told, no one cooperated with the prosecution. He was real good at judging character."

About his other co-defendants Derrick said, "Every individual said I'm not going to be a rat, it's all mental, if you go into a situation and you understand that for every mistake there are consequences and if you are a man, you can accept that. Some people fake it but when the time comes for that pressure they do something else. It is rare that 26 people get indicted and nobody flips." And that's true but Aarons' troubles were far from over. The fed case was just an uppercut to knock him off balance. Everybody knows the feds play dirty and the knockout blow was still to come.

In January 1993, Aaron Jones was convicted of first degree murder and criminal conspiracy in connection with the August 18, 1990 shooting death of Bruce Kennedy. *Jury Convict Three in Drug Gang Slaying, The Philadelphia Inquirer* headline read on January 21, 1993. Aaron and two associates, Sam "Black

Sam" Brown and James Anderson, were convicted of first degree murder in what prosecutors called the assassination of Bruce Kennedy in West Philadelphia. Assistant District Attorney Joel Rosen said the killing of Bruce Kennedy in August 1990 was an organized hit related to drug dealing by the JBM and their ever-warring factions. The night before the slaying Jones, who was in prison at the time, conspired with Black Sam who ordered two hitmen, James Anderson 20, and Chris Anderson 21, to carry out the murder contract. The gunmen, who were not related, shot Kennedy 26, more than a dozen times as he was cooking a steak sandwich inside Mommies Market on 54th Street near Master. James Anderson stood over Kennedy and fired three bullets into his head and all over his body, according to testimony. Chris Anderson testified against the threesome.

Aaron was accused of orchestrating the murder of Bruce Kennedy to avenge the death of Leroy Davis another high-ranking member of the JBM, who was believed by the organization to have been murdered by Aaron's federal co-defendant Bryan "Moochie" Thornton. Thornton was in prison at the time, so Aaron and his co-defendants were accused of plotting to kill Thornton's cousin, in order to send a message to Moochie that killing a fellow member is unacceptable. Aaron allegedly put the plan together along with arranging for the get away car and cash. Aaron was already in prison serving a federal life sentence for running a continuing criminal enterprise for his leadership role in the Junior Black Mafia. James Anderson and "Black Sam" Brown were sentenced to life in prison for the murder while Jones as the orchestrator received the death penalty.

"My federal drug case and murder case is nothing but word of mouth from a bunch of frogs (snitches) trying to find a way out. So who is the top prize, me." Aaron said. "In Philly I like to call them frogs- they leap into bed with the feds. Conspiring with them, telling infinite lies and ad-libbing as they go along mixing up half truths to make themselves sound believable. There was no other evidence in either case just hearsay evidence. I have no faith for justice in the judicial or should I say political system." Throughout Aaron's several court cases he and his lawyer proclaimed racial discrimination and improprieties as well as his innocence in his capital murder case. Through hearsay, snitch testimony, street informants, exaggerations and out and out lies, Aaron said that he was personified to represent what ills society- drugs and violence.

"Aaron Jones got the death penalty because he was a black man," James Cole said. "Nothing else. Race played a part in him winding up on death row. I'll tell you like this, Aaron was sentenced to the death penalty for the murder of Bruce Kennedy. They alleged Aaron gave an order to two JBM members to kill Bruce. He is on death row because of word of mouth. Rodney "Frog" Carson told the government that somebody told him Aaron gave the order to wipeout Bruce, because he was the cousin of another JBM member, Moochie." And James Cole had his own music to face.

JBM Connect Gets Life in Coke Case, He's Fifth in Gang to Receive Life Sentence, The Philadelphia Daily News headline read on February 19, 1994. After being caught as a fugitive after 30 months on the lam, Cole 40, was tried, convicted and sentenced to life in the feds for trafficking in cocaine. "There wasn't any evidence in this case," Cole said. "The DEA was lucky to get a fellow who lived in Harlem, NY who was a drug addict, to come to court and implicate me. The DEA paid him $17,000. The reason I say the DEA got lucky is because nobody in Philly would do that. Our case had two grand juries. The first grand jury wouldn't indict. The DEA got Sutton to implicate us. We don't know him." And just like the Jones trial there were allegations of improprieties but the charges against James Cole stuck.

Being a victim of the snitch system, Aaron knew how the game worked. "Frog" Carson snitched on him, Chris Anderson and more. Some just made up outright lies to save their own asses, playing on Aaron's notoriety. Even his own brother-in-law, the FBI agent turned on him and was key in putting him away. For most who get in the game it's only about the glory. They have no guts and when it comes time to pay the piper they can't handle the pressure. So they break weak and flip on their comrades. But not Aaron. He was ready to stare down certain death, even at the hands of the state's hired assassins, government sanctioned execution and all.

Part 8-Death Row

While serving three different sentences, Aaron was on death row in a maximum security prison, waiting to face his execution. "I have a death sentence. These people want to take me out under the premise that I was a mafia boss." Aaron said. "What's ironic is that not one white (Italian) so-called Mafia figure has ever been placed on the row here in Pennsylvania." And looking back from his cell on death row Aaron has come to some conclusions.

"Look at me, I am sitting on the row, ask me was it worth it? I tell you no." Aaron said. "I have come to terms with the lifestyle I chose years ago. My plight is a little different than most brothers. I played no part in the capital murder, this brother will not be on a bent knee trying to demonstrate a remorseful attitude to a system and society that never shows mercy itself and is built on tyranny and racial discrimination." But Aaron's detractors might say he was the tyrant himself, who never showed any type of mercy to his victims in Philadelphia. Still Aaron is a soldier, regardless of what his critics think.

"As I sit on the row to me it was never an option to take the stand on my comrades. That never even came across my mind as an afterthought, you feel me?" Aaron said. He played the game the way it was supposed to be played. He stuck to the code and embodied what death before dishonor meant. In retrospect, he came to some real thoughts concerning the drug game. "It won't last and when it comes time to pay-the money and nothing you may think you accomplished are worth your life." Aaron Jones was not the monster people would have you believe he was. He's lived on the row with a peaceful vibe of a man that has come to terms with himself and his higher power. He's a devout Sunni Muslim that long ago came to terms with his lot in life. His days and nights are very different from the lifestyle he was accustomed to on the street. Aaron's days begin and end in a cell locked down, away form the world.

"I am locked down 23 hours a day. Monday to Friday." Aaron said. "Twenty-four hours a day on Saturday and Sunday. I get one hour of exercise in the yard during the week and I may sign up to go to the law library for a two hour session once a week when it's my turn. I can have a two hour visit and a 15 minute phone call every week." And all his visits are non-contact, with Plexiglas between him and his visitor. No human contact for the convicted JBM boss. Aaron must talk on a phone to his visitor. That's the end result for being a real live street legend. There's no gangster paradise, just a jail cell to rot in or a gravestone with your name etched on it. But all that hasn't stopped Aaron's legend from spreading.

Death Sentence Upheld, read *The Pittsburgh Post- Gazette* on November 24, 1995. They reported that the State Supreme Court had affirmed the death sentence of a Philadelphia man- JBM leader Aaron Jones. Still battling, Aaron has been fighting his death sentence and first degree murder charge from the jump with the same relentlessness he displayed in the street. And he's been dogged by the same adversaries.

When State Supreme Court Justice Ronald Castille was a district attorney, his office fought to dismantle the notorious JBM and to bring Aaron Jones down. Castille was instrumental in forming the taskforce that was specifically charged with targeting Jones and his crew. Aaron Jones was the D.A.'s main objective in the probe. Then when the court unanimously upheld Jones' conviction and death sentence on November 22, 1995, Castille wrote a 59-page opinion setting down the court's ruling. In the opinion, Castille wrote that Jones had devised a murderous plot to assassinate Bruce Kennedy in 1990 and ordered subordinates to carry out the killing. Castille declined a request by Jones' lawyer, Gerald A. Stein, to disqualify himself from the proceedings, bringing up accusations of an ethical violation.

"This raises a very serious appearance of impropriety, which is made worse by the fact that Justice Castille was the author of the opinion in this case." Stein said in his petition, which asked the high court to reconsider without Castille's participation, its ruling. "The appearance of being prosecuted and then judged by the same person is an unacceptable violation of Justice Castille's responsibilities as a jurist under the code of judicial conduct, and a violation of Jones' right to a fair and impartial panel," Stein said. Assistant D.A. Norman Gross dismissing Stein's objections said the court unanimously made their decision so, "even if Justice Castille had not been on the case, it would have been upheld." Aaron Jones couldn't believe it. The guy who helped put him away, wrote the opinion denying his appeal for a new murder trial. It didn't seem very American. But this oversight of justice has kept the case alive all these years.

Execution Ordered for JBM Founder, The Philadelphia Daily News headline read on December 21, 2002. The paper reported that a death warrant was signed for the notorious JBM founder and street boss Aaron Jones. Jones was ordered to die on February 18, 2003 by outgoing Governor Mark Schweiker. It was the third death warrant for Jones since his 1995 conviction. But it was stayed and Aaron is still fighting his case. Keeping his silence despite the glorification of his deeds and legend.

Part 9- Glorification

"For years I remained in a passive mentality not wanting my voice to be heard because I know how cynical and pessimistic society is." Aaron said from his cell on death row. "Especially when it comes to brothers like myself. People contact me to try and quote me one way or another. Knowing full well how I am perceived I felt it would be foolish on my part to say anything. Regardless of how I came off they would twist it around to make me look bad." And Aaron has stuck to his guns but that hasn't stopped the world from writing about him, making movies and more.

There has been an explosion of books claiming to be about the infamous Aaron Jones and his comrades known as the JBM, all unauthorized and very inaccurate according to Jones. "I have nothing but contempt for the books written about me. These so-called authors trying to capture the psyche of my thing but all fall way short. You can't get information from none of these books about me because believe me, they don't have a clue." Aaron said that everything that has been written about him is based on speculation and gossip and the things that may have been true were embellished for drama and credibility. All the stories that have circulated, all the testimony given, has been given by third parties- snitches, wanna-be's, gossips and liars. "To this day all versions of our time have been diluted and fabricated. Stories and lies from suckers who knew full well they had to step off the scene when real brothers came on the set. So many people try to come at you with games, only to exploit you for financial purposes." Aaron said.

Teri Woods, a well known street lit author, was one of the first with her clas-

sic street novel, *True to the Game*, which fictionalized the rise and fall of the notorious Junior Black Mafia crew. The book chronicled the time period in the
late 80's that Aaron and his crew were out there. Aaron's name and Black
Mafia are even used in the book, which has gone on to sell more than 500,000
copies. "You write what you know," Teri Woods said. "*True to the Game* was
meant to represent a lifestyle, the book is leaving a piece of documented history. I don't really call what I do street fiction. I refer to it as true to life crime
and that's what my book represents. The crack era existed for black gangsters
just like prohibition for the Italians and Irish."

The Teri Woods' book kept it very real. Maybe too real. "Some of the stuff
that was written in there was real close to what really happened," Ock says.
"Stuff in the book, it was like I remembered when that happened. Someone
got shot up leaving the Chances Are Club and that was in the book. One dude
pressed up on Teri Woods, 'You wasn't around that era, how you know so
much?' He asked. 'From talking to dudes,' she told him." And Beanie Sigel, the
Philly rapper got into the JBM story too.

The *State Property* movie from Rockafella Records starred Beanie, Dame
Dash and Jay-Z. During production the movie was titled Get Down or Lay
Down. Word on the streets was that the movie was based on the life and times
of Aaron and his crew the Junior Black Mafia. Aaron has made it clear that
he was displeased with all the movies and books attempting to depict his time
on the street. With or without Aaron's input, the story put out by the media
and what could be heard from the people who lived through the era in Philly
made for a real live gangster tale. Beanie Sigel said *State Property* was about,
"The drug scene in Philly." He said it wasn't the JBM story, "It's every man's
story. It is about every guy whoever tried to make a name for himself in the
drug game." But everyone knows that's some bullshit, it's about Aaron Jones.

Part 10- Retrospection

"I've come to terms with my life and take responsibility for my actions and
choices I made," Aaron said. "I'm not going to blame the system, the environment, no one but myself. But I don't accept everything that's happened to
me especially this unjust death sentence." Aaron deals with his life and his

legend one day at a time. At times both contrite and combative, pressing to release the tension and understand all that has occurred. His legacy as a true gangster is intact though. "Whatever happens happens and whatever is going to be is going to be. One thing for sure, I will never give them the satisfaction to think I will crumble to the system looking for mercy so they can laugh in my face. I will never allow my circumstances to break my strong will as a man." Aaron said. Spoken like the stand up convict and gangster that Aaron embodies. Still he reflects on his life, his legend and his time in the game.

"The thing is, it's not just about you but how it will affect everyone around you whom loves you once things come falling down." Aaron said. "The destruction of your life and the lives of your loved ones will be affected by it. I shared some of my views of how I feel about my unjust sentence and the way I was prosecuted, but in no way do I want to come off as condoning the lifestyle. I've had plenty of discussions with younger brothers who come through and from what I usually get is that they are not trying to hear it. They aren't listening to older brothers preaching to them about the streets. I said to myself why even bother? But then I realized that would be a defeated attitude I would be adopting to. So for whoever is out there and wants to hear some harsh realities from someone they can identify with, I'm your man." Real words from a real dude. Aaron Jones isn't faking it. He wasn't no buster-ass studio gangster- he was the real, live, genuine article. And he's paying the ultimate price for being the man that he was. Justified or not, his notoriety could stand nothing less. He was a legend in his own times. A man held above the rest of the throng and now, due to that infamy, he has a date to die.

Aaron Jones being a true Don, has kept it all in perspective. Its stories like Aarons that make some people believe that real Don's- real masters of the street-were born with something that drives them to the game, no matter their environment. There is no doubt that Aaron's a certified street legend. The baddest who ever did it in Philly. Not because he amassed millions, owned luxury cars, played the broads and lived ghetto fabulous but because he has proven himself to be a man of character and integrity. Aaron made a decision to play the game and he played by the rules to the very end, "Nothing is guaranteed in this game but death and prison." Aaron said and knowing that he still did what he did. Truer words have never been spoken and Aaron Jones will go down in the gangster chronicles as a full-fledged street legend.

Chapter 5

Peter "Pistol Pete" Rollack

PETER 'PISTOL PETE' ROLLACK

Pistol Pete and the Blood affiliated Sex, Money and Murder gang were the scourge of the Soundview section of the Bronx back in the day. In his teens and into his early twenties Pistol Pete acquired a reputation as a ruthless killer, who made millions in the drug game in the late 80's and early 90's. He was known as one of the most feared and powerful men in New York during the crack era, who could get people killed with his word alone. His influence and organization stretched south from the city's five boroughs reaching out and touching states all across the eastern seaboard. Pistol Pete was one of Soundview's Original Gangsters, setting the bar high for his hood and the Northeast Bronx.

In the city and all down the coast Pistol Pete was known for bustin' his guns with no conscious. When it came to that gun smoke, the kid didn't play. He was all business. It's rumored his body count numbered over three dozen. The kid was quick to pull and quicker to blast. He lived by that NWA credo, *"It's not about a salary its all about reality."* That's why they called him Pistol Pete. He was like a gunslinger from the old west. A modern day Billy the Kid. Many of the murders Rollack was allegedly involved in were ordered from his prison cell. Even after being locked up he still controlled his set- Sex, Money and Murder, from jail, as they wreaked havoc on the streets of the Bronx and beyond. Even to this day Pistol Pete's name is revered in the South Bronx and the walls and buildings still carry the SMM markings from Pete's heyday. Because of all this, Pistol Pete has gone down as a true certified street legend.

Part 1- Growing up in Soundview

The notorious Soundview/Castle Hill sections of the Bronx were known for poverty, crime-ridden projects and rampant drug sales and abuse. This cauldron of go-hard, gully streets defined what a ghetto was and it wasn't anything nice. These same streets were where Pistol Pete grew up and came of age. They spawned the child that became Pistol Pete. "The neighborhood is good for dope and crack." Money, a Bronx native from the era says. "That area is the same like Hunt's Point. That shit is twisted. It's all the South Bronx area. Spots everywhere." And Pistol Pete was no stranger to the game. You could say he was born into it.

In court papers it was said Pistol Pete's criminal behavior stemmed from his early years in a dysfunctional family. His father, the papers pointed out, was serving a 50-year prison term for his role in a drug organization. "Pete subconsciously idolized his father," the papers said even though his father abandoned his mother and spent most of Pete's childhood in prison. His father, Leonard Rollack, was convicted of racketeering charges in the 1980's. He was allegedly connected to the Nicky Barnes organization. Gene Gotti, Angelo Ruggiero and Mark Reither from the Gambino crime family were his co-defendants. Brenda Rollack, Pete's mother, said of Pete's father, "He was in prison but I had left him when Pete was three. He hustled, he was a street person and he was violent, but not around me. That's why I left him and took Petey, I didn't want him to grow up like that." But despite Brenda's best intentions Pete was destined to follow in his father's footsteps.

"I had him in Catholic school up until high school. Me and Pete were so close, he never gave me any problems," Brenda said. But when Pete started going to public school with the neighborhood kids his outlook changed. "When I switched him over to public school, he went to Stevenson High School where he met Twin and that's when he started changing." Through his peers Pete was introduced to the wider world. He started discovering the streets and found he had a liking for them. The lure and trappings of the drug game appealed to him in particular. The money, the women, the bling-bling, the cars and most of all the power were strong temptations for the young Pete. "In the early 80's, like 81-82 Pete was a kid back then. Like 11 or 12," an oldhead from the neighborhood remembers. "He was still going to school back then. His dad was a street legend himself so Pete got mad respect for that." Being the sharp kid that he was he studied his surroundings, took note of who was who and watched how dudes were making moves and coming up. Learning from observation while at the same time building his own crew around him Pete finally decided that he was ready to get his and get his by any means he did. If Pete was anything he was a leader. And in the streets he was known to be fearless. Though not large in stature, he had a heart that was crazy big and his neighborhood peers took notice and rallied around him.

"Projects are a good breeding ground for gangs," Money says. "Kids from broken homes, poverty level areas are prime candidates. The gangs take them in, give them that family." And in Pete, the kids from Soundview and Castle Hill found a figure to look up to. To lead them. "Castle Hill projects is big." Money says. "Them twelve-story joints. It's a world of its own. The projects are something else. Soundview are smaller, but bigger inside. The way that shit was you drove in then you had to go on foot. You could drop a body over there and it'd be two to three hours before the cops showed up. The conditions is crazy." And this crazy dog-eat-dog world shaped Pete and his young cohorts. They saw the world through tinted lenses. They saw what they didn't have and they decided that they would get it even if they had to rough it off.

"The surrounding neighborhoods are middle class," Money says. "A lot of prefabricated houses, working class neighborhoods. It's a big mix of people-white, black, Spanish." And to the kids from the projects their richer neighbors provided opportunity. An opportunity to come up from the gutter. Either by robbing them or by selling them crack. It was all the same thing to Pete and his crew. They were young roughnecks and as Pete got older he grew more wild and bold. "At about seventeen I couldn't take him," his mother said. "I put him out. I sent him to George Wallace, his father's friend, who I thought would guide him in the right direction and help me out." But George Wallace, a friend of Pete's father, had ties to the drug world himself and with his connections and Pete's budding crew of youngsters, they proved to be a lethal combination in the Soundview/Castle Hill area of the Bronx and in time beyond that. The beginnings of Pistol Pete's crew were coming together just like Wu-Tang, in a diverse and intoxicating manner.

Part 2- Sex, Money and Murder

Sex, Money and Murder was the name of the murderous drug gang that was started by Peter Rollack. But the name went way back. "That's a Soundview thing," the oldhead says. "They used to say we from that area where it's about sex, money and murder. Dudes used to go to clubs, like T-Connection. 'We from Soundview where it's about sex, money, murder.' That's what they would say. 'We about that sex, money, murder.' It was a saying in Castle Hill and Soundview. He came about after us." Back in the day the oldheads from the projects held it down. And Pistol Pete's dad was one of them. "Soundview was known for sex, money, murder. When Pistol Pete was a kid all that shit was going on." The oldhead says. "The original dude can't even go in that area no more. Chicken Rob raised a lot of those guys. He was a street legend back then. He was the right hand man of the guy that ran that area back then. As time went on Pistol Pete's era came on and he took on that mantle. But that shit was always about Soundview. It was bigger than Pistol Pete."

The gang allegedly terrorized the Soundview and Castle Hill neighborhoods back in the day to maintain its grip on the lucrative crack business. "They had a nice little crew." Money says. "A lot of young kids." Sex, Money and Murder was founded by Pete in 1993. Its members and associates at various times included- George Wallace, Andre "Dula" Martin, Robinson "Mac 11" Lazala, Shawn "Suge" Stokes, Rufino "Roro" Turner, Jasmine "Total Package" Mansell, Michael "Mo" Gray, David Andino, Reginald "Big Boo" Harris, David "Twin" Mullins, Rafael "Scruffy" Moore, Savon "Yaro Pack" Codd and Emilio "Leadpipe" Romero. They were into slinging crack, robbing dudes and roughing shit off with strong arm tactics. Pete's crew didn't play. They were quick to bust their guns and Pistol Pete set the tone with his violent demeanor.

"There are three realities to this game- freedom, prison and death," Pistol Pete said. "The odds are negatively stacked against all the participants of this life but this is something we know and accept before we even get into the game." Pistol Pete set down the rules and had a "to do" list instructing fellow gang members not to use their real name and urging them to kill snitches. He told his crew to "keep the circle tight" and "to take care of all of the orders to kill." As the gang grew in the Soundview section of the Bronx their reign of terror ensued. They killed indiscriminately and basically did what the fuck they wanted, when the fuck they wanted to with no repercussions to speak of.

"They started making noise in the 90's, like 93 or so," Money says. "I first saw them in 94 when these kids came down to Hunt's Point talking about they running with Pistol Pete, like this dude is some kind of street god or something." In the early 90's, as Pistol Pete built his rep he attracted others to his crew. Savon Codd also know as Yaro Pack, who'd known Pete all his young life was one of those who threw in with the clique. Rollack was the leader of the SMM crew but Yaro Pack was making a name for himself as a money getting dude who could move a lot of weight. He joined up with Pistol Pete's gang and got Sex, Money and Murder even more engaged in distributing cocaine and crack cocaine.

"A lot of dudes were on the set with him," Rock, another Bronx native from the era remembers. "His set was known for bikes and Uzi's. They'd be flying through tearing shit up. You know Pistol Pete had the uwop on him. He stayed with an Uzi on him." And Pete wasn't one to shy away from beef. He courted it. "They'd beef with whoever. Pistol Pete didn't care. It seemed like he liked that shit. They got three buildings down there bubbling crack. If someone around the way opened a spot they'd beef with the dudes across the street, lighting their asses up every time." Money says. And if any strong opposition showed up, Pistol Pete had something for them too. One night the Sex, Money and Murder crew were outside of the Olympics Restaurant in the Bronx when they saw this local tough dude, BO. BO had a solid rep on the block and Pistol Pete knew he could get points for knocking dude off. Pistol Pete wanted to go in and kill him right then in front of all the people just on G.P. but his mans and them tried to talk him out of it. Pistol Pete wouldn't listen though. He was adamant but finally his crew convinced him to wait for the dude to come outside. BO never came out though, so Pete told all his people, "No matter what," if any of them saw BO anywhere they were to kill him. Twin ended up killing BO shortly thereafter in 1995. "When them niggas came through they was deep. They stayed strapped too." Money says. The crew was armed and dangerous. Beware any who stood in their way.

"How many people jump into this life just wanting to enjoy the fast money, the cars, the women, the event and fail to prepare themselves mentally or just refused to accept the darker side of life?" Pete asked. He was the type of dude if you were all in, then you'd better be all in. There was no halfway with Pistol Pete. And he didn't just talk it. He walked it. Rock explains, "There were times they'd be at the Tunnel, that's the club in Manhattan where Pistol Pete and his guys would rob a lot of people. It was a known stick-up spot. But Pistol Pete would front on dudes. He in there and he got a chain but he knew that them dudes from Brooklyn were stick-up niggas looking for somebody to rob. But Pistol Pete told his mans and them to let him hold all of their chains and he put them all on. This is how brazen he was."

Because in reality Pistol Pete didn't give a fuck. He liked to flaunt shit in dudes faces. "He would walk dead amongst and in the center of all these stick-up niggas." Rock says. "Just daring them to fuck with him. This was his character. This is how he carried it. This nigga got a bunch of jewelry on him. A bunch of chains. That was a brazen act. Daring these stick-up niggas to try him." But that was Pistol Pete. He courted chaos. He lived for the drama. The turmoil and dangers of the street were his domain. It was where he had to prove himself again and again. And he made his presence known too. "Nothing moved in the Boogie Down without his say," Rock says. "Dude was powerful." And one time Pistol Pete even ended up busting off on a bunch of dudes in the club, just to prove a point. Allegedly someone was killed. "History repeated itself with the club murder because his father had a similar situation in a club 20 years before." The oldhead says. Pistol Pete was destined to follow in his father's footsteps.

Part 3- North Carolina and other trips

When Yaro Pack got down with SMM he was already involved in cocaine and crack cocaine distribution in Pittsburgh, Pennsylvania. Pistol Pete saw this as a good move and started accompanying Yaro on the trips to Pittsburgh in late 1993 and 1994. They were transporting eight to ten kilograms of cocaine powder and crack at a time. At first Pistol Pete served as an enforcer on the trips to Pittsburgh and was paid $5,000 per trip. But Pistol Pete was observing, taking it all in and making plans. "He had the shit in Soundview and Castle Hill locked down, so he must of been looking for more opportunities,"

Money says. "The young kid Pete was getting that money," the oldhead remembers. "He was on the rise. He was out there putting that work in." And the trips to Pittsburgh opened up the door to a whole new world of the drug game for the young Pistol Pete.

In 1994, Yaro Pack and his associate David Gonzales met in the Bronx with Pistol Pete and other SMM members. Gonzales told them there was a gold mine awaiting them down in North Carolina. All they had to do was take the coke down there. As a result of this conversation Yaro Pack, Pistol Pete and several other SMM members began making trips to North Carolina in a leased Nissan Quest van carrying drugs. With the success of these trips Pistol Pete and his crew started to become hood rich as they say, and started sporting all the trappings of a ghetto star. SMM members were running massive amounts of narcotics up and down the east coast, expanding Pistol Pete's empire, one crack house at a time. He was franchising, but instead of Subway, it was Sex, Money and Murder. The flow of cocaine came from Pete's father's friend, George Wallace, who had taken Pete in when his mother kicked him out and another connect Pete had was John Castro, who worked as a corrections officer. By the summer of 1994 things were on the up and up for Sex, Money and Murder.

"When he was out there, dude was a millionaire when he was 19," Rock says of Pistol Pete and as the money started flowing in from the out of town trips, Pete took another unique step. He incorporated the gang name Sex, Money, Murder into SMMC, Inc. It was a phony business front that was used to lease a fleet of luxury cars from a leasing company located in Pittsburgh. Supposedly SMMC was the leasing company's number one client and kept them in business with their leasing contracts. The company served two purposes for SMMC, Inc. First it helped them lease cars and helped them hide huge car purchases. The leasing company got SMMC deals financed by doing prepaid leases. Essentially the members would pay for their leases up front, often dropping as much as $24,000 for a two year lease before they drove the cars off the lot. Second in an attempt to hide the massive amounts of money being spent on some of the vehicles the SMM crew were purchasing fully, the leasing company would make the paperwork appear that the vehicles were leased but in fact the members would pay cash for these cars upfront. Most of the vehicles leased through this company were equipped with secret compartments known as stash boxes used to conceal drugs, money and guns. Some of the vehicles obtained through the Pittsburgh leasing company were a fleet of minivans used for Pistol Pete's various smuggling operations and trips. SMMC, Inc. also had a Hummer, an NSX, Mazda RX7, Toyota Supra, Cadillac STS, BMW's and Mercedes. Many of the cars were driven by Pistol Pete himself. The crew had every hot car imaginable in the early to mid 90's and they all had stash boxes.

When Sex, Money and Murder rolled, they rolled in style. Pistol Pete made sure of that. "Them youngsters out of Soundview were doing it for sure," Money says. "Their shit was bubbling but it got fucked up somewhere along the way." North Carolina proved to be a gold mine like David Gonzales said but it would also prove to be Sex, Money and Murder's downfall and Pistol Pete would be the first to fall. On one trip that precipitated the fall Yaro Pack, Pistol Pete and David Gonzales met in New York and drove the van containing eight kilograms of cocaine to North Carolina. During this trip the men sold cocaine in Rockingham and Lumberton, North Carolina, as well as somewhere in South Carolina. They then drove to Charlotte North Carolina where Yaro Pack and Pistol Pete were introduced by Gonzales to David Evans.

Evans wanted to open some crack houses in Charlotte and he saw Pistol Pete and Yaro Pack as the perfect partners in the venture. He would run the day to day activities of the crack houses and Pistol Pete and his people would provide the coke and the out-of-town muscle if need be. Pistol Pete saw the idea as an easy way to increase his profits. He figured there'd be no bamma-ass country dudes fucking with him or Sex, Money, Murder. Pistol Pete and them examined several Charlotte neighbors hoods as possible locations to open up crack houses. After that Pistol Pete, Yaro Pack and Gonzales decided to return to New York temporarily. They left the van at the airport and flew to New York for a few days. At this time the van contained almost $70,000 and two kilograms of cocaine for the Charlotte crack houses. Yaro Pack would fly back down to Charlotte to handle the business with David Evans and to pick up the van and return to New York with their profits.

Another trip to North Carolina proved ill fated. The trip began in New York like any other. Yaro Pack, Gonzales, Pistol Pete and a fourth dude known as Leadpipe left New York in a leased van. The van had Pennsylvania plates and contained about ten kilograms of cocaine, powder and crack, designated for certain people and out of town spots. In Pittsburgh they collected money and delivered six kilo's of coke. The price of each kilo was $22,000. A portion of the drugs they distributed in Pittsburgh were Yaro's while the rest were Pistol Pete's. From Pittsburgh they drove to Lumberton to collect more money and then to South Carolina to make some more pick ups (money) and drop offs (cocaine). They were like regular traveling salesmen but they carried guns and handled sales disputes with deadly violence. There were no 'have a nice day' greetings with this crew. From Lumberton they drove to Rockingham to meet with a customer of theirs, Darious Covington.

Covington was in a bind. He owed Pistol Pete and them almost $90,000 for cocaine he had been fronted and he was unable to pay the full amount owed. Pistol Pete wasn't going for that. With him it was get mine or be mine. That was his prevailing attitude. He didn't go for any sob stories or none of that. And if it meant murder, then it meant murder. Pistol Pete wasn't adverse to killing to get his or just killing to send a message. While tapping a gun against his own head Pistol Pete told Yaro Pack and Gonzales, "Yo, I'm going in there and murder him." In response to Gonzales' pleas Pistol Pete agreed that Covington would have one more day to come up with the money and keep his life. As the four men had plans to drive to Charlotte for the evening they agreed to meet with Covington when they returned the next day. From Rockingham they drove to Charlotte for a concert and to check on the status of their crack houses. They still had two kilos of cocaine in the van and several guns. After the concert they dropped off Pipe in Lumberton to handle some BI and drove to Wilmington, North Carolina to deliver more cocaine before returning to Rockingham the next day to meet with Covington and get their money.

When they returned to Rockingham on October 21, 1994 Gonzales paged Covington in order to make arrangements as to where the men would meet.

It was agreed they'd meet in a local fast food restaurant. But Covington never showed. Unknown to Pistol Pete, Gonzales had phoned Covington and warned him that Pistol Pete was going to kill him if he didn't have all the money. Covington couldn't handle the whole ticket so he made other arrangements that didn't involve meeting up with the murderous Pistol Pete. In Pistol Pete's eyes that marked Covington for death. Wasn't nobody getting over on the Pistol. Gonzales who was playing a two sided game, which was dangerous for him as well if the Pistol got hip to it, urged Pete and Yaro to leave Rockingham because Covington wasn't likely to show and was probably scared off by Pistol Pete's intimidation tactics.

Gonzales told them to let him try and get the money but Pistol Pete refused, "Ain't nobody going to live in this world who owe me money." Pistol Pete insisted that they drive over to Covington's house, "because I'm going to murder his wife and kids. I ain't playing." In Pete's world it was all fair in the drug game. Innocence be damned. But before they could act, somebody, most likely Covington who was in fear for his life, put some shit in the game. Law enforcement officers appeared out of nowhere and detained Pete, Gonzales and Yaro at the exact restaurant where Covington was supposed to meet them and pay his debt. The officers had been tipped by an informant that drugs were being transported into Richmond County, North Carolina in a burgundy Nissan Quest van bearing Pennsylvania plates and occupied by three men. It was this tip that led to Pistol Pete's arrest as the officers proceeded to search the van. It later came out that police acted on a tip from Convington concerning the presence of drugs in the van. The local police detained all three men while they were outside the van near the restaurant and asked permission to search the vehicle. Yaro Pack gave the van keys to the officers and signed a written consent to search the van.

Pistol Pete and them all gave the officers false names. Yaro Pack used the name Corey Hines, Gonzales used David Richards and Pistol Pete used Nathaniel Tucker. During the initial search of the van the officers failed to locate the drugs, money and guns hidden in the stash box. But two drug narcotics detection canines were brought to the scene and alerted officers that there was indeed drugs in the van so the officers moved the van to another location where a search was conducted pursuant to a search warrant. The officers disassembled portions of the vehicle interior, seeking access to a secret compartment containing drugs. With the assistance of a Nissan mechanic, the officers located a secret compartment beneath the van's front seats and discovered guns, cocaine and money in the apartment. Pistol Pete and them were transported to the police station and booked under the false names they had provided to the authorities. Shortly thereafter they were released but the van was impounded until it could be searched properly. After they were released they discussed among themselves whether to wait in Rockingham until the van was released or to flee the city because the officers might locate the secret compartment that contained the drugs, money and guns. Pistol Pete thought the North Carolina country-ass police were stupid and urged them to stay and wait for the van. He didn't believe they could find the stash box. But he was wrong. While using a payphone to notify other SMM members of their plight the three were arrested again. They were taken to the Sheriff's Department and held under high bonds by the magistrate before a court date was set.

Pistol Pete's connect George Wallace and Yaro Pack's cousin quickly provided bail money and the three were out of the county jail and free again several days later before any prints could match up to identify them to their real names. Yaro Pack and Pistol Pete never returned to North Carolina to face their charges, nor did they make any subsequent trips to North Carolina. Gonzales did not return to face the charges either, but he continued doing business in the Carolinas into 1995. Gonzales hooked up with Hershel McNeil, an associate of Pistol Pete's from New York. McNeil arranged to have crack cocaine transported to North Carolina and Gonzales distributed the drugs. Pistol Pete decided not to make any more trips himself, but through McNeil and other subordinates he still supplied Gonzales and others, and Sex, Money, Murder continued to traffic in cocaine and crack in New York City, Pittsburgh, North and South Carolina. Pistol Pete was now behind the scenes pulling the strings. A position he found much more to his liking.

Part 4- Rikers Island and the Bloods

Pistol Pete's prison nightmare began in late 1995 when he was arrested at Grant's Tomb in Harlem, New York for the murder of Karlton Hines. Pete and Karlton Hines, a local basketball star who had a scholarship to Syracuse allegedly had some beef. On the street it was known that Karlton Hines had one foot in the game (drug) while trying to make his name in the other game (basketball). Pistol Pete caught Karlton outside a car stereo shop off Boston Road and killed him and wounded another individual by the name of Carlos Mestre on April 8, 1994. A couple of months later the Pistol caught Carlos Mestre coming out of a hip-hop store known as the Jew Man in the Bronx and killed him, because he was a witness to the murder of Karlton Hines. At the time Pete was arrested at Grant's Tomb for the murder he was carrying a gun and was required to do an eight month mandatory sentence while awaiting the murder charge.

"He was originally arrested in 1995 at Grant's Tomb for the murder of Karlton Hines," Brenda Rollack said of her son. "He was carrying a gun at the time. After he did the eight month mandatory for the gun I bailed him out." Police said that while Rollack had been imprisoned at Rikers Island Correctional Facility he became a member of the Bloods gang. During his eight month bid the Pistol was inducted into the gang but his induction into the Bloods wasn't an ordinary jump in. Pistol Pete was so high profile and held in such high regard on the Island, in a cauldron of super predators, that the Bloods gave him his own set. "How he first got on, how he first became a Blood was like this," Rock says. "He was a beast on Rikers. A monster. The Bloods on Rikers Island wanted to bring him in but he was like the only way I'm gonna be a Blood is if you all give me my own set. And to my knowledge that was how Sex, Money, Murder was brought into the Blood fold. He became a Blood in 1996." The oldhead reiterates this, "O.G. Mack and them tried to recruit him in. Pete wasn't a follower, he was a leader. He didn't want to get with them, but he did and when he did he turned the whole neighborhood red." O.G. Mack started the Nine Trey Gangsta Bloods, the first east coast blood set in 1993 at Rikers Island with fellow prisoner Leonard "Deadeye" Mackenzie. Recruiting Pistol Pete into the fold was a coup for them. Because when Pete did something he did it all the way.

That's not all Pete was doing. During his incarceration he was also making moves and keeping his ear to the street. He had an empire to run. Under the pretense of trying to get money for his lawyer, he played some suckers too. In early 1996 while David Gonzales was still dealing with Hershey McNeil, Gonzales spoke by phone with Pistol Pete. Gonzales owed McNeil money for some fronted coke but Pistol Pete wanted the money Gonzales owed and he wanted more. During the telephone conversation Pistol Pete let Gonzales know that the source of cocaine Gonzales was moving was in fact Rollack's father's friend George Wallace who Pete called his uncle. The Pistol explained that, "my uncle gave Hershey some cocaine to sell for me so I could pay for my lawyer." Pistol Pete then went on to explain that the kilo and a half of crack that McNeil fronted to Gonzales actually belonged to him and Pistol Pete wanted his money. The whole North Carolina deal had left a sour taste in Pete's mouth so he decided to shake Gonzales down. Gonzales was shook and agreed to pay McNeil the money he owed and to loan the Pistol additional money to pay for his lawyer. Pete ended up getting about 20 grand from Gonzales, but his shakedown would come back to haunt him.

Once the eight month mandatory sentence for the gun was up, Pete's mother bailed him out and Pete walked the streets free for two weeks. But that was it. At the time Pete didn't know this though. He went full steam ahead with his commitment to the Bloods. "When he came home he was on the Blood shit hard," Rock says. "He had the whole block in red. All his mans and them were all in red. He was real serious on that Blood stuff. They had the red converse, red everything." Pistol Pete was not joking. He turned his whole area into Bloods. Money explains, "That shit was like a wave when it happened. After that you saw Bloods everywhere. That whole joint was like that. All red. That whole area. Once a gang takes over a certain section you either in and out." And that was what Pistol Pete was preaching, "You with me or against me." He didn't go for all that fake-ass bullshit. And Pistol Pete helped that blood shit to spill over into the streets from prison. But unknown to the Pistol that would be his last two weeks on the streets. "He's been in since 95 with only two weeks on the streets," Rock says. "Dude is a mystery to people. Nobody knows him really."

When he went back to court for the murder case, which he beat because there were no witnesses, he was remanded into custody because of a federal narcotics indictment out of the Western District of North Carolina. It seems the feds had matched up Pistol Pete's prints in the NCIC computer database and with cooperation from some of Pete's old associates, namely David Gonzales, they indicted Pete for the drugs, money and guns found in the seized van they'd been left holding. Pistol Pete was subsequently transferred to the Charlotte-Mecklenberg County jail in Charlotte, North Carolina to await trial. His mother was distraught, "Two weeks after I bailed him out when he went back to court on the murder case he was remanded for the drug case in North Carolina and he's been in jail ever since. That was 1996, he was only twenty years old." But the Pistol took the whole thing in stride like the gangster he was. "A true player will accept the hand that he is dealt simply because he did not live a lie." The Pistol said and truer words were never spoken.

Part 5- The North Carolina Case

In 1996, Pistol Pete was transferred to a jail in Charlotte, North Carolina to face federal narcotics charges in the Western District of North Carolina at Charlotte before Chief District Court Judge Graham C. Mullen. Five cooperating witnesses, three Rockingham police officers, Special Agent Tadeo of the Bureau of Alcohol, Tobacco and Firearms and Sergeant Savelli of the New York Police Department Citywide Anti-Gang Enforcement Unit testified for the prosecution. The time frame of the conduct alleged in the conspiracy was only 10 months but Pistol Pete was looking at a lengthy sentence if convicted. The government pointed out that the case was not a typical drug conspiracy in that material and relevant evidence of the conspiracy included cryptic letters and codes seized from Rollack's jail cell. Such documents were not self-explanatory and their content and context were not self-evident. The court determined the various acts performed over a series of years ranging from 1993 to 1996 were intrinsic for proving the conspiracy. Evidence of Rollack's involvement with drug trafficking in the Bronx, Pittsburgh, North Carolina and South Carolina all pertained to drug distribution by the persons named in the indictment and their associates. The Feds were gunning for Pistol Pete, but how did the case come about?

"Pete was doing business with a guy named Yaro that he's known since they were kids." Brenda, Pete's mother explained. "Another guy that they were dealing with in North Carolina, who was really an operating informant for the feds told the feds about a Nissan Nautica van that they were using. The feds let the guy sell drugs and stuff and then the guy gets cool with guys that come to North Carolina to do business and he helps the feds bust them. He told the cops that the van had hidden compartments in it, so they went to the van when no one was around and got inside and searched until they found out what was in it." Testimony by co-conspirators about the transport of drugs from New York, through Pittsburgh, was an integral part of the prosecutor's case. They painted a picture of Pistol Pete as an interstate high profile drug trafficker, with a Blood gang back in New York City, ready to kill and smuggle drugs at his command.

"They found over $250,000 in cash and a couple of kilos of cocaine, but Pete wasn't even in North Carolina at the time," Brenda said. "He had left because he felt something wasn't right. So someone had to tell the feds that Pete had something to do with that stuff because he never met the operating agent." But obviously the operating agent knew about Pistol Pete. The court found that there was no evidence that Rollack withdrew from the conspiracy. To the contrary, the evidence presented at trial showed that Rollack continued in the drug trade demanding payment from David Gonzales for the drug debt owed Hershey McNeil. Also when Covington failed to pay his debt it was Rollack who made the decision that Covington was to be killed. By introducing evidence that Pistol Pete was in fact a leader the feds tried to pull out all the stops. All the alleged charges and uncharged counts painted a devastating picture for him.

Derious Covington was the informant Pete's mom referred to. Covington credibly testified that for years he had been an informant for Phil Sweatt, the officer in charge of the van search. Covington also testified that he had purchased drugs from Rollack only days before, and that he saw Rollack remove drugs from what appeared to be and sounded like a motorized stash box in the van interior. Covington identified Rollack in court as Pistol Pete. The testimony in itself was damaging and undeniable.

"After they found everything they arrested Yaro and the other guys. But then after a few days they just let them go." Brenda said. "Yaro came back saying that the cops kept the cocaine and took most of the money as taxes on the income that they would have made on the cocaine if they would've sold it." Testimony at trial showed a different story though. The rats testified that Pete was on the scene with Yaro in North Carolina the whole time and on trips to Pittsburgh and North Carolina Yaro Pack painted Pistol Pete as his enforcer. But he also testified that on the final trip to North Carolina half of the drugs in the Nissan Quest van were Rollack's and the other half were his. Yaro was a fucked up snitch, painting himself as the leader, but at the same time selling out his man. That's how some cats carry it though. The drug game can be dirty and grimy when your so-called man stabs you in the back, twisting the blade slowly.

"A year later Yaro got picked up with $500,000 and some cocaine in his car," Brenda said. "And a little while after that the feds started picking everybody up for everything and they indicted Pete while he was in jail." Yaro Pack among others, had turned snitch. To Pistol Pete it wasn't clear who was snitching at first, but it all came to light. At Rollack's trial Yaro Pack and David Gonzales testified along with others who corroborated their stories, court records indicate. "That North Carolina case fucked Pistol Pete up," Rock says. "There was a lot of snitches down there." Cooperating witnesses like Hershey McNeil had to be relocated due to death contracts put out on their lives from prison by Pistol Pete. McNeil, Gonzales, David Evans, Sebastian Mathis and Savon "Yaro Pack" Codd were the snitches on the case, who broke bread with their man the Pistol and then sold him out at the first hint of trouble. Weak dudes with weak minds who broke weak ruined the Pistol's run in the game.

Evidence pertaining to Sex, Money, Murder was relevant to the crimes charged in the indictment the court determined, because Rollack was leader of the gang and the gang specialized in drug trafficking in New York. According to the indictment, "Peter Rollack was the organizer and leader of a drug conspiracy in the Western District of North Carolina and elsewhere," and "Mr. Rollack organized a gang known as Sex, Money and Murder which later became a Blood gang." At trial, letters seized from Rollacks jail cell were introduced into evidence and Sergeant Savelli translated the documents, written in code, for the benefit of the jury. Sergeant Savelli testified as an expert witness in the field of codes and as an expert witness on the Bloods gang. Agent Tadeo testified about the interception of Rollack's mail, pursuant to federal search warrants between December 17 and December 19, 1997. The mail was seized from Rollack's jail cell. It was all written in Bloods code. Also seized was a list of Bloods codes.

Agent Tadeo described information supporting his belief that Rollack was using the mail to direct illegal activities of members of his SMM gang and had used the mail to order murders. Both incoming and outgoing mail to and from the following persons was seized: Xavier "X" Williams, Robinson "Rob" Lazala, Brian "Stone" Boyd, Edwin Vega, Corey "Little Bear" Brown, John "Baby-J" Gonzales, Shawn Stokes, Kevin "Beno" Allen, and Gisett "Lady G" Hardy. During the course of these intercepts, federal agents reviewed all of Rollack's mail and seized numerous pieces also.

Agent Tadeo testified that some of the items seized were in Rollack's handwriting, while some were not. A handwriting analyst determined that all of the letters were written by Rollack except for a letter Rollack received from Pipe and a document of which the analyst could not determine who the author was. The evidence seized from Rollack's cell corroborated the testimony of other government witnesses about Rollack's role in SMM and his continued involvement in the conspiracy alleged in the indictment.

"The letters that they got fucked Pistol Pete up too." Rock says. "A lot of shit rode on the weight of those letters." Sergeant Savelli testified as to the significance and importance of certain words and symbols. According to the Sergeant, Bloods and other gang members frequently communicated with fellow gang members in code to avoid police detection. The sergeant went on to identify Bloods and SMM salutations and expressions in Rollack's correspondence. His testimony indicated that the crossing out of the letter 'C' in the seized documents was a common practice among members of the Bloods and that Bloods communicated in codes. This corroborated trial testimony that SMM became a chapter of the Bloods during the time of Rollack's leadership. In the seized materials the writer refers to himself as Pistol which was consistent with trial testimony that the defendant was known as Pistol Pete. References to droptop referred to drugs and the reference to Pipe was consistent with trial testimony about one of the un-indicted coconspirators who made trips with Rollack to North Carolina.

At the conclusion of the government's case, the prosecutor called Agent Tadeo back to the stand to testify and summarize the contents of the seized writings and letters from Rollack's jail cell and to relate them to the testimony presented at trial. The agent, in turn summarized the contents and related them to the stories told by the witnesses at trial. The agent presented his summary testimony after Sergeant Savelli translated the contents of the writings from Bloods code into English for the benefit of the jury. On January 9, 1998, Peter Rollack aka Pistol Pete was found guilty by a jury of conspiring to possess with intent to distribute a quantity of cocaine and cocaine base and knowingly using and carrying a firearm and aiding and abetting such conduct in relation to a drug trafficking crime. Rollack was sentenced to 40 years of imprisonment on Count I and five years of imprisonment on Count II to run consecutively.

Part 6- Thanksgiving Day Murders

While Pistol Pete was sitting in a North Carolina jail cell facing trial, his crew in the Bronx was busy following his instructions to the letter. In the North Carolina case, Agent Tadeo testified about a letter sent by Rollack in September 1997 to Sex, Money, Murder associates in New York with instructions for gang members to kill David "Twin" Mullins, because Rollack believed Twin was a potential witness against him. Authorities also found out that a similar letter from Rollack was read at an SMM gang meeting in New York, during November 1997. "He definitely ran that shit with a stiff hand," Money says. "He didn't give them any room to fuck up." While in prison in Charlotte it was alleged that the Pistol continued to communicate with members of his gang and run his organization. Federal Agents intercepted Pete's incoming and outgoing mail, claiming to have found evidence that Pete was in fact using the mail to direct the illegal activities of gang members.

Imprisoned Gang Leader Ordered Killings at Neighborhood Football Game, U.S. Attorney Says, The New York Times headline read on February 10, 1998. The government claimed that through the mail in the fall of 1997, Rollack ordered what became known as the Thanksgiving Day Murders. On November 27, 1997 about 30 people had gathered for a football game which had become a neighborhood custom between residents of the Soundview and Castle Hill projects. About an hour into the game a group of men, allegedly Rollack's gunmen, walked up and began shooting, police reports and witnesses said. At least a dozen shots were fired in the burst of gunfire from handguns killing David "Twin" Mullins and Efrain Solar. The terrifying holiday bloodbath left those two dead and three others seriously injured. The target of the attack was Mullins who had joined Rollack's gang in 1993 and had a history of drug trafficking and slayings. Prosecutors said Mullins was killed to prevent him from testifying against Pistol Pete in his federal narcotics trial in North Carolina. The government also said that at the same time, Pete put a hit on Damon Mullins, David Mullins twin brother.

"They claimed he was writing letters to people in the street but what I think really happened was people were trying to make an impression on other people so they decided to do those things on their own." Brenda Rollack said. "Petey took a lie detector test and was asked if he sent the letters, he said 'No,' and passed the test." Robinson "Mac 11" Lazala and Jose Rodriguez, two known Sex, Money, Murder members were charged with the killings. "These dudes didn't even know Pete." Rock says. "They just did it off the strength." Federal prosecutors claimed Pistol Pete was behind the attacks and the killings which were called, "the most heinous of his crimes," in *The New York Times*. They've come to be known in the Soundview/Castle Hill area of the Bronx as the Thanksgiving Day Murders.

Testifying in his own defense at the later trial Pistol Pete stated that, "it is my understanding the evidence against me comes primarily from letters I wrote while incarcerated. I never wrote any letters ordering the murder of David Mullins or anyone else. In fact, I had no reason to believe that David Mullins was going to testify against me." Rollack further stated that he would like to explain the meaning of the letters he wrote in a "combination of code, rap language and street lingo. I would like to refute or correct any inaccurate or misleading translation offered by the government."

Part 7- Rap Songs and the Legend

As Pistol Pete remained in jail, his stature grew as he was celebrated in rap songs. He was slowly becoming a legend in the streets. A mythical gangster of notorious proportions. But there was nothing mythical about Pistol Pete. He was a living, breathing person with a 45 year sentence. That sentence would turn out to be the least of his worries though as authorities in New York started investigating all the murders SMM was allegedly involved in. As the chips fell they all pointed in Pistol Pete's direction. A pattern of racketeering activity emerged, according to the feds, that included crack sales and robberies, acts of intimidation, other acts of violence and murder. One murder connected to the SMM crew was the 1994 murder of Tony Morton. On August 18, 1994, Morton was driving with a passenger near the Soundview houses. Gang members became suspicious when Morton's car, with its tinted windows hiding the interior from their view, slowly drove past them. SMM members approached the car, opened its doors and dragged Morton's passenger out of the car at gunpoint while others pulled Morton out of the car and shot him. Events like this and others added to Pistol Pete's mystique even while he sat in jail.

After his arrest Rollack became a kind of folk hero to other gang members who wore T-shirts with his face silk-screened on them with the words, *'Free Pistol Pete.'* "They have reunions over there in Soundview and they put certain guy's names and faces on the shirts, like guys who've passed away," Brenda Rollack explained about the T-shirts. "So one day they put Petey's face on one, they used the most wanted photo that was in the newspapers." Pistol Pete was celebrated for being the thorough gangsta that he was.

Pete's crimes earned him the description of a ruthless killer with the government but his exploits also inspired rap songs and made him a legend on the streets. "What makes someone an All Star in this game?" Pistol Pete asked. "This is a question that people rarely ask themselves but yet they crown others with this title and give them the love and respect of the streets. Financial status, popularity with women and how a person flossed are only pieces of the puzzle that form an All Star. Maintaining your honor and accepting the good with the bad completes the picture, just as the opposite erases all the glory and respect that was once due."

Pistol Pete's image was further enhanced when Lord Tariq, a Bronx rap artist, released songs through Columbia Records in 1998 that made numerous references to Rollack and his gang. The CD titled, *Make it Reign*, by Lord Tariq and another rap artist, Peter Gunz, appeared to be devoted to Rollack and his gang. In one song *"Sex, Money, Life or Death"* a known member of the gang supposedly calls the recording artists at their studio. Another song on the album appears to be a biography of Rollack. "That's some crazy shit this nigga was on," Rock says. "He was that dude. He counted his first million at 19." And at age 20, Pistol Pete had more time than how old he was. But he was about to get more. A lot more. The feds wanted to bury him and everybody associated with him.

"Before he was sentenced they would harass and investigate anyone that came to visit Pete." Brenda Rollack said. Lord Tariq stood by his friend Peter Rollack throughout his ordeal though. Fully aware that the government was harassing everyone that associated with Pete, Tariq visited his friend in jail and stayed in contact. When it came time to pay Pete's lawyers, Tariq was right there providing whatever assistance he could, even giving Pete's mother his Rolex to sell. "Lord Tariq has been harassed by those people for visiting Petey. When Petey was arrested he gave me his brand new $25,000 Rolex watch and told me to use it to get money to help Petey." Brenda Rollack said. And Lord Tariq saluted his man in verse- *I drop a tear on this poem as I write to my dog/ Pistol, I miss you sincerely yours from the lord/ you held it down on our side of the town at any cost/ and you loved in checks by money boss-* from the song, *"Keep On."*

Pete's image had grown so large among his fellow prisoners, who spoke of him reverently, that even jailhouse guards in the federal holding jail, MDC Brooklyn, had begun giving him special privileges. In Brooklyn he was able to make telephone calls up to eight hours long, a guard smuggled letters into and out of prison for Pete and a female guard allegedly had sex with him. Pistol Pete had become more infamous in prison than he ever was on the streets and his name echoed in all five boroughs and courtesy of Lord Tariq, SMM had their own anthem titled *"One Life to Live"- You got one life to live, one gun to bust/ one nigga to save, one nigga to rush/ Its all about Sex, Money, Life or Death/ You gotta make a choice is it right of left/ Breaking brand was a big name drug nigga/ Tell me is it in my Blood, nigga what?/ I'm from Soundview projects where all my niggas from/ And uptown just respect to call another nigga dumb.*

Pistol Pete was living large but still he was locked up. His name lived on through song though, his infamy rising. And when Nas dropped *God's Son*, the song *"Get Down"* celebrated Pete even more. *New York streets where killers'll walk, like Pistol Pete and Pappy Mason, gave the young boys admiration.* But he would have to pay for his darker side. All the murders would come back to haunt him. Pistol Pete lived by the gun and he would die by the gun. The feds weren't playing. They wanted their man. Pistol Pete had a dark charisma about him. An intrigue, a mystery. Even when he contemplated murder. "He stayed smiling," Rock says. "Even when he was about to shoot you he was smiling. Crazy right? A nigga smiling before he killed you." But that was Pistol Pete.

It is said that Lord Tariq's song, *"Streets 2 Da Stage,"* is a biography of Pistol Pete's life- *Feds still looking searchin all through Brooklyn/ But in the Bronx takin paper that tookin/ Headed southbound out of town with a pound of brown/fuck the fun, I'm getting money, its no time to fuck around/ I gotta stash full of guns and we pumpin the sounds/ pack the coke in Vaseline foolin' the drug hounds/ a big nigga I'm soon to be now/ the block is hot I'm ice so I'm coolin it down/ I gained weight stepped it up stepped off the pitchers mound/I got the money the power and the pitches now/ Feds taking pictures now/ the thugs wanna get ya now/but I got something for you thugs, take this nigga, blow/shot that nigga down in his town/first round, ding, the bell ring it on/ now who's the next nigga dead in my next song.*

Part 8- Federal Case

Pistol Pete was described by the office of Mary Jo White, the U.S. Attorney in Manhattan as a ruthless killer who hung pictures of Mafia members in his bedroom and called his murders wet t-shirt contests because his victims' bodies would be soaked with blood. Rollack was indicted in 1998 with 10 others for nine murders and for trafficking in cocaine and crack in New York, Pennsylvania and North Carolina. The 28 count indictment stemmed from his role in the violent offshot of the Bloods gang called Sex, Money, Murder. The gang's members were responsible for a series of murders and attempted murders in the Bronx, prosecutors said. As the gang leader Pistol Pete was charged with the slayings as part of running his violent drug trafficking crew from his jail cell in North Carolina, according to the racketeering indictment that was unsealed in February 1998 in Federal District Court in Manhattan. The indictment contained substantial charges against Pete and 12 counts in which the other defendants were charged. He was charged with narcotics trafficking, RICO violations, five actual murders and two conspiracies to commit murder. The indictment also charged that Rollack committed these acts for the purpose of maintaining or increasing his position in the racketeering enterprise.

"Not only was Rollack willing to commit murder, he seemed to relish them, bragging about them to anyone who would listen, regaling his gang members with stories of pursuing his victims, tracking them down and killing them." Prosecutors said. Assistant U.S. Attorney Elizabeth Glazer, chief of the Manhattan U.S. Attorney's Crime Control Strategies Unit, said her office had joined a special program to eradicate gang activity from the 43rd precinct. The prosecution of Rollack's gang was part of a broad anti-gang effort undertaken by the U.S. Attorney's office in cooperation with local groups in the Castle Hill and Soundview neighborhoods. The prosecutors contended that Sex, Money, Murder as an organization engaged in numerous murders. The government contended that members and associates of SMM agreed to commit murders in exchange for money payments from others and to acquire narcotics from other drug dealers. Although the media coverage on the Sex, Money, Murder gang mainly focused on the violent murders that occurred the indictment that came down on Pistol Pete and his associates included not only murders, but violence, robbery and narcotics trafficking. The DA said John Castro, one of SMM's cocaine connections and an ex-corrections officer paid SMM to do things to people with kilos of coke, be it murder, beat downs or extortions.

From 1993 to 1995, John Castro was a drug dealer who supplied drugs to members and associates of SMM. In early 1994 he had a dispute over drugs with a dude called Totito. Castro paid Totito for some drugs and Totito never returned. Castro called Yaro Pack, Andre Martin and Peter Rollack for help in locating Totito. On March 9, they saw Totito's car double-parked on 174th Street. Rollack took a gun and exited the car. Rollack ran into the street and started shooting but Totito got away. Rollack went to Jacobi Hospital after learning Totito was there to kill him if he was alive, but the heavy police presence scared him off. Totito was later killed. Yaro Pack testified that Totito was killed for embarrassing the organization. Another SMM member, Brian Boyd, testified about the Tony Morton murder. He said that while he was occupied pulling Morton's passenger out of the car, he saw SMM member Sean Carr ride his bike up to Morton's car and shoot Morton. Another SMM member, Emilio Romero, testified similarly. Morton died of his wounds.

Rollack was in prison awaiting sentencing in North Carolina, where he was convicted in January 1998 in a narcotics case when the federal murder indictment was unsealed in Manhattan. Pistol Pete was accused of involvement in a total of five killings, the indictment said, as well as cocaine and crack trafficking and witness tampering. The indictment also said that all 10 people charged were members of the Bloods. George Wallace, Pete's father's friend and his cocaine supplier was accused of being a member of Sex, Money, Murder also and was indicted in one of the nine slayings. The witness tampering charge was related to the slaying of David "Twin" Mullins, 22, and Efrain Solar, 26, who were killed in the infamous Thanksgiving Day Murders in a burst of gunfire during a football game between residents of Soundview and Castle Hill houses in the Bronx. Prosecutors did not say what connection there might be between the Bloods and Pistol Pete's gang, which they said used cars with secret compartments to carry drugs, money and guns. The gang was incorporated as SMMC Inc. the indictment said, but did not elaborate.

"They say he murdered seven people," Brenda Rollack, Pete's mom said and federal prosecutors said Pistol Pete had become a kind of folk hero to some young gang members in the Bronx, even honored in some rap songs as a legendary crime kingpin. The government sought the death penalty against Pistol Pete. It didn't look good for the Pistol with former cohorts like Yaro Pack and Hershey McNeil lining up to testify against him again. Brian Boyd and Emilo Romero were also signed on to testify against their former leader. Both of them were willing to testify to the murders and Boyd cooperated against many others, including identifying the photographs of nearly 30 SMM members and telling the government "about guys that (he) was dealing with, that (he) was doing things with" for the gang. Pistol Pete's attorney argued that "these guys are just willing to admit what they can admit and tell what they can tell and do as much as they can to get their 5K1 letter, because if not they are going to jail for the rest of their lives." And Pistol Pete said that "it is my understanding that the evidence against me on these charges consists primarily, if not exclusively, of the uncorroborated testimony of cooperating witnesses." Pistol Pete was facing death and staring into the face of the grim reaper, but he didn't flinch. The feds put some shit in the game though.

"They threatened to put me in prison if he didn't plead guilty." Brenda Rollack said. "One day a supposed to be friend of Pete's called me and told me that he had some money for Pete, so I told him to bring it over. They were recording my phone calls and they said that I was receiving money for Pete's drug business." But it was all a sham because in reality the informant only gave Pete's mom $40. Not even enough for his commissary account and literally chump change in the drug game. A debt not even worth collecting. But the feds had Pete's mom in a bind and Pete recognized.

Rollack pleaded guilty to a massive racketeering indictment to avoid a possible death penalty trial for his crimes, the paper reported but in reality it was a little more complicated than that as the feds had their knife twisted in Pete's heart by threatening his mom. The government called Pete's plea agreement an unusual deal. He plead guilty to federal racketeering and the murders of eight individuals with the understanding that he would get life with no parole instead of the death penalty. Prosecutors agreed not to seek the death penalty against Peter Rollack as long as he agreed to the restrictive prison conditions that would limit his visits and contacts to his lawyers and his immediate family. In court Rollack listened impassively as the mothers of three of his victims addressed the court. "He should be locked up forever," Theresa Hines said, whose son Karlton, the basketball star was killed by the Pistol in 1994. "He needs to be in a coffin just to feel where my son Karlton is."

The feds had a coffin for Pistol Pete but they called it ADX Florence, the Bureau of Prisons Supermax. Pistol Pete was resigned to his fate, he faced up to the consequences of his actions and carried his weight like the champ he was. The ironic thing about it all was that the Pistol sat in the same Manhattan courthouse that his father Leonard had almost 20 years before. Like father, like son. The cycle repeated itself and the system was there to lock Pistol Pete down forever.

Part 9- The Aftermath

On January 4, 2000, Pistol Pete pleaded guilty to charges in a deal that spared him the death penalty, admitted he killed or ordered the murders of six people, tried to murder another and conspired to kill another two people who were ultimately killed by members of his gang. "Mr. Rollack you have done terrible, terrible, vile things in your young life, things that have destroyed others totally." Judge Miriam Goldman Cedarbaum said. The judge allowed the mothers of several murder victims to speak in court including Theresa Hines who said her son was a basketball player who signed a letter of intent to play for Syracuse University before he was killed. "I hope Mr. Rollack when you go to sleep that you visualize all the bodies that you murdered, that they come to you at night. That's your penalty, they come to you at night, they haunt you," she said through tears.

On December 8, 2000, Pistol Pete was sentenced to three consecutive life terms plus 105 years without the possibility of parole for his role in the murderous drug gang Sex, Money, Murder. During his jail tenure from arrest to his ultimate sentencing Pistol Pete had become a folk hero akin to Robin Hood among prisoners because of the mystique that surrounded him after he was described in rap songs. Pistol Pete was a prince of the underworld but U.S. District Judge Miriam Goldman Cedarbaum sought to strip that image of glamour and the fast life away. She said that 26-year-old Peter Rollack's prison term should be an example of the penalties faced by others who follow the ways of the leader of Sex, Money, Murder. "I hope everybody in the courtroom will carry the word back to your neighborhood that the path that you have followed leads to life in prison, without any prospect of ever being released," the judge said.

Gang Leaders Gets Life Term with Little Outside Contact, The New York Times headline read on November 11, 2000. As part of his plea Rollack agreed to be confined to 23-hour lockdown, prohibited from communicating with fellow gang members or being visited by anyone other than immediate family members and his lawyer, Judge Cedarbaum said. In exchange the prosecution dropped the death penalty. The restrictive prison conditions imposed on the defendant came about in an unusual deal that banned him from communicating with all but a handful of outsiders. Due to his status as the leader of the violent Bronx narcotics gang SMM and the federal racketeering indictment that charged him and 10 other members of his gang with multiple killings, Pistol Pete acceded to the deal. The government contended that these severe restrictions were necessary because Pete was so powerful and influential that he had the ability to continue his activities from prison. Government officials contended that Rollack was able to order hits from his prison cell via mail, written correspondence and phone conversations. Many of the murders the Pistol pleaded guilty to took place while he was incarcerated. Because of this the government said it was necessary to keep Rollack locked down 23 hours a day for the rest of his life. All his visits would be subjected to live monitoring and recording by prison officials, the judge said.

"Pistol Pete is not the Pete I raised," Brenda said defending her son. But the feds begged to differ. The federal prosecutor released a poster the government put up in the Bronx with a photograph of Rollack under the heading "Life Without Parole," and a warning at the bottom "Don't Be Next." The poster said that Pistol Pete's former turf was the Soundview and Castle Hill sections in the Bronx but that his current turf was the federal penitentiary. Manhattan federal Judge Miriam Cedarbaum guaranteed the blood thirsty gang leader would never see the light of day again with the consecutive life sentences followed by the 105 years. In effect she buried the Pistol in the guts of the belly of the beast. The judge hoped the harsh sentence would discourage other gang members from following his life of crime. The posters and the words of the judge were efforts to stem the violence, drugs and degradation in that part of the Bronx. "He's holding himself together," Brenda Rollack said of the Pistol. "He refuses to let it break him." The judge piled the time on though.

"I hope that you will spend your time in prison reflecting on how you have both wasted and destroyed your life," the judge said as she ordered Pete to pay his victims funeral expenses. "Peter Rollack became the latest poster boy in our joint taskforce campaign to eradicate the gang from the Castle Hill/ Soundview section of the Bronx," Manhattan AUSA Elizabeth Glazer crowed. She said she hoped the *Life Without Parole* posters circulated throughout the Bronx bearing Rollack's picture would discourage others from following his lead. At sentencing Rollack apologized for his crimes, "I want to apologize to my family, the community, everyone who was affected by my actions. For whatever its worth I hope the government steps up to bring the other people who was involved in this case." Pete's lawyer Abraham C. Moskowitz asked that Mr. Rollack be imprisoned close to New York so that his young son and family could visit him but the government objected.

"Obviously, the family members of Rollack's victims are unable to see the family members that they lost at his hands," said federal prosecutor Nicole LaBarbera, so it was off to ADX Florence, the Alcatraz of the Rockies for Pistol Pete. Just another street legend and gang leader among the many that the facility holds. Pistol Pete's incarceration and multiple life sentences didn't stop anything for real. Members of Rollack's gang continued to control the areas drug trade. Their presence was felt everywhere- in the shot out street lights, the bullet riddled buildings and the graffiti, which Sex, Money, Murder members scrawled memorializing their gang and imprisoned leader Pistol Pete on every available wall. The red flag still flies high in the neighborhood as well as many other parts of the city too. Pistol Pete who oversaw the violent street gang which accounted itself responsible for multiple murders and was the subject of rap songs extolling his crimes, was gone but he would never be forgotten. And his legacy in bringing Blood Sets to the streets of New York was intact.

Part 10- Looking Back

Government Hopes Life Sentence Will Tarnish Image of Gang Leader, The New York

Post headline read on November 8, 2000. But in truth the sentence and all the hoopla only increased Pistol Pete's infamy and helped to sustain his legacy as one of the baddest men ever out of the Bronx. "I am gone but never forever." The Pistol said and he knew what he was talking about. He knew the strength and importance of having a reputation. An unshakable one. The streets crown who they want as king but the person they crown must be deserving. And Pistol Pete doesn't have any love for rats who got their shine on. "Why should we embrace someone who lived by and prospered from the laws of the streets when they turned against and broke the rules that made them who they were once they were faced with doing time?" Pete asked. "A conscious player knows that he is sacrificing his life for the likes of his family and friends. We go hard so the people we care about and love won't have to follow in our footsteps and experience all the struggles and hardships that we did."

Pete's mom, Brenda Rollack, keeps it gangster also. "I'm sorry that the other mothers lost their children. I'm sorry for those women but their sons weren't angels, some of them had murder charges too. It's not my sons fault that he was quicker. Anyone of them would have killed him first had they gotten the chance." And Brenda relates how it's hard back in the neighborhood because even though it's all said and done the truth still lingers. "I run into the family members of a few of the people who told on Pete all the time in my building. We all still live in the same place and it is a constant reminder." A reminder of the death, the devastation, the murders and the violence that will always be a part of Soundview's history. But also a reminder of those that stuck to the code and played the game how it was supposed to be played and a reminder of those that broke weak when the going got tough and snitched out their mans and them. In the drug game that's just how it goes. Snitches get stitches but they also go into the Witness Protection Program and serve their crime partners life.

Pistol Pete will be forever remembered as the leader of the violent Bronx-based street gang- Sex, Money, Murder- that was once feared on the streets and glorified in rap lyrics. From his teens the Pistol was a thorough and notorious figure who was quick to kill and bust his guns. He rose out of the notorious Soundview Projects to become a big baller and trap star by the age of 19. *The New York Post* called Pistol Pete a bloodthirsty drug baron, reporting that he was hammered with a life long prison sentence that guaranteed he would die behind bars for the decade long crime spree of murders, drug dealing and violence he perpetrated.

What cemented Pistol Pete's legend was that he continued to exercise control and maintain his leadership position even after he was put in jail. SMM continued supplying kilos of cocaine to distribution points and crack houses the Pistol had established in multiple states including New Jersey, New York, Pennsylvania, North Carolina and South Carolina. Agents testified at Rollack's trial that he maintained control of SMM through letters. The letters worked twofold for the Pistol because he knew the instructions in his letters were going to be shared with associates and it was his purpose to silence those, whether it be through death or coercion, who were going to turn on him. That's just how the Pistol rocked. He played the game on multiple levels like a street legend should.

Chapter 6

George "Boy George" Rivera

Boy George was a multi-millionaire by the age of 21. A brilliant and powerfully ambitious drug entrepreneur who saw an opportunity and seized it. It's alleged he made over $15 million in his two year run. Government sources say that Boy George and his Bronx, NY based heroin organization grossed $250,000 a week. Boy George, barely out of his teens, built himself a reputation of being one of the wealthiest druglords to come out of New York and one of the youngest to be charged with the kingpin statute. At the end of the 80's while America concerned itself with the crack epidemic, Boy George was running one of the most lucrative and aggressive heroin organizations in the city. Flamboyant and charismatic, the Puerto Rican drug baron was one of a kind. Equal parts gangster, CEO and gentleman who juxtaposed street smarts, innovative marketing and ruthless efficiency to create a heroin empire, while other kids his age were still worrying about what clothes to wear or what girls to date. Boy George and the Obsession case are street legend-the exotic James Bond cars, the Christmas Eve yacht party, the harem of girls tattooing his name on their bodies, the glamour, the jewels, the stacks of money, Boy George had it all. And he had it all as a teenager. He was definitely one of the best to ever do it in the drug game.

Part 1- South Bronx

Junkyards interrupted block after block of garbage infested streets. Abandoned warehouses and fenced in lots, where wild dogs roamed, were commonplace. Garages that resembled scrap yards, mattress and tire shops and auto repair shops occupied the dwellings of the South Bronx. The buildings were dangerous and decrepit. Junkies shot up in the stairwells and crackheads smoked in the halls. The South Bronx was ghetto as ghetto could get. Walking over the Willis Avenue Bridge to the South Bronx wasn't pretty. It was real. And when reality set in, the rest of the world was left behind. It wasn't

Somalia, but this is where Boy George grew up and rose to prominence.

"I was born on January 10, 1968. I grew up in the Bronx. I lived in many areas within the Bronx," Boy George said. Chaos was the stuff of everyday life in the borough. The drug plagued neighborhoods were brutal. "There's projects, tenement buildings and private houses. The majority of the ceilings are falling in. You got rats the size of cats. Most people are on welfare, scamming for the checks or into drugs. One of the shittiest areas around." Sport, a boriqua from the Bronx and the era says. "The majority of those neighborhoods were all dominated by Puerto Ricans. Everywhere you went in the South Bronx, that's all there was. The street corners blaring salsa with the speaker in the open window." And it seemed the only money making businesses were the drug operations. Gunshots and shouts of "radar" signifying the police were regularly heard in the streets. Open air drug markets dominated the landscape. It wasn't all that nice, but to Boy George it was home.

In the mid 80's the drug trade in the South Bronx was booming. East Tremont Avenue marked the north end of the South Bronx, running east to west just off the Grand Concourse, which divided the Bronx lengthwise. "The neighborhoods were dangerous all day long." Sport says. "You wouldn't be walking down that block for no reason. If you wasn't from the block, people would know. The South Bronx is big, but everybody knows everybody. It was known for big dope. You had all brands down there making all types of money. You had a conglomerate of heron down there. Everybody was coming to cop." The dope boys stood on the corner bling-blinging it, draped in gold bracelets with chains around their necks, gold-dipped name tags hanging, charms of guns or dollar signs on medallions. It was a Puerto Rican thing. A definite and identifiable style. They served their customers, who would slink through the crowd, cop and bounce. "There wasn't a block in the South Bronx that didn't have a spot." Sport says. "You didn't have to sell drugs to make money either. Dudes would be like, 'shorty hold this, put it in your mailbox, look out for the cops.'" Tremont and Anthoney, Anthony and Echo, Mount Hope and Anthony, Mount Hope and Monroe- these were some of the busiest drug-dealing blocks in the notorious 46th precinct. "That shit was bubbling," Sport says, and it wasn't so much the drugs or the money that captivated the youth of the South Bronx, as it was the lifestyle. That *Scarface* image of coming up out of the gutter from nothing to become hood rich and a certified ghetto star draped in finery, pushing a new whip with a dime piece in tow. This was where it was at, but let Sport explain, "We walked out of our building when we were young and the local drug dealer was who you wanted to be when you grew up. They're like rock stars."

This was how Boy George came up.

Part 2- Early Days

Boy George, whose father left when he was an infant, grew up with his mother, who moved the family around frequently. They lived on St. Lawrence, on Tremont, on Prospect. They stayed in Soundview projects and had an apartment across from Woodlawn cemetery. "We were always moving around," Boy George said. The young George had a lot of growing pains and ran away frequently. The first time when he was ten. He was in the streets alone, wandering around the wastelands of Hunt's Point. "I wasn't a mama's boy no more," George said. "I was out on the street by myself. I had to fend for myself. I had to make money for myself. That taught me responsibility." This early foray into hood life taught Boy George some valuable lessons he was later to apply. He clued himself into the fact that solving the small problems that can quickly become big problems in the ghetto was important. He learned to handle his business. He showed big heart from a young age, willing to put himself on the spot and do what needed to be done for himself, for his family and friends. Boy George stayed on point at all times.

"He was always the bravest in the family," his brother Enrique remembered. "He would say to me, 'Choose what you want in life. You got to be serious when you do things.'" And George was serious from the jump. By the time he was twelve his mother couldn't handle him, so the authorities snatched up young George, taking him to a diagnostic center called Pleasantville for troubled teens. Then he was transferred to St. Cabrini's, a group home in New Rochelle, New York where he stayed for three years. "I was in a group home in New Rochelle." George said. "There I learned to fend for myself. I lived with five percenters and learned their various aspects of living and beliefs.

When you're home with your moms and stuff, it's you and your mom and your brother. I had a chance to spread out wide, like a wide angle lens I got hip to everything I would need to get hip to, and I started analyzing and analyzing."

George learned to be a man, to hide his weaknesses and to exploit others. Powerful tools that would serve him later. He developed a sharp sense of humor and became known as a practical joker. He became popular and played on the New Rochelle High School football team. He started going to parties and bringing his St. Cabrini buddies. But this led to trouble as during a party George and the other troubled youths stole some silverware. Going for broke, they burglarized a few other houses and got caught. George took the whole rap and spent 13 months at Valhalla, a juvenile prison and from there he was sent back to the Bronx, where he briefly attended Morris High School, before dropping out and hitting the streets again. But this time George had a plan.

Like most young men in the Bronx, he moved through his teenage years working as a low level street dealer selling Checkmate, a brand of heroin sold on Watson Street in the Clasons Point section for the enormous drug operation ran by the Torres family, a Puerto Rican crime organization. "I didn't need a high school diploma to do what I did. I put it on full turbo." George said. He was in the streets getting money, his thoughts consumed by street dreams, with visions of mansions, fast cars, money and faster women. Boy George dreamed big. He wanted it all. The American dream. He set no limits and reached for the sky.

He met a dude from the neighborhood named Joey Navedo aka Joey White, who ran a cocaine operation near George's mother's apartment. Joey White took a liking to the young George and put him under his wing, becoming his role model. George noticed how Joey White woke early every morning to make sure his spots were open and bubbling. His crazy, tough guy image got major respect from his sellers, runners and people in the hood. Joey White flashed mad cash and used to run down on his workers in his whip with his foot on the gas and his gun aimed out the window. Joey White liked to keep people on their toes. Word on the street was that dude was a psycho, but his act was part of the game, and young George took notes. Young George also saw how Joey White gave out Thanksgiving turkeys and bags of toys at Christmas to the same people in the neighborhood he terrorized all year long.

"I idolized the guy," George said. "He was running around in Benzes, Porsches, BMW's, he had it all. I said shit, 'I want to be just like him.'" It was even Joey White who gave Boy George his street name and his first job as a lookout at the 156th and Courtland spot that Boy George later co-opted. About his street name George said, "It's different. It's not like calling somebody Chino or calling them Red or Lefty or Fingers. When you say Boy George, you're talking about the singer or you're talking about me." With his lessons in the game and street name from Joey White, Boy George was ready to embark on his chosen career as a drug dealer, and there was no looking back.

After working for Joey White for a minute, Boy George decided to switch over from selling coke to heroin. "Less time and faster money," he reasoned. Going to work for the Torres brothers, he started as a lookout, was promoted to a pitcher and then a manager. He learned the operation from the ground up. He oversaw the brand Blue Thunder at a spot on 166th and Washington. "That nigga was from Morris. That joint was full of heron spots, crack spots, weed spots." Sport says. "86-87 Blue Thunder was killing it. That's the Torres brothers. That shit was normal activity. Nobody seen that as unusual. Officially, Checkmate too." Boy George and Joey White hung out eating breakfast at Crown Donuts and discussing business. Joey took the young George to Great Adventures in New Jersey, Victor's Cafe in Manhattan and Norels, a jeweler in Chinatown. They practiced shooting at a firing range in Mt. Vernon, went to exotic car shows, skied in the Poconos and checked out other drug dealer's expensive customized cars. That was the life for the up and coming druglord.

"Joey White, he's a piece of work," Flaco, a dude from the neighborhood says. "He looked like the Dunkin' Donuts guy, short, fat with a mustache. He looked Italian, he didn't even look Spanish. You could ask Joey for anything, he could get it- cars, bullets, guns, heroin." But unknown to Boy George and the people in the neighborhood Joey White was no good. "He was double dealing. He would never drive no car to make you think he was a drug dealer.

He drove an LTD and looked like a cop. Joey White's brother got arrested years ago and was facing life so that turned Joey to work for the feds. He had a spot at 156th and Elton too. But it was a nickel and dime operation." Flaco says. Joey White gave just enough info to keep himself in business and he would eventually offer up his latest protégé, Boy George, to the feds. But all that was in the future. First came Boy George's ascension.

The high school dropout who had a love of boxing rose quickly in the Torres brother's organization. Boy George learned to talk the talk, and walk the walk, appearing in control at all times. Smooth, criminal and beyond his years, he became the one you didn't want to fuck with. He got up early like Joey White taught him to make sure his spot was open, and under him 166th and Washington started booming, clearing 65 grand a week. George was about his business, he was on point as they say, keeping close tabs on his dealers and maintaining the flow. In a business full of losers, junkies, scammers and ex-cons, he proved trustworthy and reliable. He paid his people from his 10 percent and delivered the rest to the Torres brothers. He was known to handle any problems that occurred with gunplay, quickly and decisively like a man. But he was only 17. He recruited his old Cabrini group home friends by pulling up to the home in a Mercedes. "He knew how to present himself," a New Rochelle counselor remembered. "He knew when people were playing a con game on him."

From Joey White, Boy George learned to anticipate the sudden climatic shifts that characterized the drug game and to be prepared to act decisively when the opportunity arose. "I did what most people are too scared to do," Boy George said. "And that's to take control of something very powerful." In June 1987 when DEA agents arrested key members of the Torres ring, Boy George, hard bodied and cunning made his move. Through a Torres associate he developed a supplier in Chinatown who was able to regularly deliver large quantities of China White. He recruited his closest friends from the Castle Hill neighborhood where he grew up, and put his press game down to fortify his corner. Instead of delivering 65 grand to Torres' people Boy George set up shop himself. He bought heroin, mannitol, a glass table, six chairs, a triple beam scale and glassine envelopes. The next day 166th and Washington reopened for business with Boy George's new brand- Obsession.

"Blue Thunder falls, Obsession took over," Sport says. "Once those niggas fell he had that opportunity. He was in the right place at the right time. Obsession came in after Blue Thunder fell. That shit was retarded. The first time I heard of Boy George wasn't because of him, it was because of the dope. The dope was killing them. Everybody in the hood was like – 'Who is it? Who is it?' Dudes were all asking. 'It's that little young motherfucker that got shit bubbling. He got them dope fiends sprung. They open.' He was like an oldhead opening up mad spots, giving niggas 30 percent and saying bubble my shit. Boy George took over all the spots. He had the shit at Watson, the shit in Manhattan with Bob Lemon. He had it all on lock."

Part 3- Setting up Shop

During the 80's heroin on the New York scene was brought in and controlled by the Chinese tongs. The dope traveled through their street gangs like the Flying Dragons, to which one of George's suppliers belonged. Retail dealers like Boy George usually bought from middleman who diluted the potency of the dope, but George had the hook up to a direct source of almost raw, uncut heroin, facilitating his success with crazy profits. When setting up shop one of the people he recruited was Ward Johnson, an older Jamaican hustler who was known on the street as Six-O. He became George's top man, handling administrative details of the operation, including payroll and personal. Six-O drove a dollar cab and met George by driving him around to make deliveries when he was working for the Torres brothers. Six-O was schooled in a lot of things that Boy George didn't know and had hookups to different people who could help him accomplish a variety of things. He helped George with all types of things once they started doing business together. Such as getting phony guarantors for leasing cars, finding friends in real estate who'd rent apartments in other people's names, and obtaining fraudulent business certificates for front companies. Six-O's advice and hookups were invaluable to the young Boy George as he organized his crew and got his feet wet. Soon after Boy George launched Obsession, Six-O became his right hand man.

"Six-O had a luxury cab service called OJ's," Flaco says. "People would call and get a Benz, LTD, Land Cruiser to drive them around. They would call them, get in the cars and do deliveries. Boy George got close to the dude Six-O and he got down with the organization. They called him Six-O because that was his car number. That's why they called him Six-O."

The operation began in the spring of 1987 when Boy George and Six-O obtained 100 grams of bulk heroin. With the help of a dozen mill workers including A. Turino and Luis "Weseal" Gautier, they cut and packaged the heroin in Rivera's apartment on East 213th Street in the Bronx. They set up their crew to handle all aspects of the heroin trade from wholesale delivery to milling. Once Obsession was established, Boy George began to branch out. He opened other spots and refined his milling process. "Every known drug spot he would go to and offer his dope to get the spot." Flaco says. "That's how he got a lot of those corners. His cutting mills ran like clockwork too."

Cutting the heroin consisted of adding quinine and milk sugar to double the weight of the heroin. The cut heroin was then spooned into thousands of glassine bags that were pre-stamped with Boy George's brand name, Obsession and his logo, a red crown. The bags were packaged in bundles of ten $10 bags and given to street level dealers for sale at George's spots. Spot managers generally made 15 percent of the profit and were responsible for paying the lookouts, steerers, pitchers and runners out of their share, which was typically $1 a bag commission. Spot managers made $2,500 a week and the top lieutenant Six-O made $12,000 a week. Boy George easily made upwards of $45,000 a week. "He ran his business like it was a real business. Like he was running a corporation. Even at his cutting mills he would dock people if they missed. He didn't run his shit like a drug dealer. He ran it like a CEO." Flaco says.

"While I was in high school I was driving to school in a Mercedes Benz of the year." Boy George said and he owed his success to having a good product. If the quality was good, Boy George knew the fiends would come. During the summer of 1987, his crew distributed about $100,000 worth of heroin a week, according to law enforcement. Boy George was doing it and he was a strict disciplinarian. Just like the NWA song, *"Dope Man"* with the refrain, *Don't get high on your own supply*, Boy George never touched his product and he rarely drank. Money was his intoxication. His drug of choice. In the midst of the crack boom, he had the smarts to concentrate on heroin and with this thinking, his business thrived. "Boy George's passion was running the business," Flaco says. "Being the top dog."

Early in his murderous rise he made the Flying Dragon connect which gave him access to the Chinese wholesaler. Having made the connection to pure heroin at a good price, Boy George's brand Obsession killed the competition and made it obsolete, gaining the reputation as the best dope available in the city. It was widely available in vast portions of the Bronx and the junkies filtered in like the dope fiends they were to get it. Boy George was ruthless enough to climb up through the ranks of the local drug business, but shrewd enough to avoid touching the stuff himself. By maintaining his own special brand, he essentially locked the trade down and established a monopoly. Becoming a drug kingpin in the process. "That nigga was like the most powerful nigga in the neighborhood," Flaco says.

When Boy George first launched Obsession, his mill processed one hundred to two hundred grams of heroin a day, five days a week. The milling process was a crucial part of the operation, but it was also tedious and exacting. Bricks of heroin were diluted and packaged for retail sale at the mills. George rented apartments, or rooms of apartments belonging to his employees, their mothers, girlfriends or friends. Mills lasted from a week to several months and the workers moved along if the apartment got hot. The mill workers were paid three times the wage of a fast food clerk and were collected and delivered home by car. Boy George hired by word of mouth. He would hire a lot of his ex-girlfriends, their families and friends to process his shipments of heroin.

"He changed the entire Bronx, he was getting so much money." Flaco says. "It wasn't so much fear, but he was respected for getting money, especially at such a young age. There was a time when they were so busy at the cutting mill that one of his workers would bring sandwiches and sell them for like $150 each. The workers didn't care they couldn't leave until all the kilo's were cut. They would pay it because everybody was making so much money. Even the mill workers."

The apartments he used usually were furnished by him with carpets, a kitchen set, a bedroom set and a huge TV. Two large glass tables would be pushed together. Garbage cans filled with lighter fluid flanked each end. If police showed the heroin would be shoved in the cans and sulfuric acid, kept on hand, would be dumped on top to destroy the evidence. At one end of the table a worker crushed the brick while it was still in its package before cracking it like an egg into a metal cup and crushing the chunks into a powder. It was a very culinary process. At the other end of the table someone weighed out mannitol, precisely measuring the chalky substance on a triple beam scale. The cut had to be exact or the fiends wouldn't buy the dope. The heroin would then be ground in a coffee grinder and repeatedly stirred until it was sufficiently fine, mannitol would be added to finish.

At first Boy George paid someone $50 to deliver the heroin to his store or spot. But delivering the dope to his block managers became a full time job for Luis "Weasel" Gauteir and Ralph Hernandez. They would make trips on the regular like the postman. Spot managers broke the milled bricks into smaller bundles and dealers stored them in mailboxes, under parked cars, under a crack in a fence or in a baby's diapers- wherever they could find a good hiding spot. The street system worked like this- the lookout watched, the steerer brought customers to the dealer, the dealer took the money, another steerer sent the customer to a pitcher, who delivered the heroin.

A spot manager wanted access to several empty apartments or rooms within one building to stash dope, guns and money. They'd pay a super to look the other way or pay rent for single moms and buy their kids food or they'd just find a junkie and use their apartment to set up shop. It didn't really matter because the heroin was a means to the end. Boy George had an elaborate system set up through beepers and pagers with codes that instructed his spot managers on pick ups and deliveries. The managers of Boy George's drug crew used the street number nearest their block to identify themselves. Boy George used 666. He said he like the satanic implication of the code. Boy George would rarely call people back himself. Usually his man would call people back that beeped him. "I'm calling for Boy George," they would say.

George's mills were heavily armed. Guns rested on the table in case of stickups- .357's and .38's, a .45, Uzi's, an automatic shotgun or a Mossberg pump. George was not fucking around. He was very aware of robbers and the fact that he could get taken at any time. His mills and stash house were an obvious source of cash and robbing drug dealers in the city had become its own lucrative trade. The stick up kids were everywhere and in full force, looking to come up, and only by a show of force, clever manipulation and the rotation of stash houses and mills could they be deterred and defeated. And anyway dealers could hardly go to the police. When Boy George first set up, he had a robbery scare at his first cutting mill at East 213th Street in the Bronx. He relocated the cutting mill to the Manhattan Marriott Marquis and not a minute too soon because in September 1987 police officers acting on a tip, located the abandoned 213th Street apartment where they found glassine envelopes, heroin cutting paraphernalia, a Bowie knife, a bulletproof vest, a shotgun and a variety of ammunition.

When he learned of the seizure Rivera switched the heroin brand name to Delerious, with the logo of a crazed looking man, which spooked addicts, who refused to buy it. He folded the Delerious operation within a week and returned to Obsession, because his customers had developed a loyalty to that name. Also to keep on his toes Boy George relocated the cutting mill from the Marriott Marquis to the apartment of one of his people and it was subsequently moved to other homes and apartments. He had no problem opening up new spots either. "They heard he was making so much money that dudes would go to him to get the dope for their spots." Flaco says. "So their spot would become his spot. I don't think there was no other people that was making that amount of money at that age. Dude was official."

As his spots boomed Boy George introduced other brands like Sledgehammer, which borrowed the logo from the Arm and Hammer Company and recruited more friends like Walter "Ice" Cook, who was a classmate at Morris High School to run his lucrative 122nd Street spot. George's man Six-O asked him, "What are you trying to be? McDonald's and Burger King?" Referring to the launch of the second brand name. But George was just innovating. Obsession was his goldmine, but why couldn't Sledgehammer take off too? With more money coming in Boy George bought cars and shipped them to Puerto Rico. He sent Weasel and Six-O to San Juan with suitcases full of cash. Boy George was rolling and so were all of his workers who spent their money on cars, sound systems, fur trimmed coats and more. They lived in the projects, but they lived large. They wanted nothing more than to wear gold as heavy as that worn by Boy George.

Part 4- Blowing up

Boy George had five major spots- 166th and Washington where he got his start, 122nd and Second Avenue, the block long abandoned building on 139th and Brook, 156th and Courtlandt, a playground in a public housing development and 651 Southern Boulevard, better know as St. John's. Washington Avenue, Courtlandt and 122nd each generated 40 grand a day. 150 grand was normal for St. Johns, which had good access. In the dope game, good access meant right in the hood, but also right by an exit off the Bruckner Expressway, which made it easy for suburbanites to drop by, buy their drugs and bounce. Cars idled three deep at St. Johns and the constant flow of traffic made unannounced visits by the police almost impossible. Boy George was prepared in any case though. Four lookouts were stationed on the sidewalk outside the building and two more were on the fire escapes. Two runners steered long lines of people into the building. A pitcher was behind a cement framed, thick metal apartment door. He handed Obsession glassines out through the hole. George used to close his spots when children walked to and from the nearby schools. Even drug dealers can have morals. He was responsible drug dealer.

Boy George was running one of the most lucrative and aggressive heroin crews in the Bronx at the young age of 21. It was said he employed 50 people and grossed a quarter of a million a week. The Rivera organization operated like a corporation because of the professionally packaged nature of the heroin sold, the percentage basis on which spot owners sold it, and the central management team to which everyone reported. Boy George's management style was a combination of bribery and threat. He lorded over the mill workers like an irate factory owner. He docked his workers $300 for showing up late and fired them after one absence, although he often took them back.

He sent his table manager and productive workers on fully paid vacations to Puerto Rico and Disney World. His policies were very corporate but yielded results. By 1988, the mill regularly processed seven hundred grams of heroin every shift. "You never saw him around," Flaco says. "To think he was getting that money, but he was. He was corporate-style though. He wasn't on the block grinding."

Boy George who has been described as very charismatic and mean, was also extremely generous to his crew. He kept loyalty strong among his people with cash bonuses, gifts and free vacations like those mentioned above. Lieutenants and managers received gold belt buckles with their names scripted in diamonds. Top dealers received red and white leather baseball jackets. Progressive management, good product and brute force had won him a virtual monopoly. "That was a big crew," Sport says. "But you wouldn't see everybody together. When dudes overstepped their boundaries they would blast their guns. Being violent is the nature of the neighborhood. If you want that shit to continue to grow, you have to put your hand down. That shit is normal in the South Bronx." Those who prospered in the drug game tended to be not only ruthless and calculating, but lucky. For a minute George was all three.

"I guess my ambitions got the best of me at the early age of 17." Boy George said. "To believe that I was already in the 7 digit bracket at that young age would be unbelievable, but when you have an imagination and ambition that knows no limits, why go half-ass when you can go full steam ahead." Boy George bought heroin wholesale through his Flying Dragon connect who he referred to privately as, "Fried Rice." The bricks were the size of small boxes of soap, like the ones from the vending machines at a Laundromat. Over the telephone they referred to the bricks as girls, as in, "How many girls do you need?" The $100,000 girls brought back $240,000. After copping the dope Boy George passed it along to his lieutenant Six-O, the Jamaican hustler. Six-O passed off the heroin to girlfriends of their male associates and their friends who acted as $10 an hour workers that cut the heroin in cutting mills, which were rotated regularly from South Bronx walk up and project apartments to some hotels in Manhattan and New Jersey.

The success of Obsession owed to its potency. George was getting 87 percent pure. He compared it to the difference between dollar-store soda and coke. But like Sport says, "If the dope was whack it would still sell because of the name. He took that shit to another level. Everybody got a gimmick. His was that the dope made you drop. His shit sold on G.P. just because of the name." And the money coming in was silly. Six-O picked up the money for counting, often in shoe boxes. Even with counting machines and everyone skimming, Six-O fell garbage bags behind. George stored some of his money in safes in empty apartments. Sometimes he crammed duffle bags full of cash in the trunk of a car he'd park in a long-term garage. As Obsession continued to sell well, laundering money became a priority. Boy George worked with a stockbroker who converted sneaker boxes full of tens and twenties into bonds. He hired a financial consultant to diversify his interests and he owned shares in a water filtration company.

Through his front company Tuxedo Enterprises, Boy George leased stables of Jetta's, Maxima's and other cars for daily use. Tuxedo Enterprises appeared to be a very prosperous and fast growing Bronx company. Just what the neighborhood needed. And while running the company Boy George posed as a successful business manager. "When I'd get stopped by the police and that's if I wanted to stop, I'd present legitimate information showing the vehicle as one owned by a corporation and I was a representative of the said corporation." Boy George said. And Tuxedo Enterprises required so much firepower because of its illicit street operations, that it set up a subsidiary division to import guns into New York City through a gun store in Virginia. "They needed a lot of protection," Sport says. "And they had the paper to get the hammers they needed."

With each retail location generating 50 grand in business a week and the network behind them also shipping China White as far away from the slums of the Bronx as the upstate City of Rochester Boy George was balling. He was a *New Jack City* CEO. As he concentrated on his investments and expanding the business, Six-O managed most of the daily activities for the druglord while George attempted to open several new heroin spots in Manhattan. He set up stores on Fifth Avenue and 105th Street, First Avenue at 115th and 132nd Street between Madison and Park. He was franchising like 7-Eleven. "They called him the King of New York," Flaco says.

Business was booming and Boy George was playing the part of the gentleman drug baron. He strengthened his bond with his Flying Dragon connect "Fried Rice" during a dry spell in April 1988 when he hooked up a deal for them both. He invited the Chinese in on the deal and each put up 300 grand. They got burned on the deal and Boy George took full responsibility for the fuck up. He reimbursed the Chinese their 300 G's and absorbed the over half a mil loss himself. "Excuses are for assholes," Boy George said. But to further strengthen his ties to the Chinese he had to tie up loose ends, finding the dudes who burned them and handling it. But the money was never recovered. His Chinese contacts were suitably impressed though. They continued doing business with George, scheduling their meetings and exchanges in parking lots at Kennedy airport, on various corners and in midtown Manhattan and commercial districts all over Queens.

In the late summer of 1988, Boy George launched the Sledgehammer brand, usually more diluted than Obsession to preserve the elite brand, and appointed Walter "Ice" Cook to supervise its distribution. George used some of the proceeds of the operation to purchase a house in Puerto Rico for $145,000 cash. He extensively remodeled the house, including the installation of an outdoor pool with the words Obsession and the initials B.G. tiled in the bottom. With the help of a financial consultant he also prepared to open a fast food mall in Puerto Rico with a McDonald's, Church's Fried Chicken and Pizza Hut. He also purchased a number of customized luxury cars. In 1988 he was driving a charcoal-gray Mercedes Benz 190 but a year later he had a fleet of exotic cars. "He definitely had a lot of cars and shit like that," Flaco says. Boy George began boxing at Gleason's Gym with a dream of winning a Golden Gloves championship plus he backed several promising young boxers. "Will got him involved in the boxing," Flaco says. "Will was like his right hand. Will was vicious with his hands. Boy George really didn't trust a lot of people. Will was like his brother."

Boy George enjoyed the life of a gentleman at leisure. Enjoying trips to Hawaii and Puerto Rico and hiring limousines to take him and his crew to Great Adventures amusement park in New Jersey. "He liked to go on the rides," Sport says. "He was still a kid." In a painting Boy George commissioned he stood shoulder to shoulder with his mafia heroes Fat Tony, John Gotti and Carmine Persico. He also had a photo of him posing like Rambo strapped with guns. Boy George had imagination and he envisioned himself a Puerto Rican mafia don. "Dude was like that for real," Sport says. "He had it going on."

At the age of 20 he embarked on the biggest deal of his life, a 32 brick deal of premium China White for $1.1 million in cash. Each brick was worth $175,000 on the street. The deal took place at Whitestone Lanes in Queens and with the finalization of the deal Boy George had even more money than before. But it didn't last. With his name in lights, shining bright, he wouldn't last much longer.

His reputation was getting too big. His name was ringing loudly, he was too flamboyant and flashed too much wealth. The kid from the South Bronx was getting hot. "How many Bentley turbo's or Lamborghini's do you see in the South Bronx?" Boy George asked rhetorically. "I brought heat to myself. Just as my ambitions got the best of me, so did my ignorance." Cars were his passion though. "He was extravagant. Everything he did, he did 100 percent. That's why he had all the cars." Flaco says. "I didn't think he was making that much money. I thought it was a neighborhood myth but it was true. At first you'd think he was a parking lot attendant driving all these cars, but they were his. One time we were in front of my building and he came up with a Lincoln, then 30 minutes later he came back with a Porsche and then with another car. He was like that. He was young. He was flashy."

Part 5- The Legend

Boy George was the master of the Bronx universe. Using a management style that might have been honed in a corporate boardroom and a brand of violence common to drug dealers, Boy George carved out an empire and flooded the streets of Manhattan and the South Bronx with a brand of high quality heroin with the brand names Obsession and Sledgehammer. He was ruthless and powerful, federal authorities said and they linked him to a dozen homicides that marked his climb to the top. The 20-year-old CEO allegedly ran a $9 million a year heroin ring. "Boy George was making crazy money," Sports says. "Everybody knows that." He was known for having a temper and had been involved in several shootouts to cement his reputation in the streets yet he never missed an opportunity to intimidate. Boy George didn't fuck around when it came time to get paid either. "Don't fall for tricks about 'Oh, I'll see you tomorrow, blah, blah,' when you are dealing with someone who owes me money. You say, 'Listen homie, I want to eat today. So I'm not going to wait until tomorrow to eat. I want to eat today. I'm hungry. Pay up dude.' That's it." He said.

The authorities alleged George killed mercilessly with hired hit men, killing anyone who crossed his path, workers who came up short, anyone who stole- Boy George was merciless. The murderous and smart dealer was so young that his own lieutenants called him a prodigy. "He kept loyalty strong in this organization," Sergeant Billy Cook of the NYPD said. "By distributing cash bonuses, gifts and free vacations- the identical incentives that the head of a le-gitimate company would lavish on star performers." But investigators main-tained that behind the generosity there was a deadly face. At least a dozen homicides, investigators said, could be directly linked to George's rise to the top, which earned him a reputation that encouraged loyalty by force of death. "If you weren't with that clique they didn't really fuck with you," Sport says. And the one thing Boy George was known for, besides being calculating and violent was his cars. "The first shit was the Benz. The 190, kitted up, music blaring." Sport says. And Boy George was on some white boy shit too he liked rock and roll, jamming to Guns-n-Roses in the hood. "The first time I saw his shit I was over there on Brook Avenue. On a drive-by too. He was just pass-ing by. Everybody knew him off the rip." Sport remembers. Boy George did-n't play when it came to cars. He bought Ferrari's, Lamborghini's and a Bentley. All this only added to his legend. "He pulled up in a Lincoln Town car to show us," Flaco says. "He had the Porsche pressing buttons showing how the license plate moved and the lights changed."

Barely out of his teens, Boy George built an organization so lucrative that he registered a fleet of Mercedes, BMW's and customized Porsches to one of his corporate fronts, Tuxedo Enterprises. "The press called me the Puerto

Rican James Bond because of the gadgets in my car. I was on foot when I was arrested. If I could have gotten to my car they'd still be chasing me." Boy George said. James Bond, one of George's heroes, inspired 50 grand worth of special features added to the 190 Mercedes he had. Radar detectors manned the cars front and rear, the license plate slid into a side compartment and a strobe light blinded anyone following him. Secret compartments in the door panels and the floor hid weapons and cash. One device squirted bogs of oil from the tail while a hidden switch flipped a box in the trunk that sprayed nail-like tacks. Boy George also had a Ferrari, a Lamborghini, a Bentley and a Porsche in his garage.

His $140,000 customized black Porsche had a trunk full of stereo equipment, a telephone system, a VCR, a color TV, ebony finish, thick custom rugs, gun compartments that slid open at a touch and a host of other exotic goodies. A button in his customized BMW would cause loaded handguns to pop out of concealed apartments. Boy George spared no expense customizing his favorite cars with $12,000 ostrich-skin interiors, 630 watt stereos, 10-track CD players, televisions, VCRS and cell phones. Several of his cars were straight out of a James Bond flick with all types of features to assist in escaping in car chases. "The biggest influences in his life were probably Gleason's Gym and James Bond." Sport says.

At 21, he owned shopping malls and commercial real estate. He flaunted a lifestyle as lavish as a New York socialite or those portrayed on *Lifestyles of the Rich and Famous.* But his passion was boxing. "They used to be saying that he was into boxing," Sport says. "His whole crew was all real nice with their hands. They would give you a fair one if that's what it was. But they would beat dudes down too." Boy George's favorite charm was two tiny gold boxing gloves which symbolized the Golden Gloves boxing competition he'd trained so hard for. He trained at boxing and worked out religiously. "He'd always eat healthy food." One of his girlfriends said. "He cycled and jogged." And his trusted Lieutenant, Will "Love" Claussen, was the son of a professional boxer and helped to train George.

Handsome and debonair, Boy George wasn't that big a dude. "He's like 5-7 or something," Sport says. In the South Bronx he was remembered wearing a black leather cap that matched his black leather trench coat. He cropped his dark brown hair short and kept his goatee neatly trimmed. His brown eyes were intent. "He had a good reputation," Sport says. "Ain't nobody got nothing bad to say about him. If you bubbling you got to respect that because he took that shit there. He was doing it." Boy George dined at upscale restaurants like Victor's Cafe in Manhattan. He liked expensive silk shirts and went by many aliases. He once sent a girlfriend to San Francisco on a day trip to fetch a pair of Nikes that weren't in stock in New York. He was well-mannered, attentive and confident. Boy George had a big, echoing laugh. He loved Andrew Dice Clay, who was his favorite comedian. The in your face humor fit Boy George's style but he had a generous side too. His workers would lug bags of groceries from the Food Emporium for the families of girlfriends, of which he had many. Most were Puerto Rican girls from the poverty stricken South Bronx. It was said he kept a harem of women in the neighborhood. "He had a lot of girls. He was all over with the broads," Flaco says. George had all types too.

"One night stand girls who came back for more," he explained. "Girls who clung to me like a cheap suit. Then there were girls who were my regular jewels of the Nile, more upper class than these regular girls." Boy George's girls were bejeweled in leathers and furs, reclining on ostrich-skin passenger seats of his Benzes and BMW's. A lot of them tattooed 'Property of Boy George' on their bodies. To the girls sex was currency and they spent it on Boy George. He liked his girls customized like his cars. He demanded color coordination. He had a 50 dollar rule, nothing under $50 was to be taken off the rack while shopping. He had one girlfriend wear a twenty-two karat gold 'Boy George' name plate around her neck. And his women had to be on point. "He always liked everything spotless, house, clothing. He never liked to see anything dirty." One girlfriend said. "He'd bring home a whole lotta videos and I would just watch TV. I didn't have to get a job. I was to cook and clean and take care of things and I would get an allowance at the end of the week."

Boy George would frequent Club 371, where his whole crew hung out. No waiting in line for Boy George. He strode to the front, sat in the VIP section and sipped on a bottle of Moet. Everyone treated George like a king. "They used to pass by the clubs- Riddler, Peoples and Kamikazi on Westchester, two blocks off of White Plains Road. Two opposite each other." Sport says. "It was called herpes triangle. A lot of fucking was going on. Dudes weren't going in. The party was outside the club. The bitches used to come to see who was driving up. Boy George and them drove up in all new cars, tricked out, jeweled up. All the broads were trying to get with them." Boy George hosted several organization wide social events too including a fall 1988 party at a restaurant and dance club and the infamous 1988 Christmas Eve yacht party.

On December 24, 1988, Boy George threw a black tie party for his entire crew aboard a chartered yacht. He rented the Riveranda at World Yacht's 23rd Street dock. He and about 150 others in black tie attire set out to party while cruising around the New York harbor. George paid $30,000 in cash to rent the Riveranda, which included dinner for all and a disc jockey. He spent 12 grand to have Big Daddy Kane perform for 15 minutes and laid out more cash for Loose Touch and the Jungle Brothers to perform. The menu consisted of steak tartare, skewered lamb, prime rib and 12 grand in champagne. Boy George paid for the tuxedo rentals, dinner, open bar and entertainment, including a raffle with luxury prizes. The party goers were seated at tables organized by spot location.

The men from each spot wore bands of the same color- red for one distribution group, purple for another and gold for a third. Those that arrived together, stayed together. The managers sat among the pitchers and dealers who worked for them. It was like prom night but with an open bar and no chaperons. As the employees waited on the dock at 23rd Street in Manhattan to board the yacht and begin the party cruise, the men adjusted their bow ties and touched their gold belt buckles emblazoned with their names in diamonds. The guests arrived by BMW's, Mercedes, by rented limousines and by dollar cabs. Boy George arrived fashionably late in a silk tuxedo and Bally shoes as his tuxedo-clad troops cheered and clapped while he strode up the ramp and waved with a girl on his arm. The DJ announced, "Mr. and Mrs. Boy George." The king had arrived.

"It's good to bring them together so they know, 'Listen man you have a family here. If anything goes wrong this is the type of force that's coming behind you."' Boy George said. And the highlight of the night was the raffle. A fully loaded Mitsubishi was the grand prize, 20 grand in cash first prize, a Rolex watch second prize, a trip to Hawaii was third prize and a trip to Disneyworld was fourth prize. Boy George gave Walter "Ice" Cook a BMW 750, Six-O a gold Rolex and 50 grand in cash and gold and diamond Obsession belt buckles to his top four men, each appraised at over 8 grand. As the night went on fights erupted and during the course of the party a man was stripped on the main deck, beaten and spit on by Boy George for stealing a necklace from one of the other party goers. As the yacht made for shore at the stroke of midnight a man attempted to dive off the bow and race the boat on a bet. He was restrained. Unknown to George and his guests, there were three off duty New York City detectives aboard as part of the yacht security. However when it came time to talk to the DEA, these detectives were uncooperative and during George's trial they remained steadfast in their refusal to testify to what they had witnessed. And Sport remembers when the party went down too, it was legend in the South Bronx, "When they had the shit on the boat, niggas was talking about they was giving away BMW's. They said they had bows on them and shit."

Part 6- The Investigation

From the jump Joey White, Boy George's mentor, had tipped the cops to his protégé. Joey White had been a confidential informant for years, unbeknownst to Boy George or other South Bronx residents, filing reports with the New York Police Department and the DEA. His snitching provided him immunity on the streets. It was his cost of doing business. Duplicity was a major component of ghetto life and Joey White played both sides of the fence. As early as August 1987, the police had learned of the Rivera operation from Joey Navado aka Joey White, George's supposed man. On August 27th the rat Navado introduced Rivera as Boy George to undercover detective Joseph Mendez, who bought two ounces of 88 percent pure heroin from Rivera for $12,000. At the meeting Rivera claimed that his organization distributed two kilograms of heroin a week. On October 6, 1987 Navado and Mendez met with Rivera, Six-O and A. Turino. Mendez bought 600 glassine envelopes of leftover Delerious for $5,000. Rivera conducted no further business with Mendez after that because Six-O correctly surmised that Mendez was an undercover officer. The government then backed off so that they could build a stronger case against the suspected heroin kingpin.

In April of 1988, the government had enough information from their snitch Joey White to seek a court order to set up a monitoring device known as a PEN register and attach it to telephones widely used by members of the Obsession organization. When the devices were removed over 40 percent of the calls were to beeper numbers, a large number of those to the government snitch. On one of those telephones 2,884 calls were placed between May 1, 1988 and March 20, 1989 when the monitoring device was removed. Other calls went to five public telephones on the streets Boy George's dealers controlled. The first snitch, Joey White, soon led to three others, each yielding more info on Boy George's network- an address for a heroin cutting mill, the nicknames of George's most trusted confidants, even the kind of jewelry- a gold ring that spanned three fingers, worn by one of George's most successful dealers. This all went to the surveillance teams and undercover agents. Drugs were bought and observations made that confirmed the snitches info. The feds needed more evidence to put Boy George behind bars though. To get the whole network off the streets police had to step up. Surveillance of his mills and distribution points was intensified.

The police went in front of federal Judge Thomas P. Griesa with a ten page request for a wiretap. This request authorized by the Attorney General's office was approved by Judge Griesa after he read a forty-two page supporting affidavit by two of NYPD Sergeant Billy Cook's investigators, DEA special agent Anthony Farretta and Detective Willie Cebolleros. It summarized the results of the eleven month long investigation and showed that Boy George was running a heroin ring. On April 4, 1989, the New York police obtained authorization to wiretap Rivera's home phone at 1665 Morris Avenue in the Bronx. The tap remained for twenty-seven days. Spanish translators and agents were busy listening to the dealers transact business. Within a month federal agents realized that their wiretaps were being circumvented by the use of beepers, payphones and cellular phones. The wiretaps largely documented

Boy George's girlfriends' conversations. George was usually out and about while she spent her days on the phone, shifting people between call waiting. Police decided that surveillance and snatch and grabs were the way to go if they wanted to gather enough tangible evidence to get a conviction.

On the evening of April 30, 1989, a collection of the alphabet boys, federal agents, city detectives and state police investigators formerly known as the NYPD-DEA Drug Enforcement Task Force got the break they needed. New York police had established surveillance of a suspected cutting mill then in operation at 740 East 243rd in the Bronx. Upon leaving the apartment that evening Jaime Cuevas was arrested with 10,400 glassine envelopes of Obsession heroin. When Luis "Weasel" Gautier and Ralph Hernandez subsequently left the apartment they were arrested with 8,718 more Obsession glassine envelopes. The police had gotten their break in the case.

With these arrests Sergeant Billy Cook of the NYPD and his task force had finally reached the end of the heroin trail they had quietly been investigating. It came after two years of patient investigation that had led Cook's task force to the bitter end of the Chinese heroin trail inhabited by the black and Hispanic distribution network run by Boy George that controlled fifteen or so lucrative spots in the Bronx and Manhattan. Boy George's retail network that Cook ended up targeting was the most aggressive group of sellers in the Bronx. They bought pure heroin wholesale from the Chinese, through the Flying Dragon connect, then handed it over to $10 an hour workers who doubled its weight by adding quinine and milk sugar then measured out single dose quantities of the 50 percent heroin in plastic McDonald's coffee spoons. Spoon by spoon they shoveled heroin into thousands of glassine Obsession envelopes. The lieutenants then took the heroin back and handed it out in bundles of the $10 bags to street corner pushers who earned commission on each bag sold. One $170,000 kilo, divided up this way yielded the network a profit of $300,000. The network sold several kilos each week. And through their slow and relentless investigation, the Drug Enforcement Task Force was ready to get the big prize- Boy George.

The next step in the government's plan to bring Boy George down was a series of raids. "Okay boys, lets go wreck some zip codes," the ever smiling

Sergeant Cook told the 70 raiders as they squeezed out of the tight lecture chairs packed into the conference room to head for the Bronx buildings whose doors they would crash through. "Remember seize all the paper, paper, paper, paper. That's what we need to make this case stick." Cook told his team. Cook knew that conspiracy cases were built on little scraps of paper. In a successful conspiracy case it was the paper that tied one person to another without room for denial. The paper ultimately formed a chain of evidence that led to conviction, even if no drugs were seized. The first series of raids went off without a hitch, a tremendous success on the feds part. It was disastrous for Boy George.

At approximately, 2:30 AM on May 1, 1989, the police executed a search warrant on the 740 East 243rd mill apartment. Eleven workers were arrested and the officers seized 1.1 kilograms of heroin, five loaded weapons, over 100,000 empty glassine envelopes bearing the Obsession or Sledgehammer logo, dozens of blocks of cutting agent, a triple beam scale, four grinding machines, other processing materials and a spiral notebook containing production records for the organization's mills. Another raid resulted in 13 arrests, seven pounds of heroin, seven guns, 60 grand in cash and a set of the famed gold and diamond Obsession belt buckles. A photo album was also seized that displayed photos of the 1988 Christmas Eve yacht party. These photos led the government agents to the World Yacht Club.

A visit was paid to the yacht charters but the employees of the Hudson River concern were reluctant to help. They were afraid Boy George's enforcers would sink their boats, so the task force had to subpoena their records. The government now had evidence of all the cash that was spent, documentation of drug use on board and all the luxurious gifts and prizes that were given away. The picture a jury would need was complete- Boy George standing tall at the center of his tuxedo-clad, gun-carrying, heroin dealing minions.

Less than five months after the yacht docked and the party ended on Christmas morning, a task force of city, state and federal investigators brought a halt to Rivera's meteoric rise from a Bronx tenement building to the crème de la crème of drug dealers in the South Bronx and the whole city. With Boy George's arrest early one May morning outside his Morris Avenue home in the

Tremont section of the South Bronx, a street legend's run came to an end. The second phase of the government's raids began with Boy George and his top lieutenants being dragged in. Rivera was arrested with $7,500 cash and a warrant was then obtained to search his apartment. Police found $1,000 cash, a life size crown similar to that depicted in the Obsession logo, address books with telephone numbers of his crew, ammunition, payroll records, drug transaction records and raffle tickets from the Christmas party. Shortly thereafter Six-O was arrested and his apartment was also searched pursuant to a warrant. The search revealed detailed drug ledgers for 1987 and 1988.

"I was arrested on May 1, 1989 after the DEA concluded a two and half year investigation." Boy George said, and from the upper reaches of his organization would come the final shreds of evidence necessary to complete the box around him. From the mouths of George's lieutenants came the first hint that cooperation was going to follow. These top lieutenants gave the government the last pieces of evidence they needed to prove the conspiracy charges they were alleging. "Joey White took his story to the grand jury and that was the beginning of the end." Boy George said. The government calculated that the Rivera organization distributed almost 28 kilos of heroin in 1989 alone. It was a clean sweep for the feds.

As the feds drove Boy George through Central Park on their way to Central Booking one of the agents told George, "See that plant? It's gonna be a tree when you get out." In the month of May when federal agents arrested 31 alleged Rivera associates they recovered more than 30 weapons including shotguns, Uzi's and .357 magnums. For the feds the whole investigation was an astounding success. With the kingpin laws and mandatory minimums they knew they would be able to put Boy George and his crew away for a very long time. By June of 1989, they were planning their last set of raids. They wanted to get every shred of evidence possible and every possible cooperating witness to testify against Boy George. The government began to raid the homes of the lower level workers in the organization. The government knew that the top dealers viewed the lower level mill workers that made only $10 an hour as disposable. The government knew that they wouldn't be receiving warning calls from any bosses that may have escaped the earlier raids. The minor players very often were freed in exchange for their small bit of cooperation. They were the workers who cut the heroin, the baggers who packaged it. Their lives had little in common with the lifestyle of the young man who drove a $140,000 customized black Porsche and spent money like it was going out of style.

After questioning George at DEA headquarters agents took him to MCC in Manhattan where he joined Six-O and the rest of the Obsession crew, Six-O flipped in less than a week while agents confiscated George's money and property. They'd already found one of his Porsches and a Mercedes that he'd just tricked out to the tune of 50 grand. As word of Six-O's defection spread those loyal to George dwindled. Boy George would glare around the unit at MCC and say, "Who's next?"

Part 7- The Case

Heroin 'Boy' Trial Opens, read the *Newsday* headline on September 13, 1990. The trial being held in U.S. District Court in Manhattan marked the end of the investigation but the feds still needed to prove their charges against the kid kingpin. Wiretaps, informants and surveillance photos would give federal prosecutors the evidence they needed to convict Boy George, but it wasn't a surefire win, Boy George hired the best lawyers money could buy. He was ready to battle for his freedom. In all, more than forty people were arrested in the Boy George case. Almost all waived their right to trial and pleaded guilty to a variety of minor narcotics charges. Most of the lower level workers accepted guilty pleas. A lot opted to cooperate against their former employer, breaking the code of the streets and becoming forever branded as rats and snitches. Six-O, Weasel and Ralph Hernandez became prosecution snitches. They couldn't face the time. Of the 33 defendants originally charged in the Obsession case only George and five co-defendants rose for the entrance of Judge Shirley Wohl Kram on the opening day of the trial. With the initial and superseding indictments returned, the trial commenced on August 27, 1990 with jury selection.

In September 1990, Boy George and several of his co-defendants opted to stand trial in federal court. Boy George was charged with 14 counts, among them conspiring to run a continual criminal enterprise, drug possession and distribution, and ownership of many guns. "My case originally started with the number of co-defendants ranging from 32 to 125, Puerto Ricans and African Americans. I have some Asian co-defendants that are alleged members of the Flying Dragons from New York." Boy George said. "Since the number of co-defendants was so great the case was broken down with a main one being that of the lieutenants and managers and high seated members. The other trials were for mill workers and alleged hit men."

The fourteen-count indictment filed on June 7, 1990 charged that George Rivera, Ketty Turino, Danny "Green-eyed Danny" Delgado, Arycelis Turino and Anthony "Ant" Cruz were members of a conspiracy to distribute heroin at the street level that operated in the South Bronx and Manhattan. Count one charged them with conspiracy from 1987 to 1989 to distribute and to possess with intent to distribute in excess of one kilogram of heroin. Count two charged Rivera with operating a continual criminal enterprise from 1987 to 1989. Counts three through nine charged Rivera with distributing and possessing with intent to distribute heroin. Counts ten through thirteen charged Rivera with using and carrying firearms during drug trafficking crimes. Count fourteen charged Rivera with attempted income tax evasion for the calendar year 1988. His other co-defendants such as reputed lieutenants Willie "Love" Claussen, Walter "Ice" Cook, Bob Lemon and Michael Cole were tried separately. All were charged with participating in a highly-structured, street level heroin distribution organization in the South Bronx and Manhattan. The operation was allegedly developed by Rivera and sold heroin under the brand names Obsession, Sledgehammer and Delerious.

"I was charged with various counts consisting of both drug and weapons charges along with a $5 million tax evasion charge. I was the youngest criminal co-defendant ever to have a federal kingpin charge," Boy George said. "My trial lasted three months. It started in August and ended in November. My main informant introduced me to an undercover cop. The feds also used an underboss of mine. These individuals who played the role of die hard gangsters, with the feds the real gangsters, turned out to be true punks and female's in disguise. My main informant was an individual named Joey Navado aka Joey White. He introduced me to an undercover cop who Joey called compai (family member). I did two sales to this undercover, which I beat, thanks to Les Wolf, my investigator." The government stressed an organizational chart containing information regarding selling spots and personnel involved in the sale of the two brands of heroin.

The undercover cop Detective Mendez, the government's first witness gave preparatory testimony as an expert regarding heroin production, distribution and use. He explained that heroin was typically sold to users in powdered form and ingested in liquid form. He testified that heroin is usually bought by dealers in bulk form (bricks), reduced into powder, mixed with other ingredients (cuts), packaged and sold in glassine envelopes stamped with a brand name. He also explained and defined terminology used in the drug trade. Detective Mendez then testified regarding his two undercover purchases of heroin from Rivera on August 27 and October 6, 1987.

Ward "Six-O" Johnson was Boy George's first lieutenant and later on became the prosecutor's primary cooperating witness when the Obsession operation fell. "Aside from Joey White, the feds used an underboss of mine named Ward Johnson, a delivery boy named Luis "Weasel" Gautier and his sidekick Ralph Hernandez," Boy George said. George and his co-defendants got to witness several of their crew members reveal themselves as government witnesses. The principal prosecution witnesses were Ward Johnson, Rivera's second in command and Luis Gautier who was responsible for delivering the heroin from the mill to the street outlets and collecting the proceeds after the sales. Rivera's lawyer argued that his client had been framed by cooperating witnesses but the government maintained Gautier and Johnson were being truthful and were in fear of their lives for snitching on Boy George.

The prosecutors said they were so afraid they couldn't even look Boy George in the eye during their testimony. "You saw them turn their chairs away from George Rivera. You could infer that these people were fearful," prosecutors said. Prosecutors also brought up the alleged hit list Boy George had sent out to Angel Marquez after his indictment and imprisonment. The page contained handwritten notations which Marquez, when arrested and caught with the list, explained with the comment "were doing voodoo on them." Among the notations on the indictment, were X's next to every defendant in the case except for Boy George. Below the names was a key, revealing that X meant, "Quiet their mouths." Moreover, one of the defendant's names was circled and had three X's next to his name. "I want him quiet and I want him to pay for all he's done." Underneath another defendant's name with five X's next to it was written, "I want him more than anything." That defendant was Ward "Six-O" Johnson. Boy George apparently had it out for his former lieutenant.

Prosecutors continued asking the judge to put Six-O in the Witness Protection Program, "because Ward Johnson's truthful cooperation with this office may reveal activities of individuals who in the view of this office might use violence, force and intimidation against Ward Johnson and his family for the purpose of retaliation or otherwise, upon the written request of Ward Johnson's counsel, this office will apply on his behalf to the Witness Security Program of the United States Marshals Service." At the trial, the government introduced into evidence the photo album seized from Rivera's apartment that contained pictures of the yacht party. In an attempt to show the lavish lifestyle of the co-defendants, the Christmas Eve yacht party photos were enlarged and pinned up on the courtroom bulletin boards for the judge and jury to see during trial. The professional photographs of each table, so meticulously arranged by drug location would prove invaluable in identifying the players in the Obsession hierarchy. Photographs from the Christmas party showed "Green-eyed Danny" Delgado and "Ant" Cruz sitting together at the 156th Street table. Along with all the other conspirators at their various tables. The government introduced solid gold belt buckles into evidence at trial. Fifty-eight recorded conversations were introduced into evidence, from the wiretap on Rivera's house. These conversations provided a detailed picture of the ongoing conspiracy and Rivera's control over it. One of the most incriminating pieces of evidence was a conversation taped by the government where George and one of his lieutenants were using pig Latin in an attempt to communicate in code their intentions of opening crack locations.

In Six-O's days of testimony he matter of factly explained the drug business in punishing detail. Scores of agents, officers and experts testified.

Through their testimony it became clear to the court that the organization maintained a cutting mill or table at which pure heroin was diluted and packaged in ten dollar glassine envelopes stamped with a brand name. The location of the mills varied, from time to time but the results were the same. After packaging, the heroin was delivered to distribution locations. There were five principal distribution outlets called spots or stores: (1) 166th Street and Washington Avenue in the Bronx, (2) Avenue-St. John and Southern Boulevard in the Bronx, (3) 139th Street and Brook Avenue in the Bronx, (4) 122nd Street and Second Avenue in Manhattan, (5) 156th and Courtlandt Avenue in the Bronx. The spots were run by spot owners who employed a variety of street managers, sellers, steerers, lookouts and other assistants. The spot owners kept a percentage of the proceeds of the heroin sales, from which they paid their employees and remitted the remainder to Rivera. The government alleged that: (1) Rivera controlled it, (2) Cruz started as a worker at 156th/Courtlandt Avenue and became its spot owner in the fall of 1988, (3) Delgado started as a worker at 156th/Courtlandt Avenue and became its street manager, (4) Briggs was the spot owner of Avenue St. John/Southern Boulevard and (5) A. Turino, K. Turino, Simmons and Rodriguez were cutting mill workers.

"During the course of my trial the jurors were shown sale receipts, which amounted in the excess of one million dollars just in vehicles, a mall in development and countless pieces of jewelry. Now try to tell me how could one win a trial alleging a drug conspiracy when your assets are worth more than a few neighborhoods in New York and you're only 21-years-old," Boy George said. The prosecutors displayed piles of weapons, the flamboyant jewelry and the boxes of empty glassines with the red Obsession crown logo to the jury. Boy George's lawyer cast him as a flashy young jewelry dealer with bad luck in bookkeepers and poor taste in friends. "He is a man who likes money and we would not argue that he was drawn to those that made it," his lawyer Robert Simels said. "But we don't think the government can prove he was a drug dealer, and associating with drug dealers is not a criminal offense." One of Rivera's defenses was that Joey Navado, the government informant, had in fact been the head of the Obsession conspiracy and had used Boy George as a front man. Rivera contended that Navado and the main government witnesses at trial conspired to frame Rivera and lessen their individual culpability. The judge decided, "since conspiracy by its very nature is a secretive operation, the elements of a conspiracy may be established through circumstantial evidence." Thus putting the burden on the defense to disprove the mounds of evidence that the government had accumulated against the defendants.

During trial, Boy George focused on the larger game just as he always had. Each morning, he'd hand his lawyer a list of questions and concerns he'd devised from going over the testimony from the day before. He took notes and combed the bible for strategy. To no avail, the prosecutors were pulling out all the stops. "The prosecutors went to every car dealer I ever dealt with or real estate agent I dealt with both here and overseas to prove I wasn't a representative of any company other than the illegal one I ran." Boy George said. Despite the scrutiny and with his life on show for all comers George was helpful, respectful and appropriately dressed at the trail. But he had his trying moments. One day when his co-defendant talked with a case agent, George blew up, "What the fuck are you talking to him for? He's trying to put you away for natural life." To Boy George the line between enemy and friend was clear. He knew what the stakes were. And win or lose he knew he'd have to pay.

"When the case came down he became bigger then he was ever in the street," Sport says. "You reading the papers and you already know he was making money and then the FBI came to get him. He was like the mafia. That shit made him an icon around there. He became infamous." The informant's testimony and the evidence gathered by the government in the investigation were enough to convince a jury to convict. In mid November 1990, the jury returned a partial verdict. "The jury deliberated for two weeks on me before they finally convicted me on two of the 36 counts," Boy George said. And consequences for some of the informants was immediate. "Joey White's a witness to the saying that god doesn't like ugly." Boy George said. "He was found in someone's trunk in an airport parking lot, no one was ever charged but I assume theories were passed through the minds of the feds." And Bob Lemon, Boy George's co-defendant said this about the government witnesses,

"The government made an offer to Johnson that they would not arrest his son if he testified on any co-defendants. He testified that if he could lie to gain his freedom he would. Another government witness Luis Gautier aka Weasel testified extensively also. Ward Johnson aka Six-O and Weasel are both rats, liars and snitches." And Flaco gives the inside story on Joey White's death, "They beat him with bats, burned him and loaded him in the trunk." Clearly a death well deserved in the eyes of the streets.

Part 8- Life in Prison

Prosecutors contended that Boy George, "visited devastation on his community in the South Bronx and upper Manhattan and used people as human guinea pigs to test the various mixes of heroin before selling them on the street." Though not charged with any violence the judge took the many violent accusations into account as relevant conduct. Behind the tax evasion and conspiracy convictions were uncharged allegations of several Obsession organization murders plus the death threats Boy George allegedly made. While Boy George was only found guilty of two of the fourteen charges- attempted tax evasion and conspiracy to distribute heroin- he would still pay heavily. At sentencing there were so many spectators, that people lined the walls. Extra federal marshals had been assigned to guard the doors and block the windows should Boy George try to make a run for it 'a la his hero James Bond. Judge Shirley Wohl Kram presiding, told him that he was one of the most violent people to ever set foot in her courtroom. She said that in the long months of the proceeding she had not seen any sign of remorse. On Wednesday, April 25, 1991, George Rivera aka Boy George, then 23, was sentenced to life without parole in federal prison for running a $15 million heroin ring.

Boy George laughed upon hearing the sentence. The baby-faced heroin kingpin stood smiling after Kram read the sentence and chuckled as the judge added five years probation to the life term. "Five years probation after life?" Boy George exclaimed incredulously. *Boy To Get Old in Jail; Ex-Drug Chief Gets Life Without Parole*, the *Newsday* headline read on April 25, 1991. "I was convicted of two of the thirty-six counts- conspiracy to distribute 100 kilos of heroin and tax evasion of $5 million." Boy George said. "I was sentenced to natural life without parole."

Court records indicated that the defendant was convicted in the United States District Court for the Southern District of New York of conspiracy to distribute heroin and other offenses connected to the conspiracy. Following a jury trial Rivera et al were convicted on the heroin conspiracy charged in count one. Rivera was also convicted of the attempted tax evasion charged in count fourteen. The jury was unable to reach a verdict on the remaining counts against Rivera and the court declared a mistrial on those counts. The district court sentenced defendants as follows: Rivera to life imprisonment; K. Turino to 121 months, Delgado to 240 months, A. Turino to 135 months, Cruz to 365 months, Victor Briggs to 188 months, Andrew Simmons to 138 months and Madeline Rodriguez to 123 months. Other defendants like Bob Lemon and Walter "Ice" Cook got served life sentences by the feds also. The jury returned its partial verdicts on November 16, 1990 and the court declared mistrial on the remaining counts on November 20, 1990.

"There are some substantial legal issues here as to whether a 23-year-old boy should be sentenced to life imprisonment when the government was unable to establish the burden of proof for a jury to convict him on that charge," Robert Simels, Boy George's lawyer said. The trial cost Boy George over $200,000 in attorney fees, still he wasn't ready to give up. But with the feds seizing his property and valuables and his girlfriends going crazy with the rest of his money it didn't look good for Boy George. His street contacts shrunk with each new round of arrests. The snitches were getting everyone he knew or ever did business with indicted. And even after his appeal was denied, Boy George still acted as though a successful appeal was guaranteed. The street legend would never bow his head down in defeat. That was just how he was cut.

Part 9- Looking Back

"The government placed 10 or more people on trial, the jury listened and a spill over effect took place due to association being established, which is not a crime of conspiracy. But when the rats start telling lies you can be found guilty because evidence against one person can prejudice an innocent person based on false testimony." Bob Lemon said. The feds conducted a war and in war everything was deemed fair game, no foul. That's how the feds played. It was a dirty game. Ward Johnson aka Six-O and the other snitches on the case detailed their crimes for the jury. They sold their souls to get a shortened sentence in an agreement to testify against their comrades. "Some of the men were in the prosecutors office the second week after the arrest making up stories based on whatever the government assumed," Bob Lemon said, "Ketty and Chela, both strong Puerto Rican ladies went to trial with Boy George and never told, lied or snitched on anyone." That goes to show that some females in the game are cut harder than the men who portray themselves as solid dudes and tough guys.

"You can't read about it in books and you can't look at it in movies," Boy George said of his rapid rise in the drug game at a young age, "I was born with something inside of me that says, 'George, that's a pretty girl. Go get her. That's a nice suit, go and get it. There is something out there, it's for you.' When you get a feel that you're almost that thing, you can reach out and grab it and it's yours."

About the whole ordeal Boy George said, "This experience is not one that I'd say caused me any regret. Despite my sentence and the trials and tribulations I've encountered I have no regrets, not one." And he offered advice for those striving for fame and fortune in the drug game, "I'm not gonna portray myself as some saint coming to preach against hustling. Nah, get yours man, but use your head and study your movies like a chess master watch *Godfather* and *Scarface*. These movies are learning tools. Study others mistakes, study investigative techniques and always scrutinize everyone. No one should be above suspicion - no one." Wise words from a man whose main partner snitched him out. And of the game in general Boy George said this, "I'd never say or agree to the statement that the game is dead. Drug's are the biggest generator of money in this country, so how could the game be dead?"

Part 10- The Legend Remains

"If you grab dudes who was trying to bubble in the mid 80's, Boy George is in the top three." Sport says. "I could probably look him up at #1 because he was so flamboyant. He was driving a Rolls Royce and everything in the hood. He was a big dog." And the rapper Fat Joe recognized, putting Boy George in his song, *Sique Para Lan Te Boriqua*. Back in the day being around Boy George was like being in the gangster movies. He was the real deal. The big city standard. He was like a rock star. Even in prison he rocked the four-ounce eighteen-karat gold chain around his neck. To kids in the hood he was and still is a star to this day. "You can put all races and he'd be #1," Flaco says. "The feds still use him to say don't be like him. They're still talking about this guy 20 years later." Boy George's impact was dramatically felt.

"Twenty-two year olds coming in from the Bronx still idolize him, so young, so much money, girls, cars. He becomes like a bedtime story," a contemporary in prison said. "I feel sad by the fact that kids don't know what they are getting into. He's doing life in jail, what's the point?" Still the kids look up to Boy George and his exploits. For Puerto Ricans he is the street legend of all legends. The Puerto Rican James Bond. The kid kingpin, el managte. A real life Tony Montana. But with George if you played dirty, you died. A lot of the snitches associated with his case ended up dead. Not to say he had a hand it in. That's just how it goes in the South Bronx.

"Consider the federales the true gangsters for many reasons consistent with the authority and manipulations they've mastered in the apprehension of felons and the manner in which they take the so-called rock hard hustler or shot callers and convert them into a heap of clay for their designing," Boy George said. "True, there exists an elite group of men who did their thing and laughed in the face of adversity, but they are few and far between. And to those men and women I say it is a great honor to know that, despite our dying numbers, we are still a force that needs to be dealt with respect and admiration for we have lived lives others fell short to visualize."

Dudes from the neighborhood like Flaco give Boy George big props also. "It's like he represents a person that didn't tell," Flaco says. "That was making millions and he was Puerto Rican. He got life and he's keeping his mouth shut. That's rare. You don't want to be talking about no dude who got money and he's a rat. Boy George is the truth. He represented all the way around."

Boy George lived like a movie star, but he wasn't in Hollywood, he lived in the South Bronx. There was no glamour and silver spoons. He came up out of the gutter to become hood rich. A ghetto star whose 80's exploits still shine to this day. At the young age of 17 he seized an opportunity that men much older were not bold enough to seize. He took the proverbial bull by the horns. Boy George plied a trade that from Southeast Asia to the South Bronx, sold China White, making its practitioners notorious, infamous and rich in the process. Boy George did not equivocate, he took action. There was no hesitation in him. From the jump he personified the gangster lifestyle. He was a one of a kind legend in an era that spawned big names. From the criminal underworld and crack era, a new generation of gangsters were born. With his marketing techniques, desire to shine and flamboyancy he won himself a place in the annals of gangster lore. Young, rich, ruthless, flashy and dangerous, Boy George was a trap star before the term was even invented. Of all those 80's drug barons his star shines high in the pantheon of the romanticized American gangsters.

Chapter 1

Vibe Magazine
XXL Magazine
Queens Reigns Supreme by Ethan Brown
Feds Magazine
Cop Shot by Mike McClarey
Don Diva Magazine
Court Records
Notorious Cop by Derek Parker
The New York Times
The New York Post
New York Newsday

Chapter 2

Don Diva Magazine
The Washington Post
The Washington Times
Feds Magazine
Court Records

Chapter 3

The Baltimore Sun
Don Diva Magazine
The Washington Post
Court Records

Chapter 4

The Philadelphia Inquirer
The Philadelphia Daily News
Don Diva Magazine
Court Records
Feds Magazine
Black Brothers Incorporated by Sean Patrick Griffin
1990 Pennsylvania Crime Commission Report on Organized Crime

Chapter 5

Don Diva Magazine
As Is Magazine
Court Records
The New York Times
New York Newsday
The New York Post

Chapter 6

Don Diva Magazine
Dead on Delivery
Court Records
Random Family by Adrian Nicole LeBlanc
New York Newsday

*Also I'd like to thank all the prisoners from the respective hoods, cities and areas where these street legends held court for all their quotes, critiques and knowledge that helped me get these stories as accurate as possible from all points of views, not just the law enforcement or court record angle.

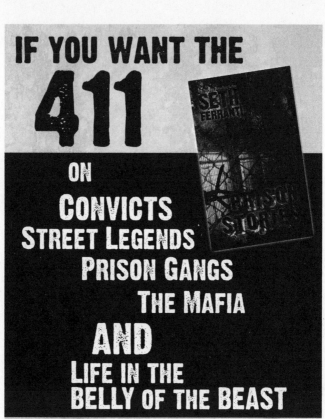

Street Legends Volume 3

The Supreme Team — the most indepth look at this crew ever. From the early 80's heyday to the RFCO Act trial to Supreme's beef with 50 Cent and eventual life sentence on a murder for-hire charge.

Street Legends Volume 4

Infamous gangsters — featuring Rayful Edmond, Lorenzo "Fat Cat" Nichols, Alberto "Alpo" Martinez, Freeway Ricky Ross and Clarence "Preacher" Heatley.

For more information on the above listed titles:
Visit www.gorillaconvict.com

To comment on this book or contact the author:
Visit www.gorillaconvict.com

Frank "Black Caesar" Matthews

In the 1970s the heroin market in the United States was dominated by one man, a black distributor named Frank Matthews who operated out of New York. He was the most notable figure on the east coast at the time and one of the first major independents who challenged the Mob for supremacy in the criminal underworld. The Black Caesar, as he was known, was a new kind of super-criminal ruling a nationwide empire of dope. He was the boss of bosses and the DEA ranks him as one of the Top Ten drug traffickers in United States history. A pivotal figure in the history of the drug trade, Matthews was one of the nation's largest narcotics dealers from the 1960s through the early 1970s, and he routinely handled multi-million dollar shipments. More importantly, Matthews was the first black man astute and confident enough to control an interstate organization the size and scope of his operation, at a time when the Mob controlled everything, illegal or otherwise. Astonishingly Matthews did it while still in his twenties.

He became a major dealer in twenty-one states with quality overseas contacts for both heroin and cocaine. Frank was a North Carolina country boy who seized control of the black rackets in New York City. The DEA said that Matthews imported heroin from Turkey by way of processing plants in Marseilles, France and cocaine from Latin America. Street legend has it that his wealth could not be counted. He had Pablo Escobar-type money in the early 1970s. It didn't go to his head. To him money wasn't but a thing. He controlled the illegal drug market in the inner-cities from the east coast to the west coast and had contacts with Cuban wholesalers who controlled vast portions of the South American coke trade to the United States. Matthews earned respect in the streets and criminal underworld by holding his own against the Mafia. When his profits became so huge that they took notice he didn't bow down, he dictated. In essence, Frank was the first black man that had the Mob shook. He was a true trendsetter and set the standard for future street legends who followed in his path and tried to earn the title of American gangster.

Part 1- Country Boy

Frank Larry Matthews was born on February 13, 1944 in Durham, North Carolina, a poor segregated town in the heart of tobacco country. His mother died in 1948 when he was only four-years-old and his aunt, Marcella Steel took him in and raised him as one of her own. The section of Durham Frank was from was called Mohead City. He lived down the street from Mohead Baptist Church and attended East End Elementary School. His whole family hailed from Durham and they called the youngster, Pee Wee.

His aunt, who was married to a cop on the Durham City Police Force, treated Frank like a son. He grew up a bright and curious kid in a family of five with his uncle the cop and two cousins. The boy called Pee Wee as a youth because of his scrawniness, would grow to full size physically and become a giant mentally. By junior high he decided that school wasn't his thing and dropped out after only a year. He knew his path would lead him elsewhere, even at that young age.

Frank was inspired by a rock-and-roll singer named Clyde McFadden who grew up in the same area and left Durham for New York City. Clyde returned twice to his old neighborhood after he made good to show off his fancy clothes, his shiny new Cadillac and his big roll of bills. Clyde made a big impression on Frank, if Clyde could do it then he could too Frank decided. In the seventh grade, before he dropped out, Frank was already dreaming big. He wrote an essay that outlined his plans to become rich and settle in South America. His future was set but first he had to make his name locally.

Little Pee Wee was a born leader, who was capable of organization and had mesmeric powers of leadership. He recruited all the neighborhood kids including his cousins and got into all kinds of mischief. Frank was the type to inspire faith and loyalty, all the young boys rallied around him and he became a shot caller at a young age. His crew plotted on the Farmer's Market, which was across the street from the ball park. Frank and his homeboys wanted to rob it. At 14, Frank's first act as a shot caller was to organize a gang of eight and nine-year-old homeboys to raid local chicken coups.

Eventually a white farmer found out Pee Wee was leading the raids and tried to teach young Frank a lesson, but Frank wasn't having it. With gangster in his blood even at that young age he threw a brick at the farmer and busted the older man's head wide open. This incident led to Frank's arrest in October, 1960 for stealing chickens and assaulting the owner of the chickens he stole. Even as a kid Frank Matthews was not to be trifled with. He served some time at the Raleigh State Reformatory for Boys on that offense and upon his release he bounced. The country boy was moving to the city at the age of 17, but he kept in touch with all his homeboys, who he'd later recruit for his drug ring.

Praise for Prison Stories, the underground hit and Don Diva bestseller.

"Seth Ferranti writes with the bluntness and slangy-ness of street lit but with a much more penetrating gaze into the world of prison." – **Ethan Brown, Author of Queen's Reigns Supreme: Fat Cat, 50 Cent and the Rise of the Hip-Hop Hustler**

"Prison Stories outlaw rawness mixes well with hip-hop's street essence. Fans of Iceberg Slim's pimp tales or HBO's 'OZ' series will really dig this." – **Elemental Magazine**

"Prison Stories is very real. I love Seth Ferranti's writing." – **Wahida Clark, Essence Bestselling Author of Payback is a Mutha**

"Don't expect a heartwarming story of redemption; expect an unbelievable addictive take of how things really operate in prison." – **Giant Magazine**

"Plenty of blood is shed in this intense record of the harsh realities of the penal system." – **Smooth Magazine**

"An episode of 'OZ' couldn't capture prison drama the way Seth Ferranti does in Prison Stories." – **Don Diva Magazine**

"Prison Stories is what 'OZ' and 'Prison Break' weren't real enough to be." – **Kwame Teague, Author of Ghetto Sam and the Dutch series**

"Prison Stories reveals a world of fearless convicts, inconspicuous snitches and deadly gang rivalry." – **The Ave Magazine**

"With Prison Stories, Seth Ferranti now finds himself among urban fiction's top writers." – **www.urbanbooksource.com**

"Ever wonder what prison life is really like? Seth 'Soul Man' Ferranti takes readers to the belly of the beast with his raw, uncut narration of Prison Stories." – **O.O.S.A. Online Book Club**

"Prison Stories gets my thug rating of about an 8, which is hard to get." – **Lamont "Big Fridge" Needum, Short North Posse**

"Prison Stories are an excellent piece of draftsmanship. Seth's style fills a great demand and the plot educates its readers to the game of life. Seth gives the readers excitement, street wisdom, prison adventures and lots of information that makes underdogs desire power. Seth takes the combination of good and evil and transforms them into a well balanced dish of delightfully dangerous episodes." – **Walter "King Tut" Johnson, New York City Original Gangster**

"Reading Prison Stories is like living in a zoo in hell." – **Vice Magazine**

"Raw, honest, and gripping. A dope read, gritty, and real." – **King Magazine**

"Prison Stories is a book about life in the joint." – **www.Gangland-News.com**

"HBO can only dream of 'OZ' being as good as Prison Stories." – **Washington Post**

"Prison Stories is good. A combination of yard gossip, speculation, and myth dressed up in story format." – **Prison Legal News**

"Prison Stories, sobre la vida en las carcelas estadounidenses." – **Gigantes del basket**

"Prison Stories is a play by play of life in the belly of the beast." – **Bonta, Author of Small World**

"Gripping and terrifying." – **Dr. John Beresford, LSD Guru**

"Written by a true convict, Prison Stories is a bold composition of prison life given to you raw." – **Jihad, Author of Safe**

"Seth Ferranti's Prison Stories is full course meal for a gangsta novel reader's appetite!" – **Joe Black, Author of Street Team**

"Seth Ferranti knows the darkness of prison. Prison Stories grabs the reader in a chokehold and shows how American prisons make bad people worse. To know Seth Ferranti's work is to know prison." – **Michael G. Santos, Author of About Prison**

"Prison Stories is vicious. Everybody should read it, it will give you an inside look at the feds. Prison is no joke!!!" – **Robert Booker, Sr., Author of Push**

"The language in Prison Stories is a dense pastiche of slangs that is very effective, beautiful and intense." – **Soft Skull Press**

"Prison Stories is engaging, readable and thought provoking." – **Dr. Stephen Richards, Author of Convict Criminology**

"Prison Stories brings 'the netherworld' to life and creates a distinct portrait." – **Cornerstone Library**

"Seth Ferranti's a talented writer and one with a unique perspective." – **The Nation**

"Seth Ferranti's style is light, involved and at times lyrical." – **Robert Gannon, Author/Journalist**

"Seth Ferranti brings to life the world of murders, dopers, sex fiends and all types of miscreants who live an insane life in the feds." – **Behind the Wire**

"Prison Stories takes the reader into the netherworld of prison life." – **Famm Gram**

"Prison Stories was great. Very gripping and suspenseful all the way to the end." – **Professor Mary Bosworth, Oxford University**

"Seth Ferranti releta en esta obra las historias en prison en las que 'el perro come perro' dentro de los internados federales." – **El Excelsior**

"Prison Stories is not a pleasant read. It's raw, honest and shows the ever present chaos and danger of the penitentiary." – **Nude Magazine**

"Prison Stories keeps it real. Read about prison drug dealers, dudes getting turned out, power tripping guards, gangbanging, psychopaths, jailhouse snitches and hustling by any means necessary." – **www.prisonerlife.com**

"Prison Stories is really excellent. Seth has a great ear for dialog and a knack for narrative rhythm. I truly could not put Prison Stories down. It just might be a classic." – **Vibe Magazine**

EXCERPT FROM PRISON STORIES BY SETH 'SOUL MAN' FERRANTI

Interludes III: Paperwork Party

"Yo, main man. What's up? Where you coming from?" Dusty asked the new jack holding a bus roll. Dude entered the unit sporting the blue slip-on skippys, the elastic-waistband khakis two sizes too big, and the soiled t-shirt that looked like it was his kid brother's, all of which marked him as in transit. Dusty knew he was straight off the bus, probably straight out the county too. The dude looked up at Dusty and gritted on him before answering.

"I was in Mecklenburg County, nigga. What's up?

"Damn, nigga," Dusty replied. "Chill the fuck out. I'm just checking you out. So you from Carolina, right?"

"Yeah, Charlotte, Newsome Projects," dude said.

Dusty's eyes lit up. "Oh, yeah? That's around my way. I'm from Crutchfield Street. They call me Dusty. What's up, homeboy?" Dusty smiled and put out his hand. Dude paused, unsure for a minute, then shook hands with Dusty.

"Alright, cool, they call me Murder," the new dude said.

"Damn," Dusty said with surprise. "Murder, huh?"

"Yeah," the dude said. "Murder."

Dusty had been in the system a minute and he'd met a lot of brothers and seen a lot of shit but he was still surprised at what dudes called themselves these days. Maybe dude thought he was straight out of a rap video or something. Dusty didn't care. At least he was a homeboy. And he was a stocky little dude too. Straight pitbull-looking muthafucka.

"So how much time you got, Murder?"

"What's it to you, nigga," Murder shot back.

"Damn, playa, don't take no offense. I'm just making conversation. I been in six years on a 15-year bid. I got busted back in 93 on the Toppy Smith case. You heard of that, right?" Dusty said.

"Yeah, I heard of that. I got a gun charge. 60 months," Murder said.

"Alright, it's all good then. I'll introduce you around to the homies on the block and on the pound. You probably know some of them. I think Popcorn and them from Newsome Projects. Anyway, chill homey and if you need something holla."

"Alright, bet," Murder said as he hit rocks with Dusty.

Dusty walked over to his man Johnny Blaze. "Who the fuck dat?" Johnny Blazed asked.

"Some young nigga outta Newsome Projects," Dusty explained.

"Oh, yeah? He know Popcorn and them?"

"He didn't say," answered Dusty. "The young brotha seem kind of high strung."

"He probably just scared, man. You know, first time in the feds and shit," said Johnny.

"Yeah, you right," Dusty said. "These young niggas always trying to go gorilla on a muthafucka and shit." Johnny Blaze nodded his head in agreement.

Later, Dusty and Johnny Blaze were in the gym balling with some D.C. cats. Popcorn came in the gym with his boys.

"Yo, Dusty, my man," called out Popcorn.

"What's up, kid?" Dusty said as he nodded to Popcorn's boys as they all nodded to Johnny Blaze. When Dusty and Johnny Blaze's team lost they joined Popcorn and them on the bleachers.

"Damn, Dusty, you let them D.C. niggas rough the court off?" Popcorn joked. Dusty and them laughed.

"You win some and you lose some," Dusty said as he and Blaze hit rocks with their homeboys. "What's up though?"

"Did you see that nigga Antawn last night? The muthafucking Tar Heels were killing them cracker-ass Blue Devils," Popcorn said.

"Yeah," piped in his man Baby. "Ain't no true nigga like Duke. It's Carolina blue all the way. MJ and all that."

"You right," Blaze said and pounded rocks with Baby.

"Did you hit or what?" Popcorn asked. "I know you took the points."

"No, man," Dusty said dejectedly. "I took the over. I didn't hit shit."

"Damn, nigga," Popcorn said. "That shit was a lock. We tore the bookies' ass up."

"Straight up," added Shane, Popcorn's other homeboy.

"Yo," Dusty jumped in. "You see that new young nigga from Newsome Projects?"

"No, man," Popcorn said. "What's his name?"

"He said it's 'Murder.' He a little dark-skinned, pitbull-looking muthafucka."

"Maybe I know that nigga," Popcorn said. "I wonder if he's on my man Big G's case. You know that nigga got life. Fucking snitches, be making people's families cry. The feds is full of them hot-ass muthafuckas. Is that cat straight, Dusty?"

"Shit, I don't know," Dusty said. "He from your hood. Said he got 60 months for a gun charge."

"Word," Popcorn said. "You seen his paperwork?"

"I ain't seen shit and I ain't co-signing either but dude seemed alright, you know?"

"Well, damn nigga, we still gotta check that shit out. Can't have no hot-ass Carolina niggas walking the pound giving us a bad rep," Popcorn said. "Introduce me to that nigga, alright?"

"Alright, I got you," replied Dusty.

"Yo," Blaze piped in. "There goes that nigga now."

Dusty looked over and saw the dude doing pull-ups.

"Yo, Murder, homeboy, what's up?" Murder heard Dusty and them and nodded. Dusty was waving him over. "Let me holla at you," Dusty continued.

Murder stopped his workout and walked over. "What's up?" Murder asked as he looked around. All eyes were on him.

"What up, man?" said Popcorn. "I'm Popcorn, this Baby, and this Shane. We from Newsome too."

"What up," Murder said while hitting rocks with them all.

"And this Blaze," Dusty said. "He on the block with us." Murder hit rocks with Blaze too.

"We on A-block. You need something, just holla," Popcorn said.

"Alright, bet," Murder said as he started to walk back to resume his workout.

"Yo, Murder," Popcorn hollered. "You know Big G and them, right?"

Murder kind of looked down at the ground before he met Popcorn's eyes. "Yeah, I know Big G. The feds did him dirty," Murder said.

"Yeah," Popcorn said. "My peeps said the nigga got life."

"That's what I heard at the county. He was over on 4 South," Murder said.

"That shit's fucked up. Fucking hot-ass niggas," answered Popcorn. "You know who snitched on him?"

"I heard some shit and read the papers but I didn't know the niggas. They said some boys down Carson Street testified against him," Murder said.

"Damn," Popcorn said. "Hot-ass Carson Street niggas."

With that, Murder took off. "Alright, I'll holla at you all."

"Alright, later."

A couple of days later Popcorn saw Dusty on the yard in the afternoon.

"Yo, my nigga, what's up?" Popcorn said.

"What up, homeboy?" Dusty answered. Popcorn took him aside and told him he wanted to holla at him.

"Check it, Dusty, I was hollering at my sister on the phone, right? And she was telling me about Big G's case. She said some nigga called Anthony Simmons was the star muthafucking snitch at Big G's trial. And she said she heard that nigga Anthony Simmons go by Murder."

Dusty looked at Popcorn, taking in the implications of what he just said. "You think it's the same nigga?"

"What the fuck do you think?" answered Popcorn.

Dusty shook his head. "That shit is fucked up, dog."

"Fuck, yeah, it is. Me, Baby, and Shane gonna check that nigga in. Unless he show some paperwork proving it ain't him," Popcorn said. "Damn, I thought that nigga was straight. We gonna find out one way or another. You down or what?"

"You gonna check that nigga's paperwork?" questioned Dusty.

"Yeah," Popcorn said. "He gonna have to show it or he gonna have to check in. We can't leave no hot-ass Carolina nigga running around the pound."

"Damn, Pop. I mean, I don't know if I'm down with some shit like that," Dusty said.

"What? You soft now nigga?"

"Don't go there, homie," said Dusty. "Cuz I'll bust a nigga's ass. But I ain't into all this paperwork shit. Why don't you just leave the nigga alone?"

"Fuck that, Dusty. You let one of them rat muthafuckas on the pound and then they'll start running shit," said Popcorn. "Snitching to the man and shit. I ain't going out like that. I represent for my hood. For Carolina, nigga. We can't be letting them other niggas think that Carolina dudes are soft. Know what I mean?"

"Yeah, I know what you mean," Dusty replied.

"So you down, right? Bring Blaze too. On the yard tonight. We gonna have a paperwork party. I'ma tell that nigga Murder at recall."

"Alright, homeboy," Dusty said.

Dusty saw Murder on the block after count. He noticed Murder was eyeing him suspiciously. For real, Dusty wasn't down with that paperwork shit. He was just trying to do his time. He didn't care what another muthafucka did. As long as it didn't concern him and his. Those Newsome Projects niggas be wilding anyhow, he thought.

"Yo, Dusty, what up?" Johnny Blaze said. "You trying to ball tonight or what?"

"No, fuck that. I ain't going anywhere near the yard. Popcorn talking about a paperwork party for Murder. I ain't fucking with that shit. He wanted you to go too. To represent for the homies." As Dusty spoke, Johnny Blaze looked at him, taking it all in.

"Well, fuck that, I ain't going out there either then," Blaze said. They both looked up to see Murder gritting on them from up on the tier. When their eyes met, Murder turned and walked away.

"That nigga shady, Blaze," Dusty said. "I ain't fucking with him."

That night, Baby, Shane, and Popcorn were in the yard with some other Carolina dudes. Not many, but enough. The 6:00 PM move ended and they started toward the gym. They saw Murder and cornered him.

"So what up, nigga," Popcorn began. "You brought your paperwork or what? My peeps from the street say a kid named Anthony Simmons snitched on my man Big G and gave that nigga life. My peeps told me Anthony Simmons went by Murder and was from Newsome Projects. So is that you, or do you got paperwork proving it ain't you?"

Murder glared around at the group that had surrounded him. They could tell he had some type of folder behind his back. "Yeah, I got some paperwork, nigga," Murder said.

"Well, let's see it, homeboy," answered Popcorn. "Because we don't like no hot niggas around here representing Carolina. And if you Anthony Simmons you need to check the fuck in or else."

Murder brought the folder out from behind his back and as the Carolina dudes looked on he ripped two nine-inch shanks outta the folder, which promptly floated to the ground. "Or else what, nigga," said Murder with a snarl. "I'm Anthony Simmons and I snitched on Big G and his whole crew. So what the fuck is up?"

Everybody jumped back and Popcorn, Baby, and Shane were definitely startled for a minute. But Popcorn kept his nerve. "What you gonna do, nigga? Stab all of us? We 10 deep," Popcorn said.

"I don't think so. I think I'm just gonna stab you three. I ain't got no beef with the others. They didn't say shit to me." explained Murder.

Popcorn looked around and saw his other homeboys backing up and then he realized that Dusty and Johnny Blaze weren't even there. Bamma-ass niggas, he thought. But Baby and Shane were still with him.

"So what's it gonna be, nigga. You think you some Big Willie shot caller. I ain't checking the fuck in. In fact, I think you the one that checking the fuck in." Murder said.

Popcorn looked at Murder's eyes and thought, this nigga crazy. He looked at Shane and Baby right beside him and realized they were thinking the same thing.

"So what up, niggas," Murder said. "You got your cutcards or what?" You ready to play? Cuz I'm strapped and I am all about murder."

He yelled the last word and lunged forward with both shanks. And with that, Popcorn, Shane, and Baby took the fuck off running for dear life. And they ran all the way to the lieutenant's office and checked the fuck into PC.

"Fake-ass hard niggas," Murder cackled after them as he watched them run. After that, Murder was the talk of the pound. Wasn't nobody fucking with him. Dudes started calling him the killer snitch. Didn't nobody want no drama. Nobody really messed with him but they kept their distance. Because for real, wasn't nobody trying to fuck with a known snitch but wasn't nobody trying to beef with him either. He had earned his respect.

Popcorn and them became laughingstocks as did the Carolina dudes on the pound. But after a while it all died down and was forgotten.

Back on the block, Murder stepped to Dusty and Johnny Blaze. "We straight, right?" He asked. They both nodded, telling him, "Yeah, we cool, Murder. We cool."

They didn't want no drama.

Seth "Soul Man" Ferranti is currently incarcerated in the feds doing a 304 month sentence for running a continual criminal enterprise. He has been in prison since 1993 and during his 15 years of doing time he has published two books, Street Legends and the Don Diva Bestseller Prison Stories.

He has also written articles for Don Diva, Feds, Street Elements, King, Slam and a bunch of other magazines. Plus his work has appeared on www.hoopshype.com, www.urbanbooksource.com and on www.gorillaconvict.com. He has been writing about this gangsta stuff, prison basketball and street lit authors from the jump. Check out all his work at www.gorillaconvict.com. And check out his blog on the same site which posts a new story every month.